SEX LIES and Stereotypes

Perspectives of a Mad Economist

Julianne Malveaux

PINES ONE PUBLISHING

Los Angeles ◆ 1994

Grateful acknowledgments are made to the following for
permission to reprint previously published material:
  —USA Today, Emerge Magazine, Essence Magazine,
  King Features Syndicate, San Francisco Sun Reporter,
  Ms. Magazine, SF Weekly, and Black Issues in
  Higher Education Magazine, Being Single Magazine.
  —Excerpt from The Year of the Woman by
  Constance Wiggins.

Publisher's Cataloging-in-Publication

Malveaux, Julianne.
  Sex, lies and stereotypes: perspectives of a
  mad economist/Julianne Malveaux.
  p. cm.
  ISBN 0-9636952-5-8
  1. United States—Economic conditions—1981-.
  2. United States—Economic policy—1981-.
  3. Labor market—United States.
  4. Sex role in employment—United States.
  5. Sex discrimination in employment—United States.
  6. Afro-Americans—Economic conditions.
  7. International relations. I. Title.

HC106.8.M35 1994   330.973'0927
                          QBI93-22654

Pines One Publishing
3870 Crenshaw Blvd., Suite 391
Los Angeles, CA 90008
(213) 290-1182
Cover and book design by Cristina C. Santos
Photograph by Jim Dennis
Printed in the United States of America

For Phyllis Wallace (1921-1993)
and Proteone Malveaux

JULIANNE MALVEAUX describes her work as "talking, writing, raising hell and trying to get paid for some of it." The economist, columnist, educator, and speaker incites, inspires, and challenges the status quo. "If Black people were content to go along to get along," Malveaux has told many an audience, "we'd still be picking cotton."

Incite. Inspire. Invigorate. Julianne Malveaux does all this and more with dignity and humor. As she does this, she explores the prickly contradictions. African American, feminist, nationalist, contrarian are all labels Julianne Malveaux gleefully claims. But with equal glee she claims her anger, her irony, and her sense of fair play. The driving force in her work is her grasp of economic issues and her sense that "everything is economic" from gender relations to job applications to toxic waste.

The compliment Malveaux most values is "you made me think." *Sex, Lies, and Stereotypes: Perspectives of a Mad Economist* is a selection of 150 of her best columns from 1988-1993 and it is certain to be thought-provoking. Her progressive, strident, "take-no-prisoners" voice will demand an audience as long as the gender gap exists, as long as people of color are perched at the periphery of our society's economic life, as long as there is political and disenfranchisement in the United States and elsewhere.

You may not agree with her, but you've got to read her:

ON SPEECH CODES: "Just like you can't shout 'fire in a crowded theater', you ought not be able to shout racial epithets on a civil campus. It is disingenuous to invoke 'free speech' when freedom isn't free, when a campus is something more than a corner, a barroom or an alley. Will the same folk fighting to dismiss campus speech codes also fight to dismiss behavioral codes, to champion the cause of students who attend class inebriated, perhaps?"

ON ANGER: "I don't mind raising hell. I thrive on it. I think of hell-raising as a useful endeavor. Of course, everybody doesn't have a stomach for raising hell. It requires you to get angry, to go out on a limb, to scream and shout, to shake trees and boggle minds, to move people from comfort zone to a place where they are able to consider change."

ON QUOTAS: "There is only one operating quota in the United States and it is this: there shall be at least one dumb man in the White House at all times. Popular wisdom would have it that the 1989-93 dummy is Dan Quayle, but if we look at the way politicians handled the Civil Rights Act of 1991, the real dummy is President George Bush."

ON LAYOFFS: "If it is in the interest of the economy for workers to have full-time, stable jobs, then we ought to reward those corporations whose workforce is largely full-time, either through tax credits or other incentives. Alternatively, we might consider penalizing those who have large part-time labor forces. Finally, we ought to make sure that part-time workers have access, at least, to pro-rated benefits, especially health care. Corporations have a responsibility to make a profit for investors. A tax and penalty structure that reflects society's need for a full-time labor force could make the shift from a full-time workforce to a part-time one simply unprofitable."

ON HOMELESSNESS: "Why have people challenged the right of panhandlers to ask people for money in subways, or the right of homeless people to loiter in libraries? The homeless, it seems, should be neither seen nor heard, lest they shatter the shaky sense of security that so many of us have. Job losses, bankruptcies, plant closings, these are the economic casualties that we fear. It is important to remember that homelessness is not a simple matter of human failure, but another economic casualty."

RECONSIDERING THE ANITA HILL EFFECT: "Was the Anita Hill effect responsible for President Clinton's lifting of the ban on importing RU486? Most working women aren't lining up to take a Concorde to get morning after pills for their personal use. The company that manufactures RU 486 doesn't want to distribute it here. Lifting the ban is a symbolic step that helps women at the top. Where is the relief for women at the bottom?"

ON THE LAPD BRUTALITY VERDICTS: "Rodney King was never on trial. Lawrence Powell, Stacey Koon, Timothy Wind and Theodore Brisenio were. So was the brutality of the Los Angeles Police Department. Instead of referring to the absurd decision that sparked a righteous frustration and sounded a racial wake-up call as the 'Rodney King' case, why don't we refer to it as the 'Lawrence Powell' case or the 'LAPD brutality' case. If Rodney King is immortalized, so also should the police officers who beat him, the police department that created a conducive climate for such brutality."

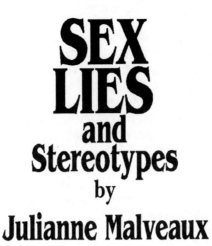

SEX LIES and Stereotypes
by
Julianne Malveaux

Contents

CHAPTER THREE: JUSTICE, PEACE AND CIVIC UNREST

CHAPTER FOUR: SPORTS AND SOCIETY: BEAUTY AND HORROR

CHAPTER FIVE: BACK TO SCHOOL IN A MULTICULTURAL WAR ZONE

CHAPTER SIX: WE ARE NOT YOUR BOTTOM LINE: AFRICAN AMERICANS AND OTHERS AT THE PERIPHERY

CHAPTER SEVEN: THE WOLF AND THE DENTIST: GOVERNMENT, REGULATIONS AND SOCIAL POLICY

CHAPTER EIGHT: THE THIRD WORLD AND THE NEW WORLD ORDER

CHAPTER NINE: AFRICAN AMERICAN HISTORY: MORE THAN A TEXTBOOK THING

CHAPTER THIRTEEN: WILL EVERY
WOMAN HAVE HER YEAR?

ABOUT THE AUTHOR 359

PUBLISHER'S NOTE 360

FOREWORD

Julianne Malveaux is the most provocative, progressive and iconoclastic public intellectual in the country. Her writings not only unsettle prevailing prejudices and undo conventional presuppositions; they also provoke passionate responses—positive or negative—precisely because she is so direct, honest and hard-hitting. Besides Noam Chomsky, Barbara Ehrenreich, Manning Marable and a few others, Julianne Malveaux is the most well-known progressive critic of contemporary American life. But she has yet to receive the serious attention she deserves. Needless to say, she has thousands of loyal fans who hang on her every transgressive word. Yet her powerful onslaught on economic inequality, white supremacy, male supremacy and just plain social meanness is gaining a larger audience in the 1990's. And rightly so, she is one of the last of a long line of American iconoclastic writers from Lydia Maria Child through H.L. Mencken to C. Wright Mills. Like them, she radically cuts against the grain of American culture and calls into question the reigning tools of American society.

Unlike most public intellectuals of our time, Julianne Malveaux possesses a Ph.D. in Economics. And unlike nearly every academic economist, she speaks to a popular audience through the print and electronic media. She also is a powerful and poignant public speaker who is quite popular on the lecture circuit. In the tradition of Thorstein Veblen, John Kenneth Galbraith and Robert Lekachman, Julianne Malveaux writes in a clear and lucid prose that stays in touch with the complex realities of everyday people. This means that she cuts through the obscure jargon and remote dogma of neo-classical economists. She knows that perfect competition models downplay the actual operations of power in the economy and that individual consumers are not sovereign in markets often dominated by transnational corporations. She also realizes that economic analysis is inseparable from politics and culture. And, of course, it is impossible to understand the American economy, politics and culture without grasping the subtle and not-too-subtle persistence of race and gender.

Julianne Malveaux differs from most black and feminist critics in that she puts a premium on economic issues. She knows that white and male supremacy are forms of social pathology—a kind of societal sickness—yet she holds that much of it has to do with economic power and material privilege. In other words, they are much more than individual prejudices and less than inborn propensities. They are sustained by institutions and structures that hide and conceal social misery and personal pain. And her courageous critiques of fellow black and feminist intellectuals add much to the debate on race, gender and justice in our time.

Last, Julianne Malveaux is unique among prophetic public intellectuals owing to her undeniable humor and fury. She is the only progressive thinker on the scene with a profound sense of the comic. This sense is shunned by most radicals primarily because genuine acknowledgement of one's own foibles seems to disempower an already weak left. Yet Julianne Malveaux's grasp of the absurd character of the human condition and American life yields a humorous treatment of serious problems that produce both laughter and lament. To put it bluntly, I detect a Chekhovian strand in her social and cultural criticism—a strand that fuels comedy and compassion. This deep comic sense is coupled with an existential fury—a kind of spiritual indignation that remains on the surface. How rare it is to see battling inside the soul of a progressive thinker an encounter of Chekhov's compassionate comedy with Billie Holiday's empathetic rage! This painful yet productive battle—that goes deeper than Du Bois' "Double-Consciousness" warring in the souls of black folk—yields a distinctive form of an informed and inspiring "madness" rarely seen in the annals of American letters. God bless the child that got its own—even in ward 6! To be a black woman intellectual with personal integrity and prophetic commitment is to catch much hell—and raise some with a smile on one's face!

Cornel West
December 1993

ACKNOWLEDGMENTS

I have a friend who says that today's column is nothing more than tomorrow's garbage liner. Since she, too, writes I like to think that her comment was designed to put a scribbler's work into perspective. Writing doesn't cure cancer, save lives, or create computer software. The most columnists can hope to do is offer a point of view, a place from which discussion departs. The folk who, over the years, have dropped a note about a note or a column, with words of agreement or dissent, or written to ask that I send a particular column have motivated me to put together *Sex, Lies and Stereotypes: Perspectives of a Mad Economist*. Now I just hope they'll buy it.

I am blessed with an opinion a minute, and a safe intellectual space from which to think and write. I am also blessed by a sense of security and audacity that has been nurtured by family, friends, and others who have convinced me that it is okay to "talk much stuff and take none." Heartfelt posthumous thanks go to my mentor Dr. Phyllis A. Wallace (1921-1993), along with thanks to my mom, Proteone Malveaux, and my siblings, Antoinette, Mariette, Marianne, and James, and my nephews, Anyi Malik and Armand Marcus. The little ones don't help me write, but they remind me why I write.

My friends are my family "of choice," as responsible for my sense of security and audacity as my family. In listing friends, one runs the risk of leaving someone special out, and I apologize for that in advance. Barbara Vance, Barbara Reynolds, Greg Lewis, Donna Williams, Ralph Wiley, Bev Smith, Brenda Spriggs, Ramona Edelin, Cynthia Barnes Slater, John Wiley Price, Cheryl Poinset, Mark Brown, Rochelle Lefkowitz, and Lulann McGriff are among those who read and react to my work regularly, encourage me when I'm lagging and razz me when I'm trifling. The examples of their lives and the work that they do, along with their random remarks that sometimes turn into columns, inspire me. I also want to thank colleagues in the San Francisco NAACP and in San Francisco Business and Professional Women's Clubs who tolerate my scatty attendance at meetings when my writing and travel schedule veers out of control.

I am grateful to the people who have published my work (including some of the pieces that appear herein) and helped nurture my voice, especially Marcia Ann Gillespie at *Ms. Magazine*, Susan McHenry at *Working Woman Magazine* (formerly of *Emerge Magazine*), Susan Taylor at *Essence Magazine*, Sid Hulbert at *USA Today*, Dr. Carlton Goodlett, Dr. Ruth Love and Amelia Ward at the *San Francisco Sun Reporter*, and Bill Cox and Frank Matthews at *Black Issues in Higher Education Magazine*. I also want to thank my editors at the King Features Syndicate, Paul Hendricks and Maria Carmincino, and also Richard Heimlich and Joe D'Angelo at King for their cooperation on this project.

Special thanks go to Tavis Smiley who virtually harassed me into this book and who has been a supportive presence throughout; to my assistant Bessie Catherine Barnes who helps my work life run smoothly and who extended herself to work nights and weekends as we completed this project; and to my publisher Denise Pines who has been alternatively prodding, firm and patient, and an utter delight to work with.

Julianne Malveaux
San Francisco, 1993

INTRODUCTION

I don't know why my siblings and I watched *The Three Stooges* when we were kids, but Curly, Larry, and Moe were folk who absorbed much of our energy. I thought them fools but my brother, the only boy of the five of us, savored their antics and even emulated them. Once he set our back porch afire and tried to stomp on it in a stooge's imitation. Another time, he ran through a plate glass window because he saw the stooges do it. He never understood why their heads survived the window intact, while his forehead was bloodied. Several stitches and a spanking later, my brother moved on to other mayhem. But I remember my incredulity that Brother (we always called him that, even before the word was some generic genuflection to racial identity) couldn't tell the difference between television and the real world. If I was shaking my head then, I'm getting whiplash now. As I read back over five year's worth of columns, I realized that one of the things I'd tried to do was record that whiplash with my pen, that sense of going back and forth, of separating images from reality, of connecting the lies with the real deal of our nation's economic conundrum.

Brother's fascination with the stooges happened a long time ago. Now there is some collective notion that it isn't real unless it is on Memorex. Young men in a small Pennsylvania town lie down on a divided highway because they saw someone do it in the film, *The Program*. Boys stick broomsticks up little girls because they saw it on television. Then their parents and their friends run around like chickens with their heads cut off, looking for someone to sue, someone to blame. If there is any lawsuit about the violence that media images bring, though, it is a lawsuit that could come, collectively, from the African American community.

The media constantly caricatures us, constantly violates our cultural integrity. If we are African American women, we are the fat, black, get-back long suffering and neglected victims of the man who was no good. We do the suffering with humor, but we suffer nonetheless. If we are African American men, we don't as much walk as glide into the nation's collective consciousness. We are homies, druggies, and fools. Such fools that we could make fools of ourselves, on shows like *In Living Color* where the jokes all too often put women on the receiving end of racial humor. Not always fools, we turn into superpeople in our dignity. For example, in his role as associate on LA Law, Blair Underwood waited four years to get a girlfriend while white folks were jumping in and out of bed with such rapidity that the rest of us couldn't keep bed partners straight.

One of the worse examples of drive-by media images was the Bill Moyers special *The Vanishing Black Family*. Though it aired more than seven years ago, the Moyers piece is significant because it was perceived as so important that it has been shown in sociology classes around the country. It is also significant because it marked a shift in the way the nation looked at African American people. The black family was vanishing, Moyers implicitly said, because black people are somehow flawed.

The program featured a young man, Timothy McSneed, who had half a dozen children by three women. McSneed seemed to swagger to the camera if one forgot the magic of editing, that the young man would not be shown halting, faltering, doubtful. The swaggering McSneed made bigger press than anything that ended up on the cutting floor. The tragedy was that white America took McSneed as a black male icon and spoke of him as if he were the rule, not the exception.

When I heard that Bill Moyers was doing a piece on *The Vanishing Black Family*, I almost panicked. Sometimes, I take television literally, too. So though I did not have a chatting relationship with my dad, I called him on the phone to make sure he was not vanishing. He was where he was supposed to be, in his real estate office making big money, somewhat amused by my call. Then I called my mom, whom I did chat with rather regularly, just to make sure that her space and place were secure. She wasn't vanishing, but she had a list of errands for me. So much for that. The rest of my siblings were not where they were supposed to be, but they were accounted for, and so my panic turned to skepticism. As I watched the Moyers show, my skepticism turned to an ugly cynicism that Moyers was guilty of televised wishful thinking. Too many people wish black folk would disappear, vanish. Too bad – the black family is not going anywhere. Our families just don't always look like the white families.

The differences are rooted in our histories. Black families are poorer, more likely to be headed by women, more likely to depend on public assistance. Moyers took these facts out of context and tried to make us demons, but he wasn't the only one. Drive-by analysis comes from almost every direction, from the hostile conservatives to the hand-wringing liberals who don't understand that the real issue is economics.

Too many analysts are caught in the sex, lies, and stereotypes of the media to make effective public policy. Too many repeat, with relish, the stories of youngsters like Timothy McSneed. Too many believe that most black people are either criminal or welfare recipients. Or, they believed the Clarence Thomas lie, that his black family was one of the few that worked hard and chafed under the yoke of segregation. When Thomas told the United States Senate that his grandmother was forced to use segregated bathrooms, I wanted to holler, "My grandmama, too." That's history, not the grounds for Supreme Court confirmation. But the United States Senate no more knew us, as a people, than a Thomas staffer "knew" Anita Hill. No more than every black woman who watched the "knowing" knew the meaning of the neck roll and the signifying. "She doesn't know me" doesn't mean an unawareness, it means an unacceptance, a lack of rapport. You broke bread with me, but you didn't know me. You sat with me, but you didn't know me. We shared office space, bathroom confidences, fingernail polish, but you didn't know me. While our knowledge of each other was once so intimate that if you said Fisk '66, I could name your classmates, our knowlege now is so diffuse that Brown '92 means little to either me or you.

Unless you are so connected that you don't ask questions. Unless you are a Senate accepting Clarence Thomas on the word of George Bush. The Senate's knowledge of black folk was so cursory that they believed the hype that Thomas was an exceptional black man, that his family's work ethic was exemplary, so exemplary that they could afford to ignore the contradiction of his own hard work and his skewering of his sister's welfare dependency. The Senate's fractured knowledge made us all want to trot out our hard-working relatives, the ones that look like they escaped from the cover of a rice or pancake box, the ones that worked, sweated, and put on unfashionable headrags to support their families even though they probably knew that their sacrifice would not be regurgitated and tailored for public consumption.

This silent sacrifice makes it clear that the black family isn't vanishing, but the Thomas case makes it clear that there are fissures in the African American community, distances and differences between black men and women, distances that are exploited by whites and the incogNegroes who do the conservative shuffle. Differences that are further exacerbated by the code word "crime," a coding that may account for the Guiliani victory over former New York Mayor David Dinkins, the victory of Virginia governor George "stop the parole" Allen over tepid challenger Mary Sue Terry (who supported a five day waiting period for handgun purchase), the passage of a "three times you're out" (or in as the case may be) initiative in Washington state that would send three-time felons to jail for life. All the criminals aren't black. But African Americans are more likely to run up against the criminal justice system. Between selective vigilance, selective enforcement of the law, selective prosecution, and biased sentencing, African Americans are disproportionately involved in the criminal "just-us" system. I'm not paranoid, just frustrated by the unfairness African Americans too often swallow as "business as usual," swallow because screaming is sometimes untenable.

It's not about crime. The real issues are economic, and the real rap on the race debate is that Americans are frightened. Most of us worry about our jobs. Most of us are petrified at the downward spiral of quality of life, whether it is real or perceived. Crime stories catch on like wildfire, and we focus on the crime but not the forces behind crime stories. Los Angeles, 1992 wasn't a riot, it was a rebellion, an uprising, a spontaneous combustion. And if there was arson behind some of the fires of 1993, there was also the urban legend that some homeless folk trying to keep warm set the fires. The issues are economic, issues of who has and who doesn't, who will and who won't. Race lurks in the background of these stories because the black middle class and the black entertainment class are visible reminders to white folk that "we've come a long way baby." Not so far that a third of the African American population isn't trapped in poverty, but so far that some whites feel there is an "in your face" quality to the incomes of the African American rich and famous. They are fascinated with the Oprah Winfreys, the Bill Cosbys and the Michael Jordans, fascinated and also comforted. "If Oprah can make it, why can't you," they nearly sneer at the poor. But if we take Oprah's income and divide it among the 10 million African American poor, they'd all have a few dollars and she'd be poor too!

Economics and images are intertwined. If African Americans are demonized in the media, our ability to participate in the economic arena is impaired. The woman who crosses the street because she feels threatened by the group of black men standing on a corner isn't going to do easy business with a black man over the conference table. The man who measures himself against superstar Michael Jordan doesn't want to go toe-to-toe with a shorter, fatter Jordan in a business negotiation. Whether the media defines us as invisible, inferior, or exceptional, it cheats us when it fails to define us as "real," as people.

The real deal is not the sex or the lies, it is the change that challenges our society, the downsizing, the layoffs, the notion of "new world order" that must move beyond "same old stuff." The real deal is the pathos in Rodney King's words, "Can we all get along?" And the real answer is that we can't find common ground unless we deal with economic inequities. In the twelve year period that began with the ridiculous Reagan reign, our nation managed to find a way to reward the rich and punish the poor, to divide the poor by setting white against African American, and to use code words and buzz words like "welfare" and "crime" to magnify differences. In the same period, the collective racial myopia of our Presidents turned tolerance into active malaise and the number of cross-burnings and hate crimes have grown with that malaise.

The real deal is economic. A skinhead is nothing but a white boy without a job, a white boy who has not been challenged to work, to grow hair, to constructively engage himself in our society. A white boy who sees "no whites need apply" whenever he reads, "We are an equal opportunity employer." A white boy who was as dropped out or put out as the homie in the hood, who might work if he thought there was employment. A white boy who joins his parents and leaders in buying into the economics of resentment and rage and finding African Americans the enemy.

At the root of this collection of columns, then, is an economic story. Whenever and whatever I write, part of my effort is to grapple with the economic issues, the real deal and the bottom line. Couched in these columns about contemporary life are the ravings of a mad economist, a writer and activist aggravated, enraged, and indignant. Once dazed by my brother's fascination with *The Three Stooges*, I am now stunned that contemporary stooges are public figures, "leaders," and liars. It's not news that the emperor wears no clothes, but neither the sex nor the lies cajole us into closing our eyes. Instead, it is the complacence of go along to get along, of don't rock the boat, that compels a collective silence and inspires my ire; that motivates the columns collected in this volume.

Julianne Malveaux
November, 1993

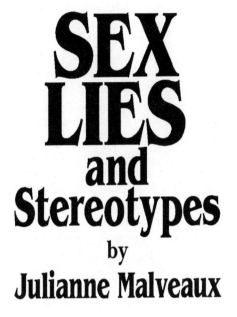

SEX
LIES
and
Stereotypes

by
Julianne Malveaux

POWER 2000 AND BLACK ECONOMIC DEVELOPMENT

*Despite inequality, African Americans represent a
$300 billion market. For some, it sounds like a
mantra to say that this amount is more than the
gross domestic product of the oil-producing nation
of Nigeria. For others, it represents an opportunity.
If more of the money African Americans earn was
spent in the black community, what would it mean
in terms of community revitalization, growth and
development?*

POWER 2000

Chicago, January 1, 2000: Although it is early Saturday morning following New Year's Eve, the offices of Power 2000, the five-year-old national black economic development consortium, hum with serious activity. Dozens of workers rush in and out of the data management station, manipulating spreadsheets, reformatting tables, and realphabetizing directories. "We'll be moving full speed until tomorrow to get the press kits ready," Booker Wilson, staff assistant to the director, tells an observer.

The directors of Power 2000 have called a press conference for the first business day of the year 2000. What better way to mark a new millennium than an announce-

1

ment that there are one million businesses owned by African Americans; that, indeed, the millionth business was incorporated during the last days of 1999? What better way to remind all Americans that self-help has always been an ethic among black people, and that last year resulted in black-owned businesses hiring more than 10 percent of the black labor force, including many semiskilled youths and socially needy single mothers who were unable to find employment in the mainstream labor market?

In fact, in the nineties, African American zeal and enterprise more than doubled the economic base of 424,165 black owned businesses. These were startlingly different from the small mom-and-pop operations of past eras and included biotech, genetic engineering, patent law, waste management, pension fund investing, home health care, textbook publishing, and other nontraditional companies. While in 1987 just one in six black-owned firms employed paid personnel, by the year 2000 that number had jumped to one in three.

What had given black-owned firms such a boost? Electoral support won by ex-Klansman David Duke so worried African Americans that several organized self-help development funds. These funds sought one-time $1,000 contributions from each of the million-plus black households with incomes in excess of $50,000, and though only a third of those approached participated, the amount collected was in excess of $300 million.

The regularity with which a generation of well-trained, talented African Americans hit glass ceilings in the labor market was another factor that fueled the black entrepreneurship surge. "If I can't be CEO of IBM, I'm going to do my own thing," groused one Harvard MBA who was among the first to win a grant from the Kuumba Development Fund. Instead of committing to repay a loan, grantees agreed to give back one percent of company profits to the fund as soon as operations were in the black. Between 1995 and 1999, the Harvard grad's company returned $1 million to KDF.

The availability of international funds also made it possible for black-owned firms to grow rapidly. The "new world order" embraced by President Dan Quayle in 1996 was little changed from that of his predecessor, who looked no further than the European Community and Japan for major US trading partners. But the fact that world manufacturers depended on metals that were available only from the African continent forcibly expanded this perspective. Trading on their monopoly power, some African nations that earned billions in metals on world markets were willing to invest venture capital with US-based African entrepreneurs.

Nor has the investment been one way. Former mayors Andrew Young and Maynard Jackson of Atlanta and former New York Mayor David Dinkins together organized an international business leadership program to expose new MBAs to international development opportunities. Many of these young entrepreneurs now work for a year or two in an African country before returning to the US, solid plans in hand, ready to do business.

Others found opportunity staying at home. As federal and state funds deserted urban coffers, the ingenious figured out ways, for example, to make garbage pay for itself. While the sanitation business had been closed to African American entrepreneurs in the past, the changing political landscape allowed some to elbow their way into waste management markets via subcontracts.

Like affirmative action, much maligned set-aside programs have been wounded but not eliminated. The 1989 *Croson v. Richmond* ruling deflated the value of set-asides for minority firms, but the research done by Brimmer and Associates in the Atlanta case meant that such programs maintained a limited viability. In cities where legislators of color were a majority, multicultural mandates made it difficult for white-only firms to do city business, and many firms solved their diversity problem by subcontracting.

Nationally, legislation authored by entrepreneurially focused senators like Maxine Waters (D., Calif.), Mike Espy (D., Miss.), and Alan Wheat (D., Mo.) revived employment tax credits, reducing the tax bill of those firms that hired disadvantaged youth. As the nation's demographics shifted, there were other tax credits available for the African American community to take advantage of–the Senior Care Tax Credit, for example, responded to the increasing poverty among older white women and offered wage credits and subsidized interest on first mortgages for those who agreed to spend two years helping to care for them. Some African American entrepreneurs had responded to the need to privatize social services by using such tax credits to capitalize service delivery businesses.

Meanwhile the Republican credo of decentralization and deregulation has trickled all the way down to child care providers and cabdrivers. The struggle between small businesses and government over a minimum benefits package for workers continues, but the passage of the Waters-Thomas Health Care Initiative sponsored by Senator Waters and Representative Mable Thomas (D., Ga.) ensured that every American had access to health care by 1995.

On this momentous New Year's Day, while Booker Wilson reviews report findings for a few members of the black press, a strategy group of African American leaders meets to finalize plans for the Monday press conference. Those present at the strategy meeting include representatives from the National Black Family Forum, the National Conference of Black Aged, the Black Feminist Collective, and the National Association of Black Lesbians and Gays. Also attending are leaders of historical organizations like the NAACP, the National Urban League, and the National Council of Negro Women, but there is a dearth of familiar faces from the early 1990s. Indeed, nearly half of those present are women, and a quarter of those in the room are under 30.

The gathering represents a range of political parties–

4

Democrats, Republicans, Rainbows and Greens. Conspicuously absent are self-help gurus of the 1988-1992 period. Glenn Loury, Shelby Steele and Thomas Sowell have all collapsed from "race fatigue" and been hospitalized. By consensus, the group agrees to send Loury, Steele and Sowell red, black and green insignia as a gesture of gratitude. After all, it was the alarm they sounded that led to the formation of Power 2000. Former Supreme Court Justice Clarence Thomas is the only person present who opposes delivery of the insignia. His suggestion that they instead send American flags draws a combination of hisses and applause in reply.

The group goes on to affirm its unanimous purpose to showcase the new black economic base, to premiere its employment program, and to announce that some Kuumba Fund proceeds will now be used to pursue a social agenda.

"The sleeping giant of black consumer power is awake," proclaims the chairperson of Power 2000 (who is a woman). "What was called the $30 billion Negro in 1969 can now be described as the $400 billion African American consumer market. Instead of spending just 6 percent of our money on our own businesses, as we did in 1990, we now spend 20 percent. More than that, as our population moves toward 15 percent of the total population, we are the profit margin for many mainstream businesses. And as we demonstrate our market clout, those who would have called us separatist just a decade ago now want to support our work and get access to our mailing lists."

Is this Power 2000 scenario just wishful thinking or a real possibility? In fact economic and demographic change can be made to work for, not against, African American entrepreneurs. In addition, despite a range of social problems faced by the black community, never before have so many been prepared to fully participate in the economy. Consider these issues:

1. Are there enough appropriately trained African

Americans to create such a surge in entrepreneurship? Though in 1986-87 the number of bachelor's degrees awarded annually to African Americans was down from its 1981 peak of 60,000, more than 55,000 of us received such degrees. By 1988 one in seven African Americans completed more than four years of college.

Today, about 15,000 of us receive master's degrees each year. Though our share of the total is dropping, a solid core of African Americans continue to pursue higher education, with more people concentrating on business, finance and economics.

2. Can black business hit the million mark? The pace of black business growth in 1982-87 was about 7.5 percent per year. At that pace, there will be slightly more than a million black-owned businesses by the end of the year 2000. It would take large infusions of capital to increase the number of black-owned businesses that have employees and operate out of the traditional service arena, where receipts are low. But labor market trends suggest the possibility of better financed, better prepared people choosing entrepreneurship over paid employment.

3. How much income will African Americans have in the future? Black people had approximately $300 billion in income in 1991, about 8 percent of the US total. If black income grows at the low rate of 2 percent per year (which it averaged in the 1980s), it will be about $370 billion in 2000. If black income grows at 5 percent a year, it will reach $488 billion by 2000.

It is clear that the black economy is not now operating at full capacity. The year 2000 isn't so far away that we can't forecast it, and organizations like Power 2000 are more than a pipe dream. It is exciting to think about a future when the sleeping giant of black economic and political power finally awakens.

Emerge Magazine, May, 1992

BLACK AND WHITE AND RED AND SWEET

This summer, like every other summer, is a summer where people who belong to organizations zip from state to state to talk and organize with others in their national groups. The NAACP met in Houston one week, the Urban League in Atlanta the next. The National Association of Black Journalists made it to Kansas City, and the National Bar and National Medical Associations were in Indianapolis. People meet, or as some say, "people *be meeting*." And dollars change hands wherever we meet.

Who gets those dollars? Usually, not black people. I was heartened to learn, at the Urban League convention, that about seventy black vendors and manufacturers got free space at the convention. And a black firm also picked up the tab for tape and video duplicating. But it was a white firm, not a black one, that duplicated those tapes and sold them at the journalist's meeting.

Whoever gets the dollars, these conventions make the point that there are dollars to be made. That was clear at the Urban League, where the organization grossed between $750,000 and a million dollars from exhibit space. Companies come to exhibit because they know convention attendees plan to spend. People come collecting resumes because they know conventioneers will look for work. And hotels compete for black convention business because they know that people spend big money at these establishments.

But when conventions are not happening, many advertisers ignore the black market. There are hundreds — Mercedes Benz, Porsche, and Fiat among them — who have never advertised in *Ebony, Essence, Jet, or Black Enterprise* and never bought thirty seconds on Black Entertainment Television. And African Americans buy their products as faithfully as they buy anything else. We give our dollars to manufacturers who will give us neither jobs nor respect.

When will we come together and demonstrate the

strength of the black market? When will we boycott some product long enough to make some corporation say "ouch." In these downsize days, many companies are settling for profit margins of two or three percent. If the black market is between twelve and sixteen percent, and we flexed our economic muscles, we could make the difference between success and failure for some companies. We ought to let them know that—first the nice way, then the hard way. We ought to boycott something. I propose catsup, because it is red and sweet.

Why red and sweet? We over-consume such products. We buy more than our share of red soda water, more than our share of barbecue sauce. And we buy more than our share of catsup. Why not boycott it? If we did, I can imagine Del Monte aching. Hear Heinz screaming. One of those CEO's would be calling Ben Hooks or some other such official black man on the telephone asking him to call us off. And the point would be to let corporate America know that we have muscles to flex.

I have been talking about the sweet, red boycott for years, and friends keep telling me it is impractical. Their children, they say, would stop eating eggs and french fries if they could not have catsup. But as long as there are tomatoes on the market, there is a way we could make our own catsup; after all, the condiment is at least marginally derived from foodstuff. If we made our own, we might even learn some lessons on self-sufficiency. And we might make a better product.

Would it be fair to Heinz and Del Monte, another group of folks asked? Who gives a good goshdarn about Heinz and Del Monte! We would be making a point, and if the point is sharp all the better. Heinz and Del Monte would survive a four quarter boycott, but maybe not a permanent one. And we'd flex a muscle.

But while we are on the red and sweet, what about the black and white? Why don't we also make a point of looking at those newspapers who don't look at us and walk on by those news kiosks that sell their stuff. I'm not biased toward the *Examiner* because they buy and run my syndicated column, but whenever I pick up the "People" section of the *Chronicle*, I want to holler "white people." They are still running antiquated society columns about ossified people in Pacific Heights called "Buffy," "Muffy" and "Fluffy" (sorry, that was the ossified cat) who give society balls and birthday parties at Trader Vic's. Other people have birthday parties, but they don't make the White People pages of the *Chronicle*. And we keep paying our thirty-five cents.

If people don't cover our community, we shouldn't pay their piper. Or when we pay it, we should flood them with letters and phone calls about their ignorance. Why didn't any San Francisco paper write about the NAACP tribute to Grandvel Jackson or the party for Dr. Zuretti Goosby? Why don't they cover the NAACP as frequently as they cover white retirement homes, mostly located in Pacific Heights? And why do we think this is okay?

Coming back from a week of what my accountant called a "junket," and what I experienced as hard work, I am more convinced than ever that black economic power is underestimated, and underutilized. We need to start flexing our flabby muscle, think about boycotting the red and sweet, the black and white.

Sun Reporter, July, 1991

THE FLIP SIDE OF BLACK POVERTY

Five hundred and fifty corporations, nonprofit organizations and government entities purchased booths in the exhibit hall at the Georgia World Congress Center in Atlanta this week. They strutted their stuff to the four thousand registered delegates and some sixteen thousand others who attended the National Urban League's annual convention July 19–24. Some say these exhibitors were there merely to "showcase opportunity." But General Motors gave its 1992 Cadillac Seville first exposure at the National Urban League Conference. And Apple Computer raffled off a Mac Classic and queried passers-by on their attitudes about technology. Exhibitors came to do business.

Some of the corporations present are laying off workers even as they exhibit. Convention manager Howard Mills explains, "In bad times, some people work harder at marketing." It's about time – the African Americans attending the Urban League Convention were consumers who have often been ignored by marketers.

Most people see just one side of the African American reality – poverty, joblessness, criminal activity. The corporations that exhibited at the Urban League convention, paying more than three quarters of a million dollars for the privilege, were responding to the flipside, the market demographics that say black people earn and spend enough to make the difference between profit and loss.

One in three black families is poor, but one in seven families has an income in excess of $50,000 per year. One can sense their economic status just by looking at the sophisticated, well clothed delegates, many of whom are junior and senior partners in corporate America. There are still few black CEO's; some of the companies exhibiting in Atlanta have less than stellar records on fair employment. But Conference Manager Mills says these companies have taken the first step toward recognizing African Americans as both potential customers and employees by exhibiting. Is a first step enough? The Urban League has its roots in negotiation, not confrontation, and so, in Mr. Mill's words, "we don't boycott, we persuade."

Economics is a major persuader. Those who are passing out gum and crackers and soda, raffling airline tickets and hotel stays, are well aware that much of their profit margin is a function of African American consumption. They are attuned to a reality, ignored by President Bush, but well stated by Coca Cola Chief Operating Officer and luncheon speaker Donald Keough. "We must open the doors to embrace our diversity. "He told those gathered." One... because it is right. Two... because it makes good sense. It is in our self interest as a nation." In other words, those who ignore a sixth of the population are ignoring a revenue base and turning their backs on a bottom line.

The poor are almost always out of sight at this convention, but they are not out of mind. For one thing, exhibitors are asked to set aside some of the goods they plan to distribute for a "community express" which benefits homeless people in Atlanta. Further, the plenary sessions and forums that draw middle class participants are influenced by concerns for the poor. Why has the government abandoned cities? How can urban education be improved? What is the responsibility of the black professional to others?

People make some of the connections here. Corporate exhibitors pay a hefty fee for space, but local African American vendors are allowed free space and exposure. Yupscale convention delegates look at new cars and computers, but anyone can pick up food samples in the exhibit hall. The link between progress and poverty is not ignored; people are painfully aware that the corporate executive's brother may well be unemployed.

Five hundred fifty-five exhibitors may not have come here to deal with these connections. They are looking at ways to secure new consumers. Attending this Urban League convention, with its pipeline to a $300 billion black economy and millions of middle class African Americans, is as good a way as any to say "let's do business."

USA Today, July, 1991

THE BLACK DOLLAR
AND THE HOLIDAY MARKET

December and January mark the peak months for

American consumer spending. First there are "the holidays" – that Christmas, Kwanza, Hanukkah celebration. For a moment, I was saying that Kwanza and Hanukkah were the only ones pure, but then I heard of people buying their kids Hanukkah presents for each night of the eight-day celebration, of Kwanza gifts that put Christmas toys to shame.

After the holidays are through, then there is the travesty of apres-holiday sales, when everything you paid $100 for in December now costs $60. Then there are "white sales" for linens, towels and sheets, fur sales, and I think last year some store had the nerve to advertise a Martin Luther King Day sale. In any case, literally billions of dollars change hands in December and January.

Black merchants simply don't get their share during these months. Black people have 300 billion plus spending power, but black owned businesses get only 10 percent of those dollars. We walk by black businesses to spend our money with whites. We act like we think the white man's ice is colder than ours is.

It's a two-way street, of course. Some black business owners can't be bothered with us as their customers. Some see you walking in the door and then double their prices. Some come up a day late and a dollar short. Some resent being asked to offer the community a corner of support. I think my favorite black business irony tale is that of a brother I ran into at an unnamed airport who had a raggedy car, no trunk, no business medallion, and wanted my business at regular prices. When I demurred, he loudly accused me of "supporting the white man over a brother," at which point I cracked up and told him I probably wouldn't even have had a conversation with a white man standing in front of such a rag.

But the bottom line is that most black businesses hire in the African American community, so that their sales turn into jobs and opportunities. Indeed, this bottom line is the rationale for set-aside policies. Minority set-asides are important, not only because they create individual entrepre-

12

neurs, but because they offer others an opportunity.

These facts, as cliché as they may be, abound in these peak spending months. African Americans have $350 billion of spending power. Probably $70 billion of that will be spent in the two months of December and January. Unless something changes about the way we spend our money, maybe $10 billion of it will hit black hands.

It could be more. Those of us who travel can use black travel agencies. Those who dress can hit the black-owned clothing stores. Those of us who read can hit black-owned bookstores. Those who drive can look for black-owned dealerships. We don't live in an all-black world. In the 1920's and 30's, the "buy black" movement was criticized on exactly those grounds. Black economist Abram Harris said he feared that if "buy black" sparked retaliation, the community might experience disastrous consequences.

But now we aren't talking about spending every cent of every dollar on black-owned businesses. It's neither "wrong" nor "right," but simply not possible, given the current configuration of ownership. Still if an effort were made to double spending in our community, it could have significant consequences.

I was thrilled to be able to spend most of my holiday money with African Americans. Much of the spending took place at an African Market held at Howard University in Washington. More than 50 vendors offered kente cloth, other fabric, T-shirts, earrings, books, art work, you name it. Among my favorite purchases (I bought several more locally at Marcus Books), was the book of days, *I, Too, Sing America.* With a lush cover, rich photographs and art reproductions, the book is chock full of moments in black history. For example, on December 26, 1894, Jean Toomer, the author of *Cane* was born. Jack Johnson won the heavyweight title against Tommy Burns in 1908. Later the loser said, "The idea of a black man challenging me was beyond enduring. Hatred made me tense." On December 27, 1956, segregation was outlawed in Tallahassee, Florida after a six month boycott. The first nationally broadcast United Negro College Fund telethon raised $14.1 million on December 31, 1984.

Here's my bottom line — people can make excuses about their spending patterns most times and get away with it. But during holiday periods, when spending peaks and goodwill is on the brain, it makes sense to make that extra effort to buy black. Products like *I, Too, Sing America,* by Paula Woods and Felix Liddell, deserve our support but also bring much to our lives. And it is this wondrous pleasure, of seeing our history delightfully packaged, our portraits staring down from the wall, the fabric from Africa adorning our bodies, that make a compelling argument for supporting black-owned businesses. In some ways, for the African American community, our very survival depends on it.

Sun Reporter, December, 1992

ALL OF IT

The organization was mostly white, mostly entrenched, mostly successful. Ordinarily they wouldn't fight but so hard about a single contract. But times were tight and economic forecasts were pessimistic. So they groused when they heard that a large contract was awarded to a minority owned firm on a set-aside contract. First it was grousing, then growling, and finally a lawsuit. And in the interim, the group, good civic players at least in their own minds, interacted with others in an attempt to explain themselves.

"The contract should be given to the firm best qualified," the grousers said. Of course they added that they were best qualified because they had a track record that went back some 50 years, years that included a time period when African Americans were not allowed to compete in their industry. They didn't take a position on the exclusion, "just went along," they said. They never discriminated, never kept blacks out. Should they be penalized now?

From where I sit, they have never been penalized, and a minority business ownership set-aside is no penalty. It is a doorstop for those who were locked out of the door for a long time. And given the utterly benign nature of the organization's discussion, it is a necessary way to keep the door open.

I remember having a conversation with one of the men from "the organization," who told me that all my anger and race baiting isn't helping black people. I get the most extraordinary advice by hanging with white men, extraordinarily strange and presumptuous advice. As if these people think I will rush back to a black people's meeting and share the advice they have to offer. "You know you need to see people as people," they say. "You people need to buckle down, work hard, and participate in the system."

When I hear this stuff, I look at those who spout it, and wonder, like they wonder about me, just what is it that they want. I asked one of them, once, what it was that he wanted. "My fair share," the white man said, without batting an eye. "What I have is my fair share. I worked hard for it, and now you are asking that I take less." "You have more than 90 percent of the city contracts, and more than 80 percent of the police and fire employees. You dominate far more than you should. What else could you possibly want," I asked in frustration. Without missing a beat the man responded, "All of it." All of it. Every drop of it.

I understand. Those who start life with a sense of entitlement have a hard time giving entitlement up. They think their gender and skin color gives them special privileges and are stunned by demands of those who don't think so. "I want all of it," the man said, and at some level it doesn't matter whether he was a member of the police or fire union or of the contractors organization. What he was, mostly, was a symbol of the status quo, a composite sketch, but nonetheless an index of some attitudes. "I want all of it," the man said. He has most of it now.

The "all of it" attitude is relevant in context of the first week of October, a week hailed by some as Minority Enterprise Development Week. Indeed, the job generating potential of the Fortune 500 have been called into question because the new economic realities suggest that smaller, not larger, businesses will generate more jobs. Those who are saying "all of it" are getting less of it, because the economy dictates it, not because, necessarily, black folk are taking theirs.

And yet some of these very people have their fingers in the equal opportunity pie. Equal opportunity? They advertise. They open up the applicant pool. But with foxes guarding the chicken coop, I am as concerned about *equal outcome* as I am about equal opportunity.

This is where the wicket gets sticky. There are folk who want all else to be equal. They want to think that color is no longer a factor in anything. They'd be content to expand the applicant pool without affecting the outcome. Because then, they could believe that everybody competed but white folk won. They were simply better.

I think we still have to count with our fingers. Outcomes speak to opportunities. If we get 2 percent of the contracts, there is something wrong with the system. The hidden biases come from the boys who want "all of it."

Sun Reporter, September, 1992

CHAPTER TWO

TOWARD ECONOMIC CIVILITY

Civility is not a word often used to discuss inequality. Yet, inequality, and the glaring nature of it, seems a form of incivility. Why build high-rise buildings a stone's throw from a dilapidated housing project, except to rub someone's face in another person's prosperity? Why park a BMW on a street full of broken down cars except to make a point? Why lay off in the name of the customer? Aren't the people who are laid off also somebody's customers? In bifurcating people from profits and economics, we have created an uncivil world where those who make $100,000 a year or more can whine that they don't make enough. For those who earn the median income of some $35,000 a year, this seems both petulant and uncivil.

TOWARD ECONOMIC CIVILITY

Dr. M. Scott Peck has written much of lives and their direction. My copy of *The Road Less Traveled: A New Psychology of Love, Traditional Values, and Spiritual Growth* is dog-eared and underlined, a reflection of the resonance I feel with his book. I awaited his new work with the same eagerness as the rest of the world and devoured *A World Waiting To Be Born: Civility Rediscovered*, which is very much a treatise for our times.

Civility is a genteel word, high minded and noble. Peck says it is more than politeness and good manners. He quotes Oliver Herford, "A gentlemen is one who never hurts anyone's feelings intentionally," to arrive at the notion that civility has much to do with awareness. "Genuine civility," says Peck, "is in part, consciously motivated organizational behavior".

In the past year, there has been plenty of direct and indirect discussion about civility in American life, and Peck's book seems to probe and reflect what has been said and implied. The philosophical underpinnings of President Clinton's "Putting People First" seem, in part, an exploration of government civility, of conscious ways to deal with people in our society. Mikey Kaus' book about public space and behavior seems also a discourse on public behavior and civility, about ways to deal with crime and other issues in a way that increases public confidence. Joel Kotkin's *Tribes: How Race, Religion and Identity Determine Success in the New Global Economy* also speaks to the fragmentation of discourse and our public space.

Yes, our social fabric is fraying. Americans aren't nice to each other. We are polarized. In public spaces and on college campuses, we black and white people separate ourselves from each other. We describe ourselves in racial terms, "black woman," "white man." Twenty five years after the Kerner Commission Report, and a year after Los Angeles burned, we are as far apart as ever.

Do good manners pull us back together? I think not, although Scott Peck is counting on a lot more than good manners. He is talking about the importance of conscious, aware behavior, underlining aware. But while many are inclined to talk about individual behavior, wringing their hands about rising crime and lawlessness, the horrors of car jackings and drive-by shootings, fewer are inclined to think and talk about economic civility, the cost of conscious and unconscious economic decisions that we make and the way that they intentionally or unintentionally hurt others. Redlining, for example, is a form of drive-by shooting, a random denial of mortgage and business credit that has enormous consequences for the vitality of neighborhoods. Bankers can justify redlining; they can call it "unintentional" discrimination. They lack the awareness Peck speaks of in his book. Yet it is their responsibility to have such awareness, in the same sense that drive-by villains are responsible for the consequences of their random shootings.

Similarly, those Republicans filibustering the President's stimulus package are guilty of extreme economic incivility. They aren't incivil because they refuse to yield to the majority party, or because they won't vote in a package that they don't believe in. Their incivility is their intentional disregard of the plight of those who might be helped by the stimulus package, especially urban dwellers and young people who might get work from the jobs package.

Too many discussions about our ripped social fabric speak about the behavioral. But if one reads Scott Peck's book with the economy in mind, it is easy to conclude that the most pressing incivility in our society is economic incivility.

King Features, April, 1993

SERVICE WITH A SNARL

My after-haircut ritual is to hit the downtown stores in San Francisco. Looking good, feeling good after a haircut is my perfect time to shop.

During this trip, though my pocketbook was willing, sales clerks just weren't able to give me help in finding what I wanted. At one store I wandered past three or four people before someone would take the hangers out of my hand and show me a dressing room. No one came to see if everything was okay. I meandered onto the sales floor wearing my pants and their blazer, hoping that might attract some attention. Not. Eventually, I was told that the smaller size I sought was unavailable. No offer was made to call another branch of the store to see if they had it.

The service was no better at two other stores I visited. At one stop, in order to get attention, I probably would have had to resort to base level shoplifting. The two sales clerks who were discussing their upcoming weekend (on Tuesday) couldn't be so bothered.

Retail stores aren't the only places consumers suffer benign neglect. At a restaurant recently, my request for a clean fork was met with a shrug, then the waiter actually wiped the dirty fork off with a napkin he'd just retrieved from another table. I know, I know they might have done the same thing in the kitchen, but at least hide unsanitary practices from me. Airline service has so deteriorated that I half expect to be asked to bus my tray. Service with a smile seems an outmoded concept.

US and Japanese leaders have recently engaged in a war of words about whether or not American workers are lazy. I don't think workers are lazy, just unhappy. In a way, I don't blame them. The average retail sales worker earned $7.00 an hour in 1991, the average service worker about $10.25. If those salaries, between $14,000 and $21,000 are contributing to household salaries, the workers are making a decent living. But if those salaries support households because spouses are unemployed or absent, then it's a struggle to make ends meet. Many service workers in the food and retail services also don't have benefits. That can't make a worker too happy!

But I wish these folks would take their unhappiness out on someone besides the customer. I'm tired of getting snapped at when I ask for another glass of water, or being given curt directions when I ask where the shoe department is. This isn't happening in fast food restaurants or convenience stores, but places where an entree runs $30 and a blazer $250. My theory is that people are angry at the economy, and at the wages that they earn; their anger sometimes bubbles over, right onto the customers they are supposed to serve. But these are the very customers some people are counting on to spend us out of a recession. That's not likely unless service with a snarl is replaced with service with a smile.

King Features, March, 1992

TAKING IT PERSONALLY

A friend of mine told me a bizarre story the other day, but then it is not so bizarre. We all have our stories, our signs of the times, our brushes with "innocent" crime. Jon's story is as ordinary as these, except for the punch line.

Jon's apartment was burglarized a couple of weeks back. Among the electronic equipment taken, there was a new portable television with a cabinet made distinctive by a flash of gold glitter and an initial. Three or four days later, he ran into a colleague watching television at his desk. "Wow, that looks just like my television that was stolen, down to the glitter, down to my initial," Jon gushed. His friend was sheepish and finally admitted that he bought it "hot" from a friend of a friend. He knew it was wrong, the colleague said, but the price was too good to pass up. It was, he told Jon, nothing personal.

Nothing personal. Those could be the buzzwords of the nineties. Too many of us are cutting corners with no notion of getting caught, much less consequences. Too many are taking the easiest or cheapest way out with not a single thought to the fact that our choice may have devastating consequences for other people. Those who looted the savings and loan industry didn't give a second thought to the millions of people they ripped off. When an older woman confronted one of those charged with savings and loan fraud in a California courtroom, the man looked as stunned as if she had slapped him. In his mind there was, perhaps, no connection between the crimes he committed and the elderly woman who is now penniless. It was nothing personal.

Nine youngsters died trying to do the right thing at a benefit basketball game in New York. They attended the game partly because it was supposed to be a benefit for AIDS education. Event organizers sold too many tickets and five thousand people tried to squeeze themselves into a gymnasium that could hold half that number. Nine people were trampled to death. The city blames the college, which blames the organization that sponsored the event. Meanwhile, parents who hoped to be organizing graduation parties are instead arranging funerals, and the stars of the benefit are hiring attorneys. Nothing personal.

Twenty-five workers died in a fire in Hamlet, North Carolina because a firedoor was locked. Employees locked the door because they wanted to prevent theft; some forty children have no parents now because of these deaths. A fine of $800,000 has been levied and all the appropriate words of regret have been spoken. Nobody knew that locking the door could have such dire consequences. Nothing personal.

And yet there is something very personal about the gains that accrue from careless, if not criminal, behavior. The man who bought a hot television saved a hundred or so dollars from his personal pocket. Owners of Imperial Foods in North Carolina used personal power to keep fire doors locked. The organizers who oversold the benefit basketball game would have received personal congratulations had their event been successful.

In the days when the old year turns to new, we will be buried in reflections and review, in lists of what is "in" and what is "out." If I had my way, the words "nothing personal" would be obsolete in this rest of the decade. Injustice happens because we ignore small acts that have great consequences. Someone has to take the locked fire door, the oversold concert, the hot television personally, very personally. When things go wrong, it is cold comfort to know that there was nothing personal to trigger the disaster.

King Features, January, 1992

PEOPLE AND PROFITS

The Bank of America Corporation earned $1.5 billion in profit in 1992. Its common stock was trading near its 52-week high, and more than 40 percent higher than its lowest price in the past 52 weeks. Good news? Not to the tellers who work at Bank of America. With the good news of a successful economic year came the stunning report that full time branch employees will find their work week reduced to just 19 hours, making them ineligible for benefits.

Bank of America's action is part of a national trend for corporations to downsize, to get lean and mean at workers' expense. This downsizing explains the mixed nature of the economic indicators, the weakness of the so-called economic recovery. One person's profit is another person's poverty. And since fewer than 40 percent of all Americans own stock, it is safe to say that most of the tellers who work reduced hours at Bank of America will not benefit from the belt tightening measure.

Corporations clearly have the right to maximize profits. Policy makers, though, must make the connection between maximizing profits and minimizing wages. Those who write tax codes must also make the connection between actions that benefit short term profit-making and actions that hurt the entire labor force in the long run.

If it is in the interest of our economy for workers to have full-time, stable jobs, then we ought to reward corporations whose work force is largely full-time—either through tax credits or other incentives. Alternatively, we might consider penalizing those who have large part-time labor forces. Finally, we ought to make sure that part-time workers have access, at least, to pro-rated benefits, especially health care. Corporations have a responsibility to make a profit for investors. A tax and penalty structure that reflects society's need for a full-time labor force could make the shift from a full-time labor force to a part-time one simply unprofitable.

The geniuses who came up with the notion of turning full-time tellers into part time workers will probably howl at my proposals and protest that they need the "flexibility." But I don't see them putting managers on part-time pay. If they needed the flexibility, why couldn't tellers be trained to do more than one job or to work new equipment? As many as 3,000 employees are being trained as disposable workers.

The California Labor Federation has the right idea. They've closed one of their accounts with B of A, and asked others to do likewise. The notion of a consumer boycott tied to the treatment of workers is an intriguing one. It challenges workers to act in their self-interest and signals the bank that they don't benefit from policies that hurt other workers. With no shortage of banks in California, and no other bank indicating that it is planning such draconian labor policies, such a boycott ought to get B of A's attention soon enough.

But in the past decade or so, workers have rarely been able to organize to act in their own interest. With the unemployment rate in California inching toward 10 percent, it is possible that many workers, instead of protesting, will compete long and hard for those 19-hour-a-week jobs. The populism that swept Bill Clinton into office has yet to be translated into a movement for an economic democracy and for labor market fairness. Too many people worship profit as if it were a deity, impervious to the people that are trampled in its pursuit.

The high corporate profits that Bank of America seeks won't turn this economy around, even if it invests part of those earnings back into its plant and equipment. People are the backbone of the economy, and despite a rising Dow Jones Industrial Average, more housing starts, and a general air of optimism, people are hurting. Coupling an announcement of a $1.5 billion dollar profit with news that people's jobs will turn from full-time to part-time is an "in your face" move that tells tellers, the unemployed, and maybe its patrons that profits come before people. A consumer boycott of the bank might remind B of A that people generate profits.

King Features, February, 1993

INSUFFICIENT FUNDS AT THE BOTTOM AND THE TOP

If you really want evidence of our nation's bifurcation, consider first the poverty statistics released in early October and then take a look at that month's issue of *Worth* magazine.

The poverty data indicate that nearly 37 million Americans (36.9 million to be exact), or 14.5 percent of us, live in poverty. That is 1.2 million more people since last year. This is the most poverty our nation has experienced since 1962 when 38.6 million Americans were considered poor.

Of course, the poverty is not evenly distributed. One-third of all African Americans live in poverty, as do nearly 30 percent of all Latinos. And despite the notion that Asian Americans are a "model minority" with favored economic status, poverty among them, at 12.5 percent, is higher than among whites, at 9.6 percent.

According to the Children's Defense Fund, for the fourth consecutive year the number of poor children also rose. Twenty-two percent of all children in the United States, and nearly half of all African American children, live in poverty.

But "child poverty" can be deceiving.

Poor children exist in the context of poor families, of unemployed parents. In many ways, a focus on child poverty allows us to forget that we cannot make public policy to help poor children without taking into account the status of their parents.

But while the poverty rate has inched up, there has been much talk of economic optimism in Washington. Gross domestic product grew by 1.2 percent in 1992 after falling the previous year. Retail sales were up 5.9 percent in 1992 ($1.9 trillion worth of goods were sold). Consumer confidence is up and housing starts are up. So why the increase in poverty?

For one thing, the rising number of part-time workers is having its effect on the economy. For another, there is the growing number of people without health care insurance who are easily bankrupted by any medical emergency. And there is the growing number of people who simply do not participate in the labor market (the unemployed).

While there may be cause for economic optimism at the top, that same optimism does not always trickle down.

Does it trickle at all?

The *Worth* magazine we mentioned earlier features a profile of that handful of families with annual incomes of $100,000 and above (4.3 percent of all families). "An income of $100,000 no longer can be considered rich," says the magazine. Pity those non-rich whose incomes are nearly triple the $35,000 median income for a family of four in this country. According to *Worth*, they save less, spend more, and feel worse. Feel worse than who, pray tell? Donald Trump? And if Trump feels badly it may have more to do with his murky personal life than his financial status.

The magazine makes it easy to understand resistance to tax increases on the rich. These stressed families who "feel worse" simply cannot understand the plight of the poor, nor feel any responsibility to them. Perhaps they do not understand that part-time employment and downsizing keep their dividend checks high.

In a nation where 37 million people (one in seven of us) live in poverty, it seems unconscionable that there are people complaining that $100,000 is not enough money to live on for one year. In this nation of high contrast, there were 608,000 housing starts in 1992 and probably three times that many people sleeping on the streets. No wonder Congress is strangled by gridlock and policy consensus is so hard to come by.

There are several definitions of "not enough money" in our country. Thirty-seven million perceive "insufficient funds" as earning below the $14,000 poverty line. Another 10 million define insufficient funds as the $100,000 earned each year. It is the whining petulance of those with six-figure incomes that has made it so difficult for our nation to tackle the poverty that has grown despite improved economic indicators.

King Features, October, 1993

THINKING ABOUT BOYCOTTS

A Black woman was pushed, shoved, and possibly beaten in a Brooklyn store this January. She was accused, it seems, of shoplifting, but to justify a beating because of possible shoplifting is like justifying a murder because someone is driving without a license.

Just as the accusation of shoplifting is incidental, so too is the fact that the shop owner was Korean. From where I sit, it is entirely appropriate that black community activists in Brooklyn are boycotting a store where owners and managers can't bother to treat people with courtesy and dignity. I fail to understand how New York Mayor David Dinkins could describe the boycott as "ongoing intimidation" and offer to mediate it.

The real intimidation takes place when black shoppers are subject to ongoing differential treatment when they try to spend their money. Maybe Mayor Dinkins, now shielded from that difference by his office, has forgotten how infuriating it can be to wait in line and have some long elbowed white man push you out of the way. How annoying it can be to stand at a department store counter and either be ignored or accused of shoplifting or tag-switching. How frustrating it can be to call these slights to someone's attention, only to be told that race is not an issue.

I have been thinking about race and boycotts, especially as I review the ways and places that I spend my money. Sometimes treatment I have perceived as racial or insulting has caused me to push a point, to write a letter, or to get in someone's face. Other times, I decide the confrontation isn't worth it, or the people are too close-minded. I vote with my feet, taking my attitude and business with me.

I have been thinking of boycotts after I stormed out of a local woman's bookstore recently. The woman at the desk wanted to take my bag, but she asked brusquely, roughly, and wouldn't listen to my explanation that my purse, though large, was my purse, not a tote. I decided to avoid the place for awhile and repeated the decision to friends. One of them asked if I'd have done the same at Saks or I. Magnin. No, I told her, I'd have asked for the manager and talked lawsuit if I thought treatment was unfair or differential. In this case, instead, I walked away and will encourage my friends to do same.

Race may or may not be an issue at the woman's bookstore. It may or may not be the issue at the Brooklyn fruitstand. All of us who spend money at commercial establishments have a right to be treated with respect. When we aren't we have the right to say "enough," to choose not to patronize a store owned by someone who doesn't offer respect. We have every right to tell friends and colleagues to do the same thing. We would be remiss if we kept silent — silence might subject another woman, another shopper, to the same kind of treatment. At some level, the woman in Brooklyn whose actions triggered a boycott is as much a heroine as Rosa Parks, the woman who would not go to the back of the bus one more time.

Bus companies in Montgomery lost money because of the Rosa Parks boycott. Greyhound has lost so much money from its picket line that it is now filing for bankruptcy. Now a grocer is losing money in Brooklyn. People aren't obliged to spend their money someplace where they can't get a minimum amount of respect and are entitled to inconvenience themselves, if they wish, by walking a few blocks out of the way to get decent treatment.

Some withdrawals of patronage are small and personal, like my retreat from the woman's bookstore one Saturday. Other boycotts are long and loud and confrontive. Either way they make a point. No one should spend their money where they are not respected.

But much of what I think about the Brooklyn boycott is amazement at "our" Mayor Dinkins. There is no way, after all, that a physical attack on a black woman can be minimized, not even by a well-meaning black mayor. No law, no mediation, can force Brooklynites to patronize a store that offers inadequate service. People have a right to vote with their feet, to put their money where their mouth is.

For a shopkeeper, shoving and jostling a customer may be no big thing. For a community pushed too long, that last shove in Brooklyn was an outrage. And for me, on a much smaller scale, a harsh word at a woman's bookstore was enough to repel me.

One of the few ways a consumer can get satisfaction is by putting her money where her mouth is, by voting on the quality of service with her feet.

Sun Reporter, February, 1989

THE POOR AND THE STATE OF THE UNION

"If you can't dazzle them with brilliance, baffle them with them bulls—t," read the sign on the door of one of my graduate school classrooms. I thought of that sign as I listened to President Clinton's State of the Union Address. Despite the bursts of applause and the standing ovations, the hour-long talk offered few surprises and little for the nation's poorest citizens. And much of the talk of shared sacrifice, belt-tightening, and "patriotism" seemed targeted squarely at the middle class, not those at the bottom.

To be sure, the bulk of tax increases will be borne by those who make more than $100,000 per year and the earned income tax credit will help the working poor. But there was little in the State of the Union Address for the unemployed poor, and little mention of those urban areas that have been ignored by federal policy for the past decade.

Yes, I heard mention of Head Start and immunization programs targeted at children. And I heard mention of greater availability of college loans. I heard about community development banks and enterprise zones. But I didn't hear mention of an increase in the minimum wage. And I thought the attack on welfare recipients represented pandering to those who blame public assistance for all our country's ills.

Public assistance costs $14 billion a year. The deficit exceeds $350 billion. Totally eliminating public assistance would not begin to eliminate the deficit, and the proposal to move people from welfare to work in a two year period seems unrealistic unless the President plans a larger public works program than he proposed in his speech.

As I listened to the President, I imagined that I was one of the residents of South Central Los Angeles that shook hands with him last May when he walked through the ruins of the rebellion that followed the LAPD "not guilty" verdicts. Was there anything in the hour-long economic message that spoke to the gang member, the unemployed youngster, the high school dropout? I didn't hear much except the notion that if the economy turns around everyone benefits. But with 10 million officially unemployed Americans, the Clinton proposal to create about 700,000 jobs seems like a drop in the bucket. How will these jobs be targeted? Why no special word to the inner city poor? Clinton certainly spoke directly to the middle class several times in his address. And he pleaded with the rich to accept a greater tax burden. But the poor, those at the bottom, seemed invisible.

I would have liked to hear the President say more about eliminating poverty in this country. I would have liked him to say more about the need for affordable child care. I would have liked to hear him talk about the eradication of bias in markets, especially in banking and in employment. Economic revitalization simply won't happen evenly. Some will gain before others will. This issue is not simply economic revitalization, but helping those who need the most help, who have been left out of the 1980's expansion.

The State of the Union Address was, by necessity, a broad brush. Many of the details will be presented before Congress in the weeks to come. Many other details will be discussed with the American people in the massive public relations effort that the President and his Cabinet have planned for the next week or so. I want to know if he will say the same things to a wealthy family in Scarsdale as he does to an unemployed youngster in South Central Los Angeles. And I wonder if he knows how many people heard his talk and wondered who he meant when he said "we?"

King Features, February, 1993

WHICH PEOPLE COME FIRST?

When President Clinton failed to mention an increased

minimum wage as part of his State of the Union message in February of 1993, I felt a sick feeling in the pit of my stomach. The candidate who pledged to put the people first had turned into the President who would rank the poorest wage earners last.

Not much has changed since that moment. Indeed, since then President Clinton has made it clear how completely he could ignore those at the bottom. His indication that minimum wage increases would have to wait suggests that poor workers are at the bottom of his list. The White House says that business balks at a higher minimum wage. But those who have no strength to balk are stuck.

About 5.6 million workers earn the minimum wage. Two-thirds of them are women; 85 percent are adults. A disproportionate number (15.5 percent African American, 12.9 percent Latino) are minority, and more than 40 percent are full-time workers. While it is true that these 5.6 million workers are a small part (5.7 percent) of the labor market, it is also true that many of these workers head households and are responsible for supporting children. The minimum wage was stuck at $3.35 an hour from 1981 until 1989, when inflation eroded the value of the wage substantially. When the wage rose, first to $3.80 an hour in 1990, then to $4.25 an hour where it has been stuck since, the increase failed to compensate for the effects of the 1981-89 period. And while the average wage has risen steadily, the minimum wage has been stuck. In turning his back on minimum wage workers, the President has indicated that their status is as secondary to him as it is to those who employ them.

Who are these minimum wage workers? They work as private household workers, as home health care workers, as chicken processors, as service workers. They park cars, pump gas, and watch children. But even as they watch other people's children, they worry about their own — as many as a third of those who earn the minimum wage are household heads or help to support families.

32

If President Clinton believes in putting people first, these minimum wage workers will be his first, not his last, priority. He won't be so quick to kick them to the curb as he curries after the favor of the business lobby. He'll earn more favor, although not more lobby dollars, by addressing himself to the 5.6 million at the bottom instead of those few thousand at the top.

USA Today, June, 1993

TIME CERTAIN OR ECONOMY CERTAIN

Welfare reform? President Clinton says he wants to change the current system to set a "time certain, beyond which people don't draw a check for doing nothing when they could be doing something." This suggests that the millions that receive public assistance are sitting around twiddling their thumbs waiting for marching orders to do, simply, something. This is absolutely not the case.

When the states have had the option of modifying AFDC rules, they've erred on the punitive side. New Jersey says it will not pay women who have additional children after they get on the welfare rolls. California proposed to cut parents with children after six months. Wisconsin's "learnfare" program would reduce the checks for families whose children don't attend school regularly. In penalizing families, have the governors of some states ignored the effect their actions will have on needy children?

Maybe they don't care. Because these children are poor children, maybe they feel distant from their fates. Or maybe they have identified the bugaboo "welfare" as a problem, without thinking about the people the system affects. To be sure, the welfare system is cumbersome and rigid, badly in need of reform. It simply is not clear to me that we need to replace one form of rigidity with another, and that "time certain" dates to find jobs really work.

The real issues here are economics, child care and

health care. Most of those who receive public assistance would not if they could find paying jobs, good health care, and affordable child care. They don't need the stick of "time certain" deadlines, but the carrot of employment opportunities and incentives. President Clinton responds to one constituency by speaking sternly to welfare recipients, but he leaves those of us who believe in labor market fairness cold when he promises to punish those who are as much labor market victims as millions of unemployed workers.

USA Today, February, 1993

THIN LINE BETWEEN UNEMPLOYED AND WELFARE

The President and Congress are just about to reach agreement that unemployment benefits must be extended yet again. A year ago, President Bush refused to sign such a measure, but what a difference a year makes! Whether it is the polls, the economy, or the pending election, President Bush seems to have changed his tune about unemployment benefits.

He hasn't changed his tune about public assistance. In the same State of the Union address where he preached compassion for the jobless, he offered little comfort for those who get public assistance. This, too, may be a result of polls and public perceptions. Too many hear the words "public assistance" and think lazy, dependent, free spending.

But a range of people receive public assistance. Some are old people who earned so little in their lifetimes that they need a supplement to their Social Security check. Disabled people, veterans, and those who receive Aid to Families with Dependent Children (AFDC) also get help from the government. In all, our government spends about $350 billion each year on all forms of public assistance (this does not include Social Security) — just 6 percent of the total gross national product.

The AFDC program is the lightening rod for the ire of politicians from President Bush to David Duke, to New Jersey Governor Jim Florio, to California Governor Pete Wilson. These men have categorized the AFDC program as one that fosters dependency and needs reform. Worse, they have implicitly suggested that the majority of those receiving AFDC are African American, giving the welfare reform discussion an ugly racial cast that obscures the fact that the majority of those receiving AFDC are poor children, not adults.

Black people are not the majority of welfare recipients — though 12 percent of the population, we are about a third of those who receive welfare. The majority of those who need a helping hand are white. Some people are on welfare because they never worked, but the majority have worked in low paying jobs and spent months, not years, receiving public assistance. Some of those on welfare can't qualify for unemployment insurance because they hold several part-time jobs to accommodate child care needs, instead of one full-time one. Some on welfare have received unemployment insurance and turned to public assistance only when those benefits ran out.

In any case, only a handful of the poor receive public assistance — 13 percent of all black families and 3.3 percent of all white families. Numerically far more whites receive public assistance than blacks.

The same is true of the food stamp program, which benefited one in ten American families in 1991. Of the 23.76 million receiving food stamps, 46 percent were white, 37 percent black, and 13 percent Hispanic. Is this a black-dominated program? Hardly.

But the governors and the President have pandered to racial stereotypes by pushing provisions that would freeze benefits and family size, implying that women on welfare deliberately have children to raise their AFDC payments by a mere $64 per month. Other provisions, which speak to "responsibility," all suggest that AFDC recipients are irresponsible. Many of them are simply unemployed people who cannot find work that pays enough to support their families.

The AFDC program could use reform, but not in the ways the new reformists suggest. Provide the very poor with access to health care, so they don't have to leave low paying jobs that don't provide it when their children get sick. Allow recipients to go to school while receiving aid, so they can learn skills that better suit them to the labor market. Of course, with unemployment rates as high as they are, skill training may not yield jobs.

This is the connection between high unemployment rates and the bulging welfare rolls. The recession has meant hard times for most Americans. But some get compassion, and others the cold shoulder because politicians need someone to blame for budgets that don't balance.

King Features, February, 1992

DO UNIONS HAVE A FUTURE?

William Jefferson Clinton was elected with the help of the labor movement, with the strong endorsement of the National Education Association, of the AFL-CIO. A year ago people were calling then candidate Clinton a pawn of labor, and the convention floor in New York City was peppered with representatives of organized labor. But those who decided that Clinton would be putty in labor's hand ignored a key fact. Arkansas is a low-wage, right-to-work state that has never put out the welcome mat for organized labor. Though Ross Perot's chicken charts drew chuckles, there was a grain of truth to his caution about the kinds of jobs Clinton developed in his home state.

Now Clinton has put the lion and the lamb together, bringing the Labor and Commerce Departments together in a late July conference on the "Future of the American

Workplace." The Chicago conference talked about labor - management cooperation, about ways to bring adversaries to the table, about the fact that "what is good for the company is good for employees." The word "empowerment" was bandied about a bit, as was the notion that workers must play a role in labor market restructuring. From the press releases I read, though, people tiptoed around key issues that will determine whether the trade union movement flourishes or dies.

Where does the profit motive go when labor meets management? Good workers mean good business in the long run, but in the short run too many managers are driven by profit and little else. If profit means cutting salaries or eliminating divisions, they'll do it. If it means finding cheap labor in the Pacific Rim or the Caribbean Basin, they'll do it. If it means sending capital abroad, to countries where there are fewer environmental regulations, they'll do it. How can a worker fight that?

"Gain-sharing," the new buzzword for profit sharing, was dangled in front of workers as an alternative to pay increases. How many executives have their pay exclusively determined by profits? I've seen too many reports of CEO's whose pay goes up while stock prices go down to have much faith in the notion that pay and profits go hand in hand for everyone. Furthermore, the gain-sharing concept says little about terms and conditions of work, an area where unions have historically been important.

A conference on the future of the American workplace is about talk and window trimming unless the conversation turns to the average worker, the guy or gal who wants nothing more than to get up in the morning, go to work, put in a good day's work, go home, the worker who wants little more than fair pay, health insurance, decent vacation and other benefits. These are workers who will buy into retraining if they have help to do it, workers who will put in the overtime if it pays well. They are workers who want no more than management does, a piece of the pie.

How much pie do workers give up when they come to the table to talk to management as if they are allies and not adversaries? Are there any crumbs left for the workers who have been, to date, locked out of the labor market, the 10 million who are unemployed, and the additional millions who are underemployed or discouraged workers? Does this new notion of gain-sharing and worker cooperation speak to the needs of those who stand at the periphery of the labor market, waiting for a chance? Will a movement forced to accept tiered wages work for the interests of those who want to enter an industry?

The Union movement has its roots in the notion that it took organized workers to stand up to management, already organized around the goal of maximizing profit. One can tiptoe around the notion that workers and management are natural adversaries when short-term profits are the ultimate goal, but one look at the status of organized labor in Arkansas suggests that workers should not tiptoe, but march and scream and shout the need for fair play.

King Features, July, 1993

EXPORTING EXPLOITATION

"Rosa Martinez produces apparel for US markets on her sewing machine in El Salvador," the ad reads. "You can hire her for 57 cents an hour." The same company produced an identical ad a year later, except Rosa Martinez's wages had dropped almost 50 percent, to 33 cents an hour. I am not sure whether to be more horrified by the low level of Rosa Martinez's wages, or by the fact that United States tax dollars paid to place the ad.

When President Bush said he'd create 30 million jobs in eight years, he didn't say where he planned to create them. Thanks to the US Agency for International Development (USAID), our country has been effective at creating jobs in the Caribbean Basin and Central America. Meanwhile, plants have been closing at home and real wages have fallen to their lowest level since 1963.

A group of US-based international trade unions came together to investigate the connection between job loss at home and job development in Central America. They were especially concerned about labor and human rights violations in Central America, and so they sent delegations of union officials on fact-finding missions to El Salvador, Honduras, Costa Rica and other countries. The results of their work is detailed in a report called "Paying to Lose Our Jobs."

In the report, the National Labor Committee Education Fund in Support of Worker and Human Rights in Central America (NLC) reveals that the Reagan and Bush Administrations have spent more than a billion dollars promoting company flight from the United States. Companies get away with paying a fraction of the wages they'd pay here, but the money they pay represents just 15 percent of a family's need in these Central American countries. Exporting poverty abroad exacerbates poverty at home, since job scarcity pushes wages downward. Manufacturing and textile workers in the United States are making less than they were a decade ago, and having a more difficult time finding employment. Meanwhile, their jobs are leaving the country with US financing.

Perry Manufacturing is an interesting case in point. The apparel assembly company employs 900 workers at two plants in the San Bartolo Free Trade Zone. Assisted by a loan guarantee from the US Overseas Private Investment Corporation, Perry imported cut fabric and machinery from the United States for the assembly, then shipped finished garments back for sale in stores like JC Penny, WalMart, and K-Mart. While expanding operations in San Bartolo, the group that owns Perry Manufacturing, the Marcade Group, put 1,499 US workers out of work, closing plants and reducing operations at several US locations.

Workers at home aren't the only ones hurt. Workers in free trade zones chafe at oppressive working conditions and are threatened with blacklisting when they complain or attempt to organize. Ninety-five percent of those employed in free trade zones are women. More than half of them are under 18. Average pay for a 44 hour week is about $22; gross annual income runs about $1,300. Most of the women employees say they work hard to keep up with their quotas and if they fail to make that quota, they're punished, including by physical beatings. More than three-quarters of the women received no sick pay, and all suffered ailments caused by pollution in the factory.

While minimum wage laws prevent United States employers from offering as little pay as companies do in free trade zones, our failure to enforce health and safety laws have caused conditions in some factories at home to resemble conditions in Central America. As I read about the conditions under which Honduran women labored, I could not help but think of the brutally inhumane conditions under which food processing workers are employed in the United States. Carpel tunnel syndrome is common at the Delta Pride catfish manufacturing plant in the Mississippi Delta, while the safety conditions at Imperial Foods in Hamlet, North Carolina caused the death of 25 workers. We seem to have exported more than poor working conditions with our investment in Central American free zones, though. We have exported an attitude that work is to be devalued, and that workers cannot earn a living wage. Is there any wonder President Bush has refused to sign family and medical leave legislation here? After all, no such provision exists for Central American workers.

King Features, October, 1992

WHATEVER HAPPENED TO URBAN POLICY?

Does America need cities? The Economic Policy Institute, a DC based think tank, asked this provocative question in a report it issued. Since the report was partly supported by the US Conference of Mayors, it is not surprising that it concentrated on the strengths that urban areas bring to the United States economy. What was startling was the decreasing amount of support that cities get from the federal and state government. Federal support of cities dropped by more than half between 1978 and 1987 — from 9 percent to less than 4.2 percent. State support of cities has also dropped, though not as dramatically. No wonder most cities face fiscal problems, with more than 60 percent expecting spending to exceed revenue this year.

The words "urban policy" have barely been spoken in this Presidential campaign. I don't expect to hear those words pass President Bush's lips. After all, his definition of urban policy has been to sell housing projects to current tenants, to ask for more money for crime prevention, and to fete Los Angeles Police Chief Darryl Gates at the White House. But cities are part of the Democratic coalition — they are blacker, browner, more female, and poorer than the general population. Those who provide city services are on "overload," serving more people in dire straits than they did a decade ago. Three quarters of all Americans live in metropolitan areas, either central cities, or suburbs. Nearly all of us are affected by the state of our cities, which provide "cultural, medical, recreational, and educational facilities" used by those who don't live inside cities. So why has so little been said about urban policy by Democrats this time around? Is it because when more people think of cities, they think of crime and drugs, and not the positive things cities bring to our lives?

To be sure, Rev. Jesse Jackson has preached about the status of cities, and marched through cities that face bankruptcy to draw attention to their plight. Aspects of his focus on infrastructure investment have been incorporated into candidate Clinton's stump speech. But as the candidates approach the New York primary and campaign for votes in New York City, it is clear that despite rhetoric, they are targeting little of their message to urban areas. Do they think the "middle class" they've pandered is solely a suburban middle class? Think again! More than half of all African Americans with incomes over $50,000 live in central cities, as do about a quarter of all whites with similar incomes.

Maybe Democratic candidates have ignored urban issues in favor of overall economic policy, figuring that if the economy improves and people get back to work, then the economic status of cities will improve. But if the 80's didn't teach us anything else, they taught us that a rising tide doesn't lift every boat. That's why the National Urban League talks about an Urban Marshall Plan, a massive investment in human and physical capital. They say their proposal isn't a social program, but "an economic investment program." Spend money on sewers and solid-waste disposal, on education and training, says Billy Tidwell of the Urban League.

Where will the money come from? Both the Urban League and the Economic Policy Institute speak of a "peace dividend," but the Urban League goes further and says that it isn't a matter of funding, but a matter of priorities. The investment pays, they say, and they have the numbers to support the argument.

Democratic candidates Clinton and Brown are giving urban policy the cold shoulder, even as they plunder through cities for votes. If these candidates believe we need our cities, they need to say so.

King Features, April, 1992

HOMELESSNESS IS AN ECONOMIC CASUALTY

The man is as much a fixture on his corner as a lamp post or a hydrant. He stands muttering a muted mantra, spare change, spare change. You don't have to hear the mumbled phrase to know he is looking for money — his hands are cupped and from time to time he jingles the loose coins in his palms.

Around the corner, a woman sits next to the piece of cardboard that tells her life story. The word "homeless" stands out on the piece of soiled cardboard, so does the word "baby." The woman holds a Styrofoam cup in her hand but, like the man with the mantra, says little. If she catches your eye she may ask, "Do you have any change?" but she is as likely to simply move the cup an inch or so in your direction.

There are thousands of men and women who make a few dollars panhandling each day, hundreds of thousands who sleep in shelters or on city streets each night. Some people see them as urban blight, others as mental health casualties. Why are so many people homeless, and why have the numbers seemed to grow so much in the past decade? Ball State University economist Cecil Bohanan, looking at variations in homelessness across 60 cities, says the main cause of homelessness is economic.

According to Bohanan's study, which appeared in the *Social Science Quarterly* in December 1991, the cities with the highest levels of homelessness were those with the highest rents and unemployment rates. Other factors, like climate and the availability of public assistance, didn't explain homelessness at all. Bohanan noted that the poor might have more mental health problems than others — cities with higher levels of mental hospital institutionalization had lower levels of homelessness. But the mental health variable explains much less homelessness than unemployment and housing costs. Bohanan concludes, "Although the ranks of homeless may disproportionately contain those with profound personal and mental health problems, the evidence suggests that they would respond to general changes in the economic environment."

Cecil Bohanan's study offers policymakers both good and bad news. The good news is this narrows our focus—if we worry about housing prices, housing stock, and jobs instead of the attitudes and behavior of the homeless, we'd go a long way toward solving their problems. But the bad news is that some politicians enjoy the behavioral rhetoric, especially in the context of economic stagnancy. With most cities crying "broke," and with Congress and the President at loggerheads over domestic policy, there is little money to increase the housing stock (thus lowering rents) in cities with lots of homelessness.

It's easier to suggest that homeless people have personal problems than economic problems. If they have personal problems they are different from the rest of us, flawed somehow in a way we are not. But it they have economic problems then they have much in common with the 10 million people who are officially unemployed, the additional millions who are underemployed. If their problems are economic, they have much in common with all of us, and for some that seems a disturbing thought.

That's why, I suppose, people have challenged the right of panhandlers to ask for money in subways, or the right of homeless people to loiter in libraries. The homeless, it seems, should be neither seen nor heard, lest they shatter the shaky sense of security that so many of us have. Job losses, bankruptcies, plant closings, these are the economic casualties that we fear. It is important to remember that homelessness is not a simple matter of human failure, but another economic casualty.

King Features, April, 1992

WHAT'S A SENATOR WORTH?

Should a US Senator be paid $125,000 a year, instead of the $101,900 pay earned before Wednesday night's vote? It depends on your reference point. The average full-time experienced male worker earned about $800 a week in 1988, or about $42,000 a year, about a third of what a Senator earns. Does a Senator do the work, or have the worth, of three experienced men? Based on the mess they have made of our budget, the way they averted their gaze from the spiraling S&L mess, the answer would have to be a resounding "no."

On the other hand, Senators made a little less than Congressional representatives until the pay adjustment, and both the Senate and the House do the same kinds of work. Should Senators make less than their colleagues, even though they could make up the difference in speakers' fees?

Members of both the Senate and the House of Representatives make much less than industry leaders, who collect salaries that make $125,000 look like peanuts. Corporate CEO's had an average 1989 pre-tax salary of $612,800. Whether their companies made money or lost it, multi-million dollar salaries and stock market options were not unusual.

Athletes, too, earn sums that dwarf political pay. Ricky Henderson didn't want to report to baseball training camp this spring until his $3 million plus salary was adjusted. Mike Tyson has earned $20 million for spending seconds in the ring. Michael Jordan gets $2 million to leap at a can of Coca Cola on television. If the market will bear $2 million for a soda commercial, ought it not provide $125,000 for a Senator?

But then this question is relative. Senators aren't only paid in dollars. They collect prestige and perks. They pay a few pennies for a haircut, get a gym and a health plan thrown in for free. They don't pay for their mail, using the "frank" instead, to build up name recognition and secure their incumbency for the next election. The $125,000 they collect may be the least of their benefits. And if the pay is too little, they can always resign and let the challengers biting at their heels have a chance.

Not only a relative question, Senatorial pay is also a question of relatives — like Rockefellers, Kennedys, Gores and Qualyes. The Senate is one of the largest millionaires' clubs in the country. Why not ask them to serve for a dollar and all the prestige they can handle?

As politicians say, timing is everything. With the budget going bust and thousands of American workers facing pink slips, this seems a strange time for the Senate to vote itself a pay raise, and an appropriate time for all of us to ask what a Senator is worth.

USA Today, July, 1991

TAX THE LAYOFF LINE-UP

A year ago, at the beginning of the recession, I didn't know anyone who had lost their job. Sure, I knew the jobless, the homeless, and folk on the periphery. But I had not had a conversation with a soul who had experienced paycheck interruptus, the shock that happens when that periodic paycheck stops.

This time last year, I knew we were in a recession. I am, after all, an economist, one of those folks trained at tracking trends. Recession, the numbers said, and I believed it. But it had not hit home.

A year later, some economists are talking recovery. Tepid, yes, and a little stale, but a recovery nonetheless. Like them, I see the numbers, but this year I hear the people who work at Apple and IBM and General Motors and the Post Office. The nightly news has become the "layoff litany," with words like "downsize" and "streamline" substituting for the ugly reality of "pink slip." This year, I not only know people who have lost their jobs, but there is a buzz buzz buzz among those who have jobs. Will I keep it? Can I secure it? If I am asked to work twice as hard for half the pay, am I up to the task?

This time last year, there were half a million of our troops in the Persian Gulf. Now, most of those troops have come home, and some have resumed life as they knew it. How many, though, came home to stand in an unemployment line? How many were casualties of this recession?

When companies announce their layoffs, they make

an appeal to their bottom line which is, after all, profits. They need to cut back, they say, because people aren't spending, people aren't buying, because they need to be responsible to their stockholders. And it is true that if they lower their wage bill they'll lower their expenses, increase their profit, and stockholders will rejoice.

But before they get out the tambourines, it makes sense to ask about the long term effect of the layoffs that have taken place in the past month. More than half a million workers lost their jobs and the hardship they experience will send ripples through our economy. If they can't work, they can't pay rent, or buy food or Christmas presents. Instead of buying a pair of socks, should not our President send a stronger signal about this recession and the path to recovery?

For starters, those firms who have lined up their layoffs should be taxed to reflect the damage they cause our economy. And then, those who hire the long-term unemployed should receive tax credits to reward them for solving a problem. Finally, if our President wants to send a signal, he should hire someone who has been laid off, instead of buying socks that he probably doesn't need.

President Bush says he will address economic issues a month or so from now in his State of the Union address. In a month another half a million people may have lost their jobs. A big part of our recovery will be consumer confidence, the extent to which people feel good about our economy's future. But it's hard for workers to feel good when they know others who have been laid off, when they fear layoffs themselves.

If our President floated the idea of a layoffs tax, he might slow the rate of layoffs and assure workers he is in their corner. Or, he can spend the holiday season playing golf, buying socks, reminding us how distant he is from our ordinary, about-to-be-laid-off lives.

King Features, December, 1990

47

CONSUMPTION TAX IS A BAD IDEA

The tax burden shifted in the 1980's, with corporations paying proportionately less, and the middle class shouldering proportionately more, of the tax burden. The number of rich people (with incomes over a million dollars a year) paying the minimum tax plummeted by 85 percent between 1986 and 1989, according to Donald B. Bartlett and James Steele in their prize-winning book, *America: What Went Wrong?* Murray Widdenbaum's proposal to tax only consumption spending continues the trend to force those with the least means to pay the greatest share of the tax burden. It is both regressive and wrong.

Those with lower incomes say less and by necessity consume more. Many went into debt to survive the lousy hand the economy dealt them in the 1980's and early 1990's — pay cuts, unemployment, uninsured health expenditures. These families are burdened, not assisted, by a proposal that excludes investment from taxation.

The average American family of four has an income of about $35,000 a year. Real weekly wages have been stagnant or falling in each of the past five years. As admirable as an emphasis on investment is, it is out of step with the economic reality that many families face, and with the struggle that some shoulder to make ends meet.

To be sure, the poorest of families can be shielded from this notion of consumption tax with a combination of exemptions and deductions. But then the Weidenbaum proposal has the potential of becoming as burdened and confusing as the current tax system. There are many ways that we can alter our income tax system to make it more fair to individuals and to encourage long-term growth. But we needn't hurt the poor and middle-income through a consumption tax to achieve that end.

USA Today, December, 1992

WILL NAFTA FAIL BECAUSE LABOR DISTRUSTS GOVERNMENT?

When President Clinton visited Northern California for the AFL-CIO convention, he argued that the North American Free Trade Agreement would create high-wage American jobs. Since California's economy is experiencing doldrums, one might have thought that his remarks would be welcomed. But few were swayed to support NAFTA by the President's remarks. Indeed, organized labor has provided the most stringent opposition to the trade agreement.

The President says he understands. He told the AFL-CIO that "people are so insecure in their jobs, they're so uncertain that the people they work for care about them, they're so uncertain about what their kids are looking at in the future, that people are reluctant to take any risks for change." He might have added that Labor Secretary Reich's opposition to providing adjustment assistance to workers affected by NAFTA may partly fuel labor's opposition to the pact.

To be sure, Reich says he prefers to develop a "comprehensive" employment and training program that will help displaced workers make the transition between obsolete industries and those that are growing, and provide unemployed workers with the training they need to find new jobs. His proposal represents an improvement in government employment and training policy, but for many in labor, it is simply not enough, and for those who will lose jobs because of NAFTA, it does not recognize their unique predicament.

Mary Greene, a former Braniff flight attendant who lives in Manhattan, Kansas, scoffs at government promises as simply nothing more than empty rhetoric. "Why should we rely on them for displacement assistance, when they have yet to meet promises to displaced airline employees?" Greene says that government promises were a joke to displaced airline workers. When Braniff folded, Greene be-

lieved that workers like her would get first hiring preference at other airlines. Instead, her life has been an uphill
struggle, and she now works as a substitute teacher. No
one paid attention to the employee protection provisions
of the Airline Deregulation Act of 1978, says Greene. Why
will they pay attention to adjustment assistance provisions
related to NAFTA?

Greene's point is reinforced by business opposition
to President Clinton's appointment of William Gould IV to
chair the National Labor Relations Board. Gould, a prolific
and highly regarded Stanford professor, is perceived by
many to be too "pro-union." According to a representative of nearly half of the Fortune 500 companies, Gould is
"nowhere near mainstream." But most Fortune 500 companies describe the "mainstream" as hostile to labor. Indeed, the National Labor Relations Board was the source
of several organizing setbacks in the Reagan/Bush years.
While Gould's work indicates that he will not turn a chilly
shoulder to labor, it seems unreasonable to suggest he will
unfairly interpret the law.

The tendency of corporate America to define labor as
enemy, combined with the economic insecurity that comes
from restructuring, has created the labor antipathy toward
the North American Free Trade Agreement. If it is good
for corporate America, many in labor reason, it must not
be good for us. If the Fortune 500 want it, then they must
see some way to hurt us with it. If government promises
relief, we can't count on the promises, based on a historical record of broken promises.

The future of NAFTA may hinge on the President's
ability to turn labor attitudes around, to make workers feel
that they have a place at the table. But people like Mary
Greene have long memories, and corporate opposition to
stellar nominees like Bill Gould reminds them that labor's
interests differ sharply from those of management. If management favors NAFTA, what's in it for labor?

King Features, October, 1993

STATE BUDGETS IN A RECESSION

Is economic recovery imminent? President Bush has been saying so ever since government economists confirmed a recession. When the unemployment rate dropped from 7 percent in June to 6.8 percent in July, the President gleefully announced the economy's forward movement.

Little of his glee has been mirrored in state legislatures, since more than half of all states began their budget process with projected deficits. Most have had to balance their budgets by juggling higher taxes, worker layoffs, loans from state employee pension funds, and spending cuts.

And, though most state fiscal years began July 1, some legislatures are still hammering out budget compromises. For example, the California legislature is considering a measure to repeal the tax on snacks and newspapers it just passed in July. California's budget also hinges on an $800 million cut in workers pay, but unions have not agreed to mandatory furloughs. Georgia's governor has also faced union opposition to the furloughs he proposed. State legislators and public employee unions are on a collision course if the alternative to furloughs is layoffs.

Legislatures have become imaginative when it comes to proposing new budget-balancing taxes. Alabama will begin taxing medical prescriptions, while New York will tax computer software and dating services and impose a monthly fee for the use of cellular telephones. Pennsylvania will tax long distance telephone calls, while New Mexico will tax "amusement services." Massachusetts Governor William Weld was only able to keep his "read my lips, no new taxes" promise because a diligent part-time budget worker found that the federal government owed the state hundreds of millions of dollars.

Some states facing deficits hiked "sin" taxes on alcohol and tobacco, even though the federal government raised those taxes a year ago. If people did the right thing and cut back on their use of these products, legislatures would be in the same boat they started out in, collecting less revenue despite the higher tax. But states have to pay their bills somehow, and income and sales taxes have been the main way to pay these bills.

The burden of payment may not be equitable, and indeed may slow the pace of any recovery that economists project. According to the Center for Tax Justice, the burden of new state taxes falls heavily on the poor. The richest one percent of our population pays just 7.6 percent of their income in state and local taxes. The middle fifth, with average income at $39,000, pays about 10 percent, while the poorest fifth pay nearly 14 percent of their incomes on state and local taxes. None of the eight states that impose the heaviest relative burden on the poor and middle income – Nevada, Texas, Florida, Washington, South Dakota, Tennessee and Wyoming – have state income taxes. And most of the states that do tax personal income do so at a flat rate that imposes a heavier burden on the poor and middle income than the wealthy.

In addition to tax hikes, states have explored ways to cut spending that place workers at a disadvantage. Beyond forced furloughs and layoffs, at least three states have trimmed benefits in workman's compensation programs, while several have reduced their contribution to state pension funds in order to balance budgets. State educational, medical and social services have also been cut.

With so many states singing the budget blues, it is ludicrous that the President's economists forecast an imminent economic recovery. Those state legislatures that have wrangled over budget issues into the dog days of August have done so because they could not see the light at the end of recession's tunnel.

USA Today, August, 1991

LABOR DAY IMAGES AND REALITIES

For most of us, Labor Day is the signal that the summer has faded back to business as usual. For millions, though, Labor Day is about just that, organized labor and its role in improving the lot of workers. Workers — they are the people whose lives aren't televised, the people who empty garbage cans and bedpans, who type and take dictation, who flip burgers and fry chicken. These are the folk who earn pennies a minute, a little bit less than five dollars an hour, the people whose lives don't turn up as chic situation comedy work experiences.

If the only information you got about work came from television, you'd think that most people are doctors, lawyers, or writers, with a few private investigators thrown in for good measure. In truth, these folk represent less than a fifth of the labor market. If managers are thrown in, we're talking something still well under half. The majority of Americans work in those blue and pink collar jobs that defy television shorthand. They type and paint and fry and sweep. They combine incomes to get the $35,000 average income for a family of four. They worry about the economy, about taxes, about crime. Their stories lack the drama of drive-by shootings and abductions. They live their lives, devoid of the drama that rivets us all. Theirs is another drama — if the interest rate falls, does it make sense to refinance? If the crime rate rises, what does that mean to the sanctity of lives? If libraries or parks are open fewer hours, what does that mean to the way children spend their time? These are dramas that cannot be televised because there is no guts and glory in the story of everyday lives.

And yet, I think Labor Day reminds us of the dignity of everyday labor, of the way people work, and that they work, often at wages that cannot support a family. It reminds us of the hospital workers of Local 1199, of the clerical backbone that comes from unions like AFSME (Association of Federal, State and Municipal Employees). It reminds us not only of teachers, but also teacher's aides, who

53

provide services to youngsters trapped in underfunded urban schools. It reminds us of the women and men who deliver our mail, who rush our express packages to us in 24 hours. This day's work is as important as the work spotlighted by a television screen. But in this post-industrial era, we are eager to forget that group of workers who produce things, who manufacture steel, glass, and cars, or who work in textiles and food processing.

The image of work that we get from television is that of wisecracking, lip smacking jokesters who spend more time at pranks than production. That's an image that is at clear odds with the way most people work. While fewer than one in five workers belong to unions this Labor Day, many find the dignity of their work improved by the labor movement. More than the message of summer's end, Labor Day is a reminder that many Americans not only work hard for their money but are ignored when we think about work and working.

Hard work is something that is difficult to televise. But it's the backbone of our society. Somehow the lofty talk about job creation has to be paired with nitty-gritty talk about the kinds of jobs that are created. Do they pay $6 an hour, $8 an hour, $10 an hour, or more? Can those who hold new jobs support their families? Does the distance between workplace image and reality explain the way public policy takes blue and pink collar workers for granted?

King Features, September, 1993

DON'T BURDEN THE ELDERLY POOR

Sacrifice, President Clinton said, in his inauguration speech. Everybody nodded because we were willing to watch the other fellow suffer, not ourselves. But we're learning that there are no sacred cows for Bill Clinton. He's tackling entitlements like public assistance and Social Se-

54

curity as part of his budget balancing plan.

While I think we will all have to sacrifice, the proposal to freeze Social Security cost of living increases and perhaps to raise the retirement age to 67 is a mistake. It treats older people as if they are homogenous group, each equally able to shoulder a cost of living freeze, each equally able to work an additional two years.

It takes a professional to come up with the plan to raise the retirement age. Most lawyers, professors, and executives remain vigorous, active, and professionally involved even after mandatory retirement. But blue collar workers who do heavy physical labor breathe a sigh of relief at retirement time. Forcing them to work two more years is cruel.

African American men have a life expectancy of just 66 years. Thus the average black male workers will not live long enough to collect Social Security. I don't think these differences have been considered in the proposal to raise retirement age. The proposal indicates a certain occupational myopia and is insensitive to the millions of Americans whose jobs are physical. It's not just laborers that I'm talking about, but waitresses and home health workers who stand on their feet all day, sales workers and truck drivers whose jobs are physically taxing. Containing Social Security costs by focusing on these workers hardly seems fair.

Nor does it seem fair to freeze cost of living increases for all workers, without somehow taking the poorest of our elderly into account. About 10 percent of our nation's elderly live in poverty. Most of them are women, and a disproportionate number of them are women of color. Many of them have Social Security as a sole source of income and will be hard hit by a check that is frozen while prices rise.

It makes more sense to give all Social Security recipients a cost of living increase, then tax Social Security at the same progressive rates that other income is taxed. Those who receive other income along with Social Security will end up paying a few more dollars a year in taxes, while those whose sole support is Social Security will not be adversely affected. Advocating a freeze perhaps sends the signal that everyone, even the elderly, will be affected by our deficit, but the elderly poor, more than any other group in our population, need to be protected.

The deficit clearly threatens Clinton's programs of social reform. But it is both important and useful to remember where the deficit came from. Ronald Reagan managed to quadruple the deficit during his administration, borrowing heavily to expand the military budget. Our deficit has ballooned because of the savings and loan bailout, not social programs. Some say it makes no sense to point fingers, the deficit has to be reduced, no matter what its source. I say tax those industries that benefited most heavily from deficit spending. And leave the nation's elderly, especially the elderly poor, alone.

King Features, January, 1993

BOYCOTT JAPANESE PRODUCTS

Here they go again. Once a year the Japanese government lets loose with a racial slur. Once a year African American people get angry and get to hollering. Ads have been taken out in the *New York Times* (1986) in the spirit of "cooperation". Discussions and trade missions have been held to explore possibilities. Apologies have been requested and occasionally granted. And the dust clears. And they do it again.

About three weeks ago they compared black people to prostitutes, saying that when we move into neighborhoods, we, like prostitutes, cause property values to fall. Of course, we were outraged, and folk were about marching up to embassies and demanding apologies. But if anybody was demanding an apology it should not have been the NAACP, or any other set of civil rights organizations. It should have been the President or the Congress requesting this apology.

But they didn't, because they share the Japanese belief that African American people are inferior. They didn't because it wasn't a big thing to them. If a foreign justice minister had slurred Jews, Italians, or some other group, it might have sparked a response. But the bashing of black people happens so frequently that few find it alarming.

Even our so-called Rainbow allies are silent in the face of slurs. Asian-Americans are quick to tell us that they aren't model minorities, that they too sing America, that they have been baited and slurred and murdered for racism. Even as we share their pain over the killing of Vincent Chin, over the doors that slam in their face, we wonder why their voice doesn't ring out against this latest Japanese slight.

Obviously African Americans have no allies when it comes to these kind of slurs. Obviously we are fair game and will have to figure out an effective response to the racist nonsense that spews out of Japanese government mouths. Is racism a requirement to hold high office in Japan? Is that why they are doing so well as they "come to America," because they say some of the things that racist whites badly want to hear?

From where I sit the response to Japanese slurs needs to be a well-focused selective buying campaign. Black people need to stop buying Nintendo, Hitachi, Mitsubishi, Suzuki, Honda, Toyota, Sony, and all the rest of that mess. Otherwise we are funding the fools who feel free to slur us. Not only should we boycott, but we need to ask others who oppose Japanese racism to do the same thing, to bombard embassies with letters that include receipts of things we bought that were NOT made in Japan.

We also need to look long and hard at the way we are subsidizing the Japanese by our involvement in the Middle East. The subsidy is a direct one—from African American troops to Japanese soil. You see, the Japanese get more than a third of their oil from the Middle East, while the US gets just 20 percent of our oil from there. The Army protecting a "way of life" for those who slur us is disproportionately Black. Those who say that we cause property values to drop need to be reminded that but for our presence they might freeze in their precious property. Reminded? They need to be arm-twisted into acting as if they have sense.

But of course, it requires some sacrifice. It requires that African Americans draw some lines and stop this rhetoric. It requires that Asian Americans take some leadership and initiate a dialogue that we may find difficult with Japanese nationals who insist on bashing. It requires that the United States government treat African Americans like any other valued population group in this country and make it clear that off-the-cuff racist remarks are unacceptable, and an impediment to future trade relations.

I don't want any apologies from the Japanese government. I want the bashing to stop, and I want a fair share of their trade directed to the African American community in this country. Or, I want them to feel it in the economy, the only language they seem to understand. If they can't watch their lips, they may have to stop counting the yen that come from here. From where I sit, the Japanese can take their Sonys and shove them!

King Features, September, 1990

CHAPTER THREE

JUSTICE, PEACE AND CIVIC UNREST

License and registration are ugly words, especially if you are black and driving in the wrong place at the wrong time with the wrong set of flashing lights beckoning you to pull over. License and registration could mean a civic interaction or a beating, and despite protestations that the police are just doing their jobs, most African Americans have a police story to tell. That's why law abiding folk identified with Rodney King. That's why black folk who crave law and order also look askance at those charged with "law enforcement." That's why millions wonder about the "just" in justice.

THE LANGUAGE OF CIVIL UNREST

Rodney King was never on trial. Lawrence Powell, Stacey Koon, Timothy Wind and Theodore Brisenio were. So was the brutality of the Los Angeles Police Department. Instead of referring to the absurd decision that sparked a righteous frustration and sounded a racial wake-up call as the "Rodney King" case, why don't we refer to it as the "Lawrence Powell" case, or the "LAPD brutality" case? If Rodney King is immortalized, so also ought to be the police officers who beat him, and the police department that created a conducive climate for such brutality.

59

The language that we have used to discuss the LAPD brutality case has been the vehicle through which we have expressed our biases. Presidential candidate Pat Buchanan calls those who hit the streets "looters and lynchers." President Bush calls them criminals. I call them freedom fighters. Had a spontaneous eruption of outrage in the face of oppression taken place in Eastern Europe or in the Soviet Union, Congress would have sent a check by now, and President Bush would have applauded their courage. But the people who chafe against the yoke of oppression are mostly African American, and live in the USA. Their outrage, then, is not understandable, according to most whites; it is simply illegal.

You could hear it in the voices of the news anchors who covered the rebellions and uprisings (not riots) in Los Angeles. Those who are supposed to be impartial wrapped themselves in righteous indignation and opined that those beating passers-by were "animals." Yet there are a million ways to beat somebody, and some of those whose frustration turned to violence have been victim of vicious economic and social beatings. I've never heard a news anchor express such horror about poverty or unemployment, only the deadpan delivery that suggests that these acts of violence are business as usual. No outrage flowed at the savings and loan crisis, no indignation at the involvement of the President's son, Neil Bush. Some violence prompts outrage; other acts, acceptance.

I not only accept the rebellions in Los Angeles, I identify with them. Were I there, I am not sure how I might have reacted. I can't see myself looting, but I've never had as few choices as had Latasha Harlins, the young black woman who was shot in the back by a Korean American shopkeeper (who was sentenced to community service for her crime) over an argument about a 16 ounce container of orange juice that cost $1.79. The same carton sells at a major supermarket for at most half that price. This is another crime that seemed to escape the editorial outrage

60

that the rebellions last week generated. The absence of outrage sent a message – black life is cheap.

Those government actions that have supported black life have also been cheapened by the political rhetoric that has surrounded the LAPD brutality case. President Bush distorts the truth when he blames Great Society programs for the Los Angeles rebellion. For example, a quarter of our nation's children lived in poverty in 1960. The child poverty level dropped – both because of Great Society programs and economic expansion – to about 14 percent in 1973. From 1973, the rate rose to hit about 21 percent in 1990. This poverty isn't evenly distributed. Forty-five percent of all black children live in poverty, as do nearly forty percent of all Hispanic children and sixteen percent of all white children. Instead of blaming Great Society programs for the outpouring of poverty's frustration, President Bush might well blame the myopic policies of his administration.

The language of unrest exposes our differences. Your looters are my freedom fighters, your rioters my rebels. Your programmatic fiasco was an essential component in my community's progress. If we cannot find common ground in language, is there anyplace for common ground? The LAPD brutality case demands an answer, but you are so busy seeking "law and order" that you haven't even heard the questions!

King Features, May, 1991

THE LAPD VERDICTS AND
THEIR EXPECTED AFTERMATH

Hardly a day passes in Los Angeles without someone speculating about what will happen after the jury returns the verdicts in the trial of the four police officers – Lawrence Powell, Stacey Koon, Timothy Wind and Theodore Bresinio – who brutally beat motorist Rodney

King on March 2, 1991. The newspapers report the preparedness of the police in case there is civic unrest. Television reporters interview every one from the police chief to mayoral staff about the police presence that will be expected when the verdicts are announced. We have learned that the verdicts' announcement may be delayed to allow the police and national guard time to get in position. We have heard that the federal government will send millions of dollars to pay for a National Guard presence in Los Angeles. We also know that Mayor Tom Bradley has instituted a "Neighbor to Neighbor" program to suppress the possibility of insurrection by reminding people of their interest in their neighborhoods. From everything I've heard, I think that people in South Central Los Angeles are being set up to respond to the LAPD civil rights violation verdicts (not the Rodney King beating verdicts) whether they are so inclined or not.

Those who approach this question least delicately are asking, aloud, "what if they riot." A recent *Los Angeles Time* headline read, "LA Stepping Lightly as It Braces for Threat of Riots." Who are "they," and when have "they" threatened to "riot?" Did "they" send the newspaper a letter with the threat? While it is prudent to prepare for the possibility of civic unrest, I think it unwise to continue the "us" versus "them" speculation. Given the tone of that thinking aloud, who would be surprised if African Americans, driving though the "wrong" neighborhood, might not be greeted with violence, perhaps by "accident."

Would the accident be justifiable? A canny lawyer might make such a case, in light of the hype that is now going on. Some people are arming themselves to protect themselves from "looters." While personal safety concerns may be justified, what is the difference between self-protection and vigilantism? Are discussions of the dangers likely to give birth to a new breed of gun-toting citizens? And who will pick up the pieces when the actions of power packing amateurs backfire, as they inevitably do?

62

Instead of asking—"what if they riot?" why aren't people asking what has happened in a year since the uprisings? What has Rebuild LA done? How much progress has gone toward revitalizing neighborhoods and addressing the social problems that led to the uprisings in the first place? Have the gang members that became media celebrities in the wake of uprisings been mainstreamed? Have they been offered jobs or opportunities, or do they feel as distant from the system as they did a year ago?

Congresswoman Maxine Waters has focused on a group of young men, those unemployed dropouts between 17 and 30 who hover at the periphery of the economic system, who should be the target of social programs. Unfortunately, most of the money for summer jobs and after school jobs is focused on "youth," those under 19 or 21. There's a gap here, a gap that can be addressed by public policy. But far fewer people are talking social policy than are speculating about action after the verdicts are announced.

The verdicts in the first LAPD brutality case were matches on the dry timber of decades of social neglect. It will take more than a "Rebuild LA" program to deal with the timber, and perhaps much more than a second set of verdicts to light another match. It seems to me that there are some who are eagerly preparing for unrest because it serves their purposes to view urban dwellers as lawless. The thinking aloud — "what if they riot?" — pulls people apart instead of bringing them together.

Discussion about ways to bring the excluded from margin to center, about concrete programs (not door-to-door gabfests) that have addressed long-term urban neglect, would seem to do more to discourage unrest than the constant "what if" talk. Has anything actually changed in a year? If something has, I'd like to hear about it.

King Features, April, 1993

BROKEN PROMISES, CRIPPLED DREAMS

Comparisons between the 1965 urban rebellion in Watts and the recent outpouring of frustration in South Central Los Angeles are inevitable. The similarities between the two disturbances transcend geography, and include a reaction to police brutality, a physical area that has been neglected, and empty rhetoric on the part of public officials. But the rhetoric of 1965 may have been more substantive than it is today.

In 1965, large segments of white America could claim ignorance about black rage. The civil rights movement had been, until then, "civil", polite, and charged with moral imperative. People had turned the other cheek and submitted to hosings and dogs to make the point that African Americans deserved full citizenship rights. By 1992, more areas than Watts had burned. Racist incidents in Bensonhurst and Howard Beach had commanded headlines, but so had the political use of racial images (like Willie Horton and "welfare queens"). In 1965, the Watts rebellion introduced white America to black rage and induced political promises of future fair treatment. By 1992, thanks to hate-mongering politicians and a faltering economy, many whites had not only wearied of the rage, but worked up a rage (and a distorted sense of fairness, as in the use of the term "reverse discrimination") of their own.

President Bush fed that rage when he blamed Great Society programs for the Los Angeles rebellion. As hundreds of social science studies show, many sixties programs made a difference.

A study of the Job Corps program, for example, found that the job training program was successful in making many black men "job ready" and able to enter the labor market. Instead of finding private sector jobs, though, many were drafted and sent to Vietnam.

Many of the students who enrolled in college between 1965 and 1975 would not have had the opportunity were it not for educational grants and loans. If these students

64

have less fortunate cousins who want to go to college today, they are more likely to be offered loans than grants for their education.

The President himself has made a "Great Society" program, Head Start, a centerpiece of his own education reform proposal. In early January, he frolicked on the floor of a Maryland Head Start Center, surrounded by the black children he said would be "the best prepared four year olds in the world." He didn't say what would happen to these children at age five or six or ten or fifteen, and he failed to request a level of funding that would fully address children's needs.

Great Society programs tried to address those needs through a range of programs that included not only Head Start, but employment programs for teens and adults, and housing development for blighted urban centers. The programs worked! The child poverty level dropped — both because of Great Society programs and economic expansion — from 25 percent in 1960 to about 14 percent in 1973. But from 1973, the rate rose to hit about 21 percent in 1990.

Ronald Reagan cut social spending drastically in 1980, but except for job training programs, the mandate for poverty programs weakened after President Johnson left the White House. Richard Nixon preferred to address racial economic issues through his "black capitalism" programs, and President Carter was hampered both by an inflationary economy and political pressure to institute welfare reform. His proposed "Program for Better Jobs and Income" was uncannily similar to Moynihan-inspired workfare programs.

Great Society programs didn't cause the Los Angeles uprisings. But the crippling of these programs represented a broken promise, a breach of faith that may have contributed to the frustration people felt when they heard the LAPD brutality verdict. That verdict represented another broken promise if "justice" is, indeed, promised.

The history of government programs and social justice that developed between 1965 and 1992 has both hopeful and disappointing episodes. In the aftermath of the Watts rebellion of 1965, there was some notion that opportunities would be offered to those who needed them. By 1992, it was clear that opportunities would be few and offered grudgingly, that rhetoric would be plenty and insulting, and that nothing short of spontaneous combustion would bring as much attention to neglected urban areas as actions like those that caused us to look at them once, a long time ago.

San Francisco Bay Guardian, May, 1992

JOBS, PEACE AND JUSTICE, MORE OR LESS

Excitement built for months before the first time people marched on Washington for civil rights. Not that the hotels would be filled by African Americans from all over the country — in those days segregation was so rigidly enforced that African Americans didn't expect to be accommodated. Somehow, though, we were all absorbed into the city, and somehow the 1963 March on Washington went well. So did the 20th Anniversary March in 1983. What will happen in 1993?

To let the *Washington Post* have it, there won't be but 35,000 people at the march. They may not be far off— insiders are saying they'll consider it a massive victory if 100,000 show. But 100,000 represents less than half of the number that showed up in 1963, and less than half of one percent of the 30 million African Americans in this country. One hundred thousand people is only a victory in the context of a march that has not been planned. In truth, the presence of just 100,000 people marching for Jobs, Peace, and Justice in Washington represents a hollow endorsement of the march's purposes.

To be sure, at the last minute, organizations like the NAACP and AFL-CIO have donated staff, office space, telephones, and other things for the march. And, at the last minute, some African American leaders are getting off their butts and on the telephones to guarantee some turnout. But it's this "last minute" that is part of the problem. Former congressman Walter Fauntroy, who is coordinating the march, didn't come on board until April. To turn out a quarter of a million people with just four months worth of effort would require far more skill than he brings to the table.

And whether the organizer was Fauntroy or the world's best organizer, part of the problem is the notion of marching in nebulous commemoration. The issues — jobs, peace and justice — are clear to some, not to others. And the civil rights agenda has changed. The signs don't say "white" or "colored" anymore and people aren't as compelled to push an African American cause as they were a generation ago. It's no longer a question of whether we have to sit on the bus, but whether we can afford to ride the bus, or own it. And many who would march for us to sit won't march for us to own.

The march has had an ambivalent reaction from some who feel the civil rights coalition is too broad, that folk use the term "civil rights" interchangeably with human rights and other rights. Some who will march for African Americans won't march for gays and lesbians (and after the gay community's rather shameful and hateful treatment of Rev. Eugene Lumpkin that sentiment is understandable). Some of the members of the "civil rights coalition" are having an uneasy time with each other. And that uneasy time translates to muted enthusiasm for the march.

In truth, many people are having an uneasy time with African American people right about now. The press covers black issues poorly, obsessed with crime and violence, but not with discrimination and institutional racism. In the wake of the LAPD brutality verdict and the uprisings, there has been a search for common ground, a desire to embrace that which is redemptive, like the message Cornel West puts out in his book *Race Matters*. There is extreme discomfort with black anger.

The economy has caused an upswing in white racism, and few white people are preaching racial tolerance. The bully pulpit on race is empty, abdicated by a President who said he wouldn't use Willie Horton as a symbol, but instead turned lawyer Lani Guinier into one. Because there is no bully pulpit on race, there is no national enthusiasm for the march. Indeed, the reaction is something like "ho hum here we go again."

This is even the case in the African American community, where reactions to the 1993 March also make the economic distance in our community much more clear. Those who can afford to march, those with incomes over $50,000 a year, probably won't march because they don't need to. They have jobs, a little bit of peace, and as much justice as they can pay for. They don't need to march. Those who need to march, those with high unemployment rates, those who live in cities abandoned by federal funding, probably won't march, either, because they can't afford to. The distance between haves and have nots, and the lack of identification between the two groups, may contribute to the low turnout so many anticipate.

If the march flops, it sends the national signal that civil rights issues are not important issues, and that the traditional civil rights movement can't pull off an event. That's the wrong message to send, but is marching really the right way to send a message in 1993?

Sun Reporter, August, 1993

BLACK YOUTH AND THE
MARCH DOWN MEMORY LANE

Dr. Martin Luther King, Jr. was 34 years old when he gave his "I Have A Dream" speech during the historic March on Washington that riveted our nation and was largely responsible for the passage of the Civil Rights Act of 1964. Three decades later, discussion of passing the civil rights torch centers around the new leadership of Rev. Ben Chavis, the 46 year old newly selected Executive Director of the NAACP. In the generation since the 1963 March, young African Americans have not been as compelled as King and his compatriots were to be involved in the civil rights movement, and the notion of "young leadership" has aged so considerably that a middle-aged man is being considered "a breath of fresh air" for the civil rights movement.

In some ways this is a move backward for the civil rights movement. The 1983 twentieth anniversary march was coordinated by then-23-year-old Donna Brazile, who had just graduated from Southern University when she was asked to pull the march together. Brazile remembers walking her first precinct at age 9 or so, and after the 1983 March went on to hold several organizing roles in Presidential campaigns, including those of Rev. Jesse Jackson, Walter Mondale, Dick Gephart, and Michael Dukakis. The youthful energy that Brazile brought to the 1983 organizing effort seems missing in the 1993 March.

Civil rights activists are among the first to talk about youth and the future, but the absence of young people in the leadership of the civil rights movement (or in line to catch the baton) may have some correlation with the tepid response that many have had to the *notion* of a 30th anniversary march. For too many marchers, a 30th anniversary event is nothing more than a promenade down memory lane. Those who weren't born when the first march took place aren't clear that they have any reason to march.

When African Americans of the thirtysomething gen-

69

eration make headlines it is less for their work in the civil rights movement, and more for their prominence in sports, music, politics, or other arenas. To be sure, young politicians like Louisiana's Cleo Fields and Georgia's Cynthia McKinney have garnered some attention as they moved from local public office to the United States Congress. But the words "young, black, and successful" elicit images of Arsenio Hall and Wesley Snipes, not Alan Wheat (a Missouri Congressman) and Curtis Tucker (a Los Angeles Congressman). Where is the young Jesse Jackson, Ben Chavis, or Dorothy Height, the 34 year old who will give a speech and do the work that rocks the nation as surely as Dr. Martin Luther King's speech did? Will it take a rapper to catalyze young African Americans? Until there is an answer to this question, and until young people gain more leadership and more visibility, the civil rights movement wears an unfortunate mask, one of being old, staid, and stuck in the tactics of the past.

In some ways, the civil rights movement suffers from its success. The signs don't say "white" or "colored" anymore. The issue isn't whether African Americans ride on the back of the bus, but whether we have bus fare to get on the bus, or enough capital to buy a bus company. Those issues don't as easily reduce to sound bites as eliminating segregation once did.

The more complex issues, like economic inequality, the proliferation of drugs in black communities, police brutality, and black-on-black crime don't distill into bumper stickers or T-shirt slogans, and aren't easily fixed by a rally or march. After the 30th anniversary march down memory lane, the civil rights movement faces the fight of its life — the fight to define issues, to attract young people, and to reclaim the vitality of King's dream and his movement.

King Features, August, 1993

70

KING'S ECONOMIC MESSAGE

As the nation prepares to commemorate Rev. Martin Luther King, Jr.'s birthday, I expect to hear the great man misquoted as conservative thinkers remind us of the color blind society King dreamed of. Essayist Shelby Steele lifted a line from King's August 28, 1963 "I Have A Dream" speech, titling his book that argued against racial awareness, *The Content of Our Character*, but he's not the only one who would focus on only one dimension of King's philosophy.

While it is true that King said, "I had a dream that my four little children will one day live in a nation where they will not be judged by the color of their skin but by the content of their character," King did not believe we could click our heels three times to realize the dream.

Indeed, King's speeches suggest that he was a legislative and judicial activist with strong ideas about economic justice. Why is he remembered for "having a dream," but not for talking about economic redistribution? "If the world is two-thirds water," King once challenged, "why should we pay water bills."

Most politicians fail to make the connection King once made between racism and economic injustice. Said King, "Many white Americans of good will have never connected bigotry with economic exploitation. They have deplored prejudice but tolerated or ignored economic injustice. But the Negro knows these two evils have a malignant kinship."

Few others made the connection between high unemployment rates and high pay for our nation's leading industrialists (who earn more than 100 times the average worker's wage). None of the Presidential candidates talked about the connection between our nation's failure to develop labor policy with the low wages that so many workers are earning. With nine million people officially unemployed, and with 25 million having experienced unemployment in 1991, King's voice on these issues is sorely missed.

In 1968, he noted, "New laws are not enough. The emergency we now face is economic and it is a desperate and worsening situation for the 33 million poor people in America . . . there is a kind of strangulation in the air. In our society it is murder, psychologically, to deprive a man of a job or an income. You are in substance saying to that man that he has no right to exist."

A generation after King made his comment, there are more poor people, more joblessness, more people being told that they have no right to exist. Dr. King probably could not have guessed that three million homeless people would roam the streets thirty years after he spoke about his dream. Nor could Dr. King have predicted that government would ignore the needs of so many people. And King would not have been likely to predict the racial meanness that has affected so many in this country.

For all he said about color-blindness, King also advocated affirmative action. "It is impossible to create a formula for the future which does not take into account that our society has been doing something special against the Negro for hundreds of years. How then can he be absorbed into the mainstream of American life if we do not do something special for him now, in order to balance the equation and equip him to compete on a just and equal basis," said King.

In his Nobel Prize acceptance speech, Dr. King laid out an economic program when he said, "I have the audacity to believe that people everywhere can have three meals a day for their bodies, education and culture for their minds, and dignity, equality and freedom for their spirits."

It is comforting and convenient to remember King for a dream he had. Those who celebrate the civil rights leader's birthday ought to probe the economic meaning behind his words. Our nation has yet to take the kind of action that would make King's dream come true.

King Features, January, 1992

SOMETIMES ICE CUBE SPEAKS FOR ME

The rapper Ice Cube has been getting a bad rap for the lyrics of his songs, lyrics sometimes best described as angry, violent, anti-Semitic, homophobic, and misogynist. And as I listen to the rapper's music, I have to admit that I cringe at his boorish and sexist references to women, his brutal comments about gay people. Beyond that, I don't support death threats against individuals who are directly or obliquely named in his album.

But I absolutely share Ice Cube's outrage at the cash register conflict that has claimed too many black lives, conflict that comes about because of a clash in cultures. And in the wake of the murder of a black teenage girl at the hands of a Los Angeles Korean shop owner, I am about where Ice Cube is in demanding that those who depend on African American customers for their livelihood treat their customers with respect or risk boycotts or other retaliation.

Fifteen year old Latasha was shot by Son Ja Du in an altercation over a $1.79 bottle of orange juice. A videotape of the incident indicates that Harlins was shot in the back. Son Ja Du was convicted of manslaughter, but despite a probation report recommending a 16 year sentence, a Los Angeles judge opted to sentence this woman to a mere 400 hours of community service and a $500 fine. What does this say about the value of the life of a black teenage girl? It says her life is cheap. It says that any black person who exchanges words over commerce can expect a bullet, quick and swift, and a judge who approves of that execution. Latasha Harlins' murder, Son Ja Du's indifference, a judge's contempt for life, all combine to make me angry enough to consider retaliation. Or at least to find comfort in Ice Cube's belligerence.

"Don't follow me up and down your market, you will be the target of a nationwide boycott," the rapper sings, and I agree with him. I do not understand why there has been so little outrage at the murder of a youngster, at the uneven quality of justice in this case. "Pay your respect to the black fist, or we'll burn down your store to a crisp." No, I don't have my molotov cocktail ready, but I feel like I'd like to see something burn, someone pay for this loss of black life.

Of course there is a bigger picture – neither blacks nor Koreans are fully empowered, and conflict between these two minority groups does little to reduce the stranglehold of economic control that a small group of capitalists have maintained. But the big picture does not speak to the way black life has been so thoroughly devalued that recent immigrants, in behavior that is clearly imitative of that of whites and reflective of media messages, feel free to physically assault, maim and kill African Americans over a bottle of juice or a can of beer. And the big picture does not speak to the anger that so many African Americans must swallow when we find the value of our lives devaluated.

I can't swallow justice that is a bitter pottage served from a broken plate. No one should be surprised that the constant ingestion of injustice results in hate. Ice Cube's angry words are the natural output from this bitter brew, his anger a lightening rod for mine. If Son Ja Du can kill and walk away, I must warn other Korean grocers that Latasha Harlins' death will be remembered. Yes, Ice Cube speaks for me.

King Features, December, 1991

MANDELA AND A FREE DC: STRUGGLES INTERTWINED

The struggles for black political, civil, and economic rights in South Africa and in the United States have been intertwined since apartheid was declared policy in 1948. Rev. Martin Luther King railed against apartheid at a speech at Columbia University in 1962; both he and Nelson

Mandela were jailed in 1963. King was released and assassinated, but Mandela remained imprisoned for 27 years.

Black trade unionists joined political activists in pressuring the United States government to bring its influence to bear in ending apartheid. Longshoremen in San Francisco refused to unload cargo from South African ships, while legislators in state capitols like Sacramento and Albany passed laws to remove state pension funds from companies doing business with South Africa, The demands were simple: the end of apartheid, the release of Mandela, full political rights for black South Africans.

But some of the most passionate fighters for a free South Africa have little political freedom of their own. Residents of the District of Columbia, like the Rev. Jesse Jackson, the Hon. Eleanor Holmes Norton, Transafrica's leader Randall Robinson, and more than six hundred thousand others, don't have the same voting rights they'd like their South African brothers and sisters to have. The principle of "one person, one vote" has been violated in the District of Columbia just as it has been in the Republic of South Africa. Indeed, with a nonvoting member in the House of Representatives, and no representation at all (except for unpaid, nonvoting "shadow Senators") in the United States Senate, residents of DC have less power than South African President DeKlerk is proposing that black South African be granted.

Mandela has been in the United States for the past ten days, pleading the case of black South Africans before the United Nations and in meetings with President Bush and other leaders. In the same sense that he supported the PLO's right to exist during his June, 1990 visit, it would have been appropriate that he mention the cause of equal voting rights in our nation's capitol. Couldn't the man whose freedom was partly the result of agitation in this country advocate a Free D.C. in the same way his allies advocated a Free South Africa?

Many would argue that Mandela was on a diplomatic

mission with bigger fish to fry than the statehood issue in DC. Had African American leaders taken that position, Mandela might still be imprisoned. A statement from Mandela on a Free DC would have been a wonderful way of acknowledging the connection between black South Africans and African Americans.

USA Today, December, 1991

CRIMINAL JUSTICE COLLISIONS — THE UNIVERSAL BLACK MALE EXPERIENCE?

The news ran in the upper left hand corner of Saturday's *New York Times*. "Forty two percent of young black men in capital's justice system." The article went on to refer to a study by the National Center on Institutions and Alternatives that showed that in 1991, 15 percent of Washington, DC's black men aged 18 to 35 were in prison, 21 percent were on probation, and 6 percent were out on bond or being sought by the police.

Does this mean that more black men are criminal than in 1989, when a comparable figure was about 25 percent? Only if we assume that everyone in the capital's justice system is guilty. I am most concerned with the plea bargaining system, with the way the innocent are often pressured into doing a little time instead of a lot. Granted, sometimes a guilty person gets a break plea bargaining, but it seems to me that the scales are tilted against the person who lacks the money to afford the best legal advice and who, as a result, ends up rolling loaded dice instead of trusting in a judicial system that hardly works.

The real news about the DC study was buried further in the *New York Times* article. The fourth paragraph noted that "as many as 70 percent of black men in Washington are arrested by the time they turn 35, and about 85 percent are arrested at some point in their lives." If this many black men are formally arrested, how many go through the informal detention, the stopping on the street, the showing of identification that too often takes place. The unspoken news in the DC study is that a collision with the criminal justice system is the universal reality for African American men!

How many of the arrests are baseless? The study doesn't say. But the gap between the men who are arrested for cause and those arrested because of their skin color represents the measure of antipathy that African American people have toward the criminal justice system, the extent to which they believe it is unfair, and the extent to which they are alienated by it.

Every "boy in the hood" has a story of unreasonable police action, but it is frightening when police officers themselves tell similar stories. A good friend's father retired from the police force after a career of lifetime service, yet he tells the chilling tale of being stopped, handcuffed, brought into a station, and nearly processed for a petty crime before some brother officer asked the rookie who detained him why he was bothering another officer. The rookie pretended embarrassment, the veteran black officer was unshackled, and as far as every white person in the station house knew that was the end of the story. But it didn't end for a black man who was humiliated, hazed. Years after the incident, he still refers to it with rage.

I saw a small slice of the rage and frustration that many young black men feel when I visited the Ella Hill Hutch night ball league last week. I wanted to talk about entrepreneurship; the young brothers wanted some jobs. The conversation bobbed and weaved and was buoyed, more than anything else, by the frustration so many young brothers feel because they are not "getting paid," because so many people who come to talk to them refer to fast foods jobs, not career building opportunities. These young men knew the criminal justice system more thoroughly than any researcher; they were eloquent about double standards and thwarted justice. And they were angry, but then again, any Black person who isn't angry is flirting with full fledged insanity.

Part of me doesn't see how Lefty Gordon does it. While he is fighting to provide recreational alternatives inside, the police circle outside the Ella Hill Hutch Community Center, prepared to hassle or hustle young men who leave the premises. One of the guys who sat speaking of finding work one minute was now being questioned about gambling or something. But fewer than two or three minutes had passed between; he had no time to start gambling. It was police officers who had a microscope trained on a facility that serves the black community.

Right, the police were just "doing their job" in asking questions. They are always doing their job scrutinizing the black community. Would they do it the same way, as harshly, if they were driving through the streets of Pacific Heights? Then again, the youngsters of Pacific Heights don't need community centers. They have large living rooms, all the amenities that go with them, and jobs waiting for them when they get out of high school.

Some won't see the DC study as a cause for black rage; they'll see it as proof of increasing criminality. The right will get to advising black people to work on our moral values, to solve our criminal problems. But that's because they are looking at the 42 percent of black men who are under justice system supervision, not the 70 percent arrested by age 35, 85 percent arrested in a lifetime, perhaps 100 percent stopped at some point.

There is, of course, a feminist perspective to this. Too many black men view their collision with the criminal justice system as a "male thing" that black women may not understand, an occasion that marks them as endangered, peripheral, in need of special attention. But the fact is that if fracas with the law is part of the black male experience, then the need to play "clean up woman," to pick up the pieces of the fracas, is almost uniformly relegated to black women. For black men to run an endangered rap on black women is to place another burden on already weary shoulders. Law enforcement policy offers us ways to deal with the criminal treatment of black men (and of black women); but jamming black women doesn't solve the problem.

Really, this is a societal problem. As long as a collision with the criminal justice system is part of the universal Black male experience, African American people have the right to look askance at the men in blue who patrol our streets. The challenge for the criminal justice system is to prove itself fair and able to distinguish between a criminal and someone who has melanin in their skin. To date, in DC, Los Angeles, San Francisco, New York, the challenge goes unmet.

Sun Reporter, April, 1992

GIVE ME MY 40 ACRES AND A MULE!

I am in complete support of the proposal that Japanese-Americans be paid reparations for the time they were interred in concentration camps during World War II. I support the reparations because the internment of Japanese-Americans was wrong, wrong, wrong. But I also support reparations for them because I think there should be reparations for about 30 million other people, notably the black Americans who are descendants of slaves.

Black people's labor laid the foundation for this country's infrastructure, first as slaves, and later as sharecroppers. But laws were passed to prevent us from working in some occupations, from attending some schools. Institutional racism, pervasive and encompassing, restricted black people's access to transportation, to education, and to other services. "Separate but equal" schools provided black people with an unequal education, with spending per pupil for blacks only half as much as spending per pupil for whites in most Southern states.

We were the victims of racial violence and intimidation, lynched for daring to walk on the same sidewalk as white people, jailed for being unable to pay fines that exceeded a year's wages. Many a southern white landowner had his fields cultivated, his crops harvested by inmates. Some landowners even requested the services of certain inmates, by name, for the length of their term. In order to get hard workers, some even engineered the arrest of certain black people.

We were the "reserve army of the unemployed" during the industrial revolution, hired when union workers were out on strike, or when white men were off to war, but fired when strikes were settled or when wars were over. Although there was a labor shortage during World War II, trade unionists in Seattle (among other places) said they would do anything for the war effort, anything except work with black workers! A. Philip Randolph had to threaten a march 100,000 strong in order to get the President to form the Fair Employment Practices Commission to stop discrimination in wartime industries.

Between the FEPC and labor shortages, blacks made decent wages for a minute. But when World War II ended, far too many black workers found themselves jobless again. Discrimination before, during, and after World Wars I and II was condoned, if not encouraged by the federal government. If apologies for past wrongs are being passed out, black people in this country should be standing in front of the line.

We should get first crack at any reparations distributed, as well. We didn't get the 40 acres and a mule promised at the end of slavery, and we've been denied the opportunity to earn and invest since slavery ended. Even when we did equal work, we earned unequal pay, and the reparations Black Americans deserve are in lieu of back pay.

It would take more space than this column offers to list the reasons Black Americans deserve reparations. And it would take more space than this to convince many of the fairness of such a proposition. Politicians like Mario

Cuomo would like to compare slaves to new immigrants, making parallels between the inhumanity endured by immigrants and slaves. There are obvious differences, though, and those begin with the act of slavery and continue through the black codes and Jim Crow laws that prevented black participation in facets of American economic life.

Black people aren't the only ones who deserve reparations. California used to belong to Mexico. The United States was once the domain of Native Americans. And working Japanese were interred during World War II.

The roots of the "land of the free" are slavery and thievery, and these wrongs must be corrected, through legislation and reparation. Only, when the apologies and the settlements are passed out, Black Americans should get their forty acres, a mule, plus interest.

Sun Reporter, April, 1988

CASTRATING RAPISTS SENDS THE WRONG MESSAGE

A Texas man accused of sexually assaulting a child was given the choice of more than 20 years of incarceration or castration by Judge Michael McSpadden. The accused first chose castration, "after consulting with his wife." Later he changed his mind, and questions were raised about coercion, his competence to choose between prison and castration, and whether castration is the appropriate punishment for an assault accusation (there has not yet been a trial) as part of a plea bargain.

Using castration as a punishment for rape suggests that rape is solely a sexual crime, and that therefore a sexual penalty must be extracted. But rape isn't a crime about sex, it is a crime about power and violence. It is entirely conceivable that a man who feels his power is diminished by castration may commit further crimes of abuse.

Secondly, castration assumes that the sexual organ is the only weapon used in rape. But victims of sexual abuse have been brutally violated with other body parts, and with external objects — with sticks and bottles and even worse.

If the notion is — mistakenly, by the way — that castration removes the instrument of rape (castration is removal of the testicles, not the penis), are we prepared to cut off men's hands and tongues when these are used as weapons? Are we prepared to permanently revoke drivers' licenses for those who raped in a car? Should we prevent those who abducted a victim and took her home from ever renting an apartment or buying a home again?

Would we lobotomize computer buggers and inside traders because their incredible intelligence made it possible for them to commit their crimes? Would we lop the hands off robbers, cut the feet off those who try to escape from prison, and so on? While those who break the law should be punished, and while some crimes are more heinous than others, do we prevent inhumanity by practicing it?

To be sure, if castration were the standard penalty for rape, it might well serve as a deterrent against this awful crime. On the other hand, if the ante is raised, will juries be prepared to "ruin someone's life" with a guilty verdict in cases where clever defense attorneys portray women as "asking for it." Further, if the penalty of castration is differently imposed, will race and class determine which rapists pay the ultimate price, and which rapists receive a lesser penalty?

In the biblical context of "an eye for an eye," castration seems a just response to rape. But rape is a crime of power, not of passion. Castration neither stops rape nor recognizes its motivation.

USA Today, March, 1992

DOES THE FIRST AMENDMENT PROTECT THE KLAN?

Will somebody give the First Amendment a break? In the name of "free speech," a Ku Klux Klansman is demanding the right to wear his hood, an open violation of Georgia state law. But, as history chillingly reveals, most hooded Klansmen have not free speech, but unfettered terrorist behavior on their minds when they don the their regalia. The Klan is responsible for the murders and lynching of thousands of African Americans, for the destruction of tens of thousands of homes and businesses, and the rapes and beatings of countless more people. Their intimidating presence at the turn of the century made it difficult for black people to demand and pursue their right to fair wages, equal treatment, and the vote. The 1951 law that made it illegal to wear a mask except on holidays or for use in sports, theater, or in other specific cases is still seen as important in weakening the Klan in that state. Now, when hate crimes are on the rise, and racism is making a disgusting resurgence, the Klan wants to reclaim its masks.

This is in no way a civil liberties issue. The Klan wears their masks not for free expression, but to conceal their identities when they are involved in criminal activity. Under hoods they can kill and avoid prosecution, but in the light of day they can hardly force cars carrying college students off the road, hang young men from trees, or bomb people's homes. I'm not invoking ancient history here. Some of these events happened a quarter century ago, but others happened in the last decade.

When legislators can anticipate a negative outcome from a certain activity, it is responsible leadership for them to do whatever they can to prevent such outcome. That's why some rap groups aren't allowed to perform in certain urban coliseums. The issue isn't their First Amendment right to rap, but the possibility of gang violence at their performances. Ditto the Klan. There may be, though I truly can't imagine it, perfectly law-abiding members of the Ku Klux

Klan. But the fact of the matter is that when these hooded citizens come together, it is reasonable to anticipate that some life threatening crime will be committed. The 1951 law the Klan seeks to overturn was written in response to that expectation.

The Klan is hiding behind the First Amendment just like it hides behind those pointy hoods that could be better used covering up somebody's mattress. They have no right, First Amendment or otherwise, to hide and to terrorize. And they need to give the First Amendment a break.

USA Today, April, 1990

WHEN SHALL WE OVERCOME?

I don't know how many times I've heard the song, how many times I've sung it. "We Shall Overcome," the Negro National Anthem, is used to open meetings and to close them, as a source of hope, of inspiration, an article of faith. But lately when I hear the words, I'm a lot closer to despair than to faith. With the economy making headlines, issues of racial justice have been pushed to the periphery of the policy sphere, and there just isn't much concern about overcoming discrimination against African Americans.

Instead, studies that document the extent of differential treatment have become commonplace. For example, a story in the *St. Louis Post Dispatch* reported that insurance coverage for homeowners in predominantly black areas is far more limited than insurance coverage for homeowners in predominantly white areas. Further, black homeowners in poor neighborhoods paid about $6.15 for every $1,000 in insurance coverage, compared to $4.70 for white homeowners in poor areas.

It didn't surprise me to learn that in revealing the disparity, the director of the Missouri Department of Insurance noted there is no clear evidence of illegal discrimination. Jay Angloff said, "We're not here to call anybody names or to accuse anybody of violating the law." Pretty much the same thing was said when the Federal Reserve Board revealed differences in mortgage lending so pronounced that upper income African Americans were less likely to qualify for mortgages than poor whites. Or what was said when the study of automobile prices revealed that black women were more likely to pay the sticker price for a car, while white men were more likely to get a "good deal."

Study after study of the banking and insurance industries reveals racial disparity in treatment. But when called upon to comment, too many bankers talk about disparity as distinct from discrimination. In other words, the differences in insurance rates, or in mortgage levels "just happen."

And because these things just happen, I've started to think of "We Shall Overcome" as more plaintive plea than call to action. While the singing and swaying certainly serve a purpose, I'd feel alot better about "We Shall Overcome" if we say, "We shall overcome today" instead of "We shall overcome someday". It just seems to me that someday is a day we never calendar, a day that doesn't get pencilled in on the filofax. Thus reports like the Missouri insurance report are treated as so much business as usual, something that little can be done about, something we study instead of change. Singing "We shall overcome today" reminds that each of us has a responsibility to do something about race discrimination every day, not just some unspecified day in the distant future.

I started thinking about this because Sunday, April 4 is the 25th anniversary of the assassination of Dr. Martin Luther King. Too many people would like to remember King for his "I have a Dream" speech that catapulted him onto the national scene. But King didn't die dreaming, he died trying to help raise the wages of garbage workers, black and white, in Memphis. He is remembered for saying, "I have a dream that my four little children will one day live in a nation were they will not be judged by the color of their skin but the content of their character", but he is not as well remembered for his criticism of our economic system, for his statement, "If the world is two-thirds water, why should we pay water bills".

Even though he has been gone for 25 years, Dr. King probably sang the verses of "We Shall Overcome" many more times than I ever have. But he made the distant "someday" happen each time he grabbed injustice by the throat. It will take more of that audacity to achieve racial justice. More of that audacity. Less singing and swaying.

King Features, April, 1993

CHAPTER FOUR

SPORTS AND SOCIETY:

BEAUTY AND HORROR

Sports is a conundrum for this African American feminist, a hodgepodge of conflicting feelings. On one hand, African American men, disproportionately represented in sports, are well-paid gladiators who are often caricatured in the media. Their excellence in one arena is often dwarfed by the paucity of opportunities in others. On the other hand, conventional sports organization puts men in the center, women at the periphery. And finally, as cities scramble for tourist attractions, sports issues elbow their way into the policy arena through tax initiatives and publicly financed stadiums. The games men play in football, baseball, and basketball arenas unfortunately reflect the games they play in life.

BLACK MEN IN SPORTS:
THE BEAUTY AND THE HORROR

There really ought to be music
More like ballet
Than a game you play
Long sleek bodies
Swift gazelles
A syncopated motion

Or a poised, tense still
Graceful jugglers with the ball
Jumping, stalking, charging —
    fall
Heads up, running
Ten giraffes
In fluid rhythm
Choreographed
Muscles taut
There really ought
To be music

The title of the poem is *Game on West Fourth Street.* It comes from my days as a basketball junkie, the days when I thought there was no better way to blow a nice Saturday or Sunday than to sit in a park with a book, some cheese, and a bottle of wine, watching the brothers play ball. Not every player had the grace of a gazelle, but it was amazing that amateur players in school yards did something in Addidas and with a ball that could put the best pro player to shame.

That was part of the problem, though. Everybody could play ball, or thought they could. Every brother who had a hook shot played with a vengeance, dreaming of the day a recruiter would drive by the playground and make him an offer. Every brother with some shoulders and a block expected to see someone from the NFL knocking on his door. Every brother who hit a school yard home run waited for the baseball scouts to call his name.

Some dreams die with adolescence, but some linger with alarming persistence. And to this day you can find brothers in playgrounds, brothers in their late twenties and early thirties, waiting for discovery. Let me not be the one to dash fond hopes with the icewater of reality. Miracles do happen. But sports sociologist Harry Edwards has written time and time again about the odds that a playground product will make it to the big leagues.

And now the headlines scream with the odds of making it THROUGH the big leagues once you get to them. One by one, the gladiators have fallen, to sudden death from drugs, to tarnished images, to pressure, to racism. If the gladiators manage not to fall, the sports establishment does whatever it can to make sure they don't rise. Al Campanis' statements on Ted Koppel's show last Monday night are an example of the barriers that black men face when they try to leave the playing arena and move into management. Campanis described black men as lacking what it takes to be managers. Fleet of feet, and with "good musculature," but with no buoyancy, black men make good players but poor managers.

Of course, Campanis apologized. Of course, baseball executives condemned his statements. Of course his resignation was requested, and of course he tendered it, with regret. And the beat goes on. After the resignation, there are no more black men managing baseball teams than there were before.

But the position of blacks in baseball management is reflective of the position of blacks in law, in medicine, in corporate America. There are too few of us at the top and too many at the bottom. We are the most vulnerable corporate players, last hired and first fired. We are the least likely to be promoted to "the top," mainly because we don't "fit in" to the upper echelons of white America. When we make it to the top, unless we are most careful, we are labeled "arrogant," "cocky", as if humility was the vehicle to get us where we were going.

And at the top we are no less immune to the petty racism that resulted in the police harassment of Dwight Gooden in his hometown, the petty racism that focuses on Willie Brown's cars and clothes but not his positions, the petty racism that exposes every black man who dares achieve to a public scrutiny far more intense than any scrutiny his white counterpart faces. The presumption, of course, is that if he is black and an achiever, then something must be wrong with him.

No wonder young brothers like Dwight Gooden and Chris Washburn turn to drugs or something to allow them to turn off the pressure of being who they are. No wonder older brothers like Willie Mays sometimes publicly express bitterness at their lack of post-retirement opportunities. No wonder Joe Barry Carrol wouldn't talk to the press for the longest time.

For white America, of course, there is a wonder. These black men are, after all, the lucky ones. They can make millions from their skill at sports, far more than the brother shooting hoops on the corner can ever hope to see. They can have fine clothes, nice cars, and even (gasp) white women. To let white America tell it, these brothers need to fall to their knees at every opportunity to thank them (not God) for their good fortune.

If the man's relationship to his sport is a fruitful one, then thanks should certainly be given. For there is nothing more beautiful than the visible use of talent, the near-ballet some brothers play when they are at the top of their sport. But on the field and off, if Al Campanis' comments are any indication, racism is pervasive. And that's the horror that can take a sportsman's dream and turn it into a nightmare.

Sun Reporter, March, 1988

TAKE ME OUT TO THE BALL GAME

Three strikes or a touchdown. Three cheers and a bowl game. For sports fans, this is the stuff that games are made of. Don't forget the dollar signs, though. Players, owners, leagues and television networks make millions on professional sports. Their profits are higher if they can convince cities to spend public dollars on their private pastimes. That's why greedy owners are threatening cities with the loss of teams if stadiums aren't rebuilt. Ballot initiatives have appeared in some cities; mayors pressured in others. Own-

ers are taking taxpayers for a ride, not out to the ballgame. I say the public shouldn't pay.

Granted, stadiums are a magnet for revenue. Fans come to watch a game, and drop dollars for parking, dining, and shopping along the way. But shopping malls and movie theaters also attract spenders. Should tax dollars pay for these, too?

Owners are looking for public dollars at a time when there are few public dollars available. More than half of all cities face fiscal problems this year. To balance budgets, most have cut services and increased parking fines. Taxpayers are being squeezed for necessities; must we tighten our belts for luxuries, too? Those people who are making money on the sport – the owners, the players, the networks – ought to pay for new stadiums, not overstressed taxpayers.

Mayors send a distressing signal when they try to keep a team at all costs, implying that sports are more important than harsh urban realities. I've never heard a mayor say he would keep libraries open "at all costs," that he would generate jobs "at all costs." A team at all costs? Give me a break. I love sports as much as anyone, but I like solvent cities, too. Mayors ought to ignore these schemes to extract dollars from taxpayers. Take me, don't tax me out to the ballgame.

USA Today, July, 1992

IN SPORTS AND SOCIETY: MAY THE BEST ONE WIN

"May the best one win." I watch two fellows face off in a game of basketball one-on-one, and furiously shoot hoops for awhile. I'm the kind of basketball fan who likes the game largely because the men have enough of their clothes off to be appreciated, but not so many as to be indecent. So I half watch, half read until the hoop shooting winds down, the brothers towel off and shake hands, and then two, winner and loser, walk away from the court.

Though there was no animosity at the end of the game, there was also no denying the way competition drove two friends to jump up in each other's faces, snatching, bouncing and dunking the ball, yelling an expletive or two to break the tension. And, because sports is often the mirror in which we see life, there is no denying the way that competition drives education, income, and employment in our society, the way we assuage ourselves, after the fact, that the "best one won." Sometimes the best one never gets to play.

The hottest contests aren't over two points in a one-on-one on a basketball court. Instead, the biggest fights are fights over markets and monopolies, over employment and images. And the way the rules are written, the players are all too often all white, the pawns in the game all black.

Just a trickle of black students were admitted to predominantly white universities prior to 1968. Most times, students entered because organizations like the NAACP filed suit to pave their way. For example, Supreme Court Justice Thurgood Marshall was turned away from the School of Law at the University of Maryland. When black students were admitted to white schools, they came one by one, loner to the Noah's ark of higher education. Despite the subtle harassment and exclusion they experienced, most held their own with white colleagues, or did better. The achievements of those black men and women who graduated from places like Yale, Princeton, Harvard, and the University of California are exceptional given the bias they faced in admissions, housing, sports, grading, and every other aspect of campus life. And, in general, because these black folk were invisible to their white colleagues, their exceptional accomplishments were ignored.

There has not often been open competition in education, or in business, or in sports. The rules have been written to lock out the open competition of black people, to deny us the opportunities that lead to opportunities, and then to lament at the fact that "we can't find any qualified." But those qualified can be found, heads bent over books in any classroom, standing on an employment line in any city. Those who can't find any qualified haven't looked, letting racist stereotypes blind their vision. Afraid of the competition, they've convinced themselves, with logic much like that of Jimmy "the Greek," that blacks have been "bred" to be subhuman, denied the right to fair competition.

Jimmy "the Greek" got fired because his racist sentiments are intolerable. Every person who has asked that Jimmy "the Greek" be judged with compassion forgets the black men and women who never got compassion or a second chance. Black men and women went to law school and didn't pass bar examinations because some states required them to submit a photo along with their examination. Black men and women majored in the sciences, but had to walk by scientific careers because laboratories would not hire them. Black people were not allowed to compete because white people like Jimmy "the Greek" were afraid of the outcome of such competition.

Despite the barriers erected by racist institutions, there are black people that achieve. And, for white racists, that must be the scariest thing of all. The "dynamics of tokenism" suggest that a black or two ought to succeed so that the rest of us will have some hope in the system. So the successes placate blacks and frighten racist whites. Racist whites see black success as a repudiation of their existence. I call it the "Diana Ross syndrome." They see one successful black person and decide that all black people (we all look alike) must somehow be successful. And then they blame it on affirmative action, social programs, whatever else they can blame black success on.

Nothing but sweet success and competence could be credited last Sunday, with the Redskin's victory in Superbowl XXII. There were those who said a black quarterback didn't have the brain power to lead a team to Superbowl victory. I wonder what they were saying when the score, at the end of the first half, was 35-10. There were those who said that John Elway, the epitome of a "great white hope" could pull it off in the second half. They chilled victory bottles of champagne, bottles that no doubt went flat while they waited for a miracle.

"May the best one win," they say when the game starts. The best one can't win in business when regulations prevent open competition. The best one can't win in education, when the potential best one is denied admission. And the best quarterback can't lead his team to victory when coaches won't even make the best one quarterback. The best one is very often a black one. White America will come to grips with this or drown in their own racism.

Sun Reporter, January, 1988

BOXING

I don't know what it is about boxing that causes thousands of people with seeming good sense to pay cash money to watch two men pound the stuffing out of each other. But then, I don't really understand why millions watch grown men in tight pants hit small balls with big sticks, or why so many of us are hooked on the Sunday-Monday ritual of watching football teams play demolition derby with their bodies. But millions are drawn to boxing, football, baseball, and basketball, and nearly as many are hooked on sports like hockey and soccer. Participation in all these sports carries some risk — men have actually died on football fields. So why does the American Medical Association want to ban boxing?

Granted, boxing has its pitfalls. Repeated blows to the head can obviously be hazardous to the health, as can too frequent fighting. And in the wake of Mike Tyson's loss of the heavyweight championship, there have been renewed allegations of favoritism, corruption, and general sleaze. Indeed, current medalist Evander Holyfield has called for a federal investigation of aspects of boxing. And that makes sense. If there's something wrong with boxing, fix it, don't ban it.

Make the fighters play with helmets on their heads if head injury is a problem. Require periodic medical examination if the question of fitness to fight is at issue. Stiffen the penalties and enforce existing laws if corruption is a problem. If drugs are an issue, there are dozens of drug laws that can be enforced to eliminate that scourge from the sport. In other words, regulate boxing if necessary. But don't even think about banning the sport unless you are willing to ban other sports.

It strikes me as incredibly hypocritical that the mostly white upper class American Medical Association would propose banning boxing, a sport that has been the ticket out of poverty for dozens of black and working class men. Granted, only one of a thousand men trying to make his mark as pugilist will have even modest success. If the AMA is just looking for sports that cause injury, what about hockey, soccer, or football for that matter. Hundreds of men are badly injured, some so severely that they will never run again after a few years in these sports. Is it the injury, the visible display of violence, class, or big ticket paychecks that bother the AMA?

You won't find me in the cheering section for the next big fight – I'm a relative pacifist who can't stand the sight of blood. But you'll certainly find me firmly opposed to schemes to ban boxing. If the AMA is really concerned about injury in that sport, let them help regulate it to minimize the possibility of injury.

USA Today, January, 1990

TYSON—VILLAIN, NOT VICTIM

Men and women, especially in the African American community are divided on whether boxer Mike Tyson should have been convicted of the rape of a young beauty contestant. Whenever a black man collides with the justice system, questions of bias come up, and in the wake of William Kennedy Smith's acquittal the mumbles are that a white man can get away with it, while a black man can't. But the cases are hardly comparable – they happened in different jurisdictions, and both the accused and the victims had different degrees of credibility. Tyson gave contradicting grand jury testimony; Smith didn't. To beg the bias question is to suggest that a black woman should be raped to shore up the judicial chances of a black man. Hogwash.

It is troubling that black clergy came to that conclusion, sponsoring a prayer rally for Tyson in Indianapolis, as if his accuser were not also deserving of prayer. The black Baptist leader who called the rally seems to be saying that a man's word is worth more than a woman's, no matter what the circumstances. These very ministers rail against Tyson-like behavior from their pulpits, but are so dazzled by his celebrity (or the possibility that he might make a contribution) that they suspend all judgment in his favor.

More troubling than the ministers are those who think that the victim's behavior somehow justifies a rape. They think women "ought to know better" than to talk to people with dicey reputations. Women "ought to be careful" of dangerous places and times. These folk would probably swath women in veils, shade our eyes, bind our feet, and keep us off the street after dark. Whether a woman is careful of place, time, or space or not, she still has the right to say "no."

I have this damn fool theory of crime. Just because you are a damn fool doesn't justify crimes committed against you. If I leave my open purse on the seat of my unlocked car in a busy parking lot, I'm a damn fool. But if somebody takes the purse out of my car they are a robber, plain and simple. My foolish behavior doesn't justify a robbery, nor does it make the robbery "consensual" or less serious. Tyson's accuser may have been foolish or naive to meet someone with a lewd reputation at two in the morning, but that doesn't jeopardize her right to say no or justify her rape.

The jury got to the bottom line in the Tyson case. Too bad so many others are stuck blaming the victim, not the villain in this case.

USA Today, February, 1992

BAD SPORTS

San Francisco's Joe Montana has switched uniforms, moving to the Kansas City Chiefs, who gave up a player and a couple of draft picks for the right to dapper Joe. Ordinarily this would be as interesting to me as the invention of an enzyme that contains pond scum, but the headline — taller than that of presidential victory — dominates the local paper, the news section, and the sports page. And it reinforces the point that sports plays such an important and pivotal role in our society that it is important to get a handle on gamesmanship and the way it shapes and influences all of us. This is what Betty Lou Haragan tried to do in her book, *Games Mother Never Taught You*, what Rev. Jesse Jackson has tried to point out in his boycotts against baseball. The game and all its layers, which go beyond owners and players, is a white male province that has disproportionate influence in the way Americans live.

How many cities have floated bond issues to finance a stadium? How many, like San Francisco, have offered teams submarket rents to keep them in town? How many mayors, like Washington, D.C.'s Sharon Pratt Kelley, have said they would "do anything" to keep a team in town? Has anyone ever said they'd go out on such a limb to keep a library open or a youth employed? How does sports get to be so all-important?

And how do sports metaphors worm their way into our language? "May the best man win." "It doesn't matter if you win or lose, it's how you play the game." The sucker punch, the triple team, they are all part of our jargon. And those men, Jack Kemps and Bill Bradleys, who have spent time playing some kind of ball look back fondly on those days and refer to them coyly. These were the days when they learned about black and white and wrong and right and values. Their sports prowess sends a signal. They are what we consider "real" men.

But what do these men really tell us? White men can not only jump, they can leave the playing field and do public policy. Black men jump and run and rock and roll and then disappear into oblivion with few opportunities for management, ownership, or electoral office stemming from their athletic days. White men's athletic prowess is an asset, black men's a liability. How many black men, after all, leave the sweat of the basketball game or the shoulder pads of football to be real players in our society? How many manage more than a car dealership or a soft drink franchise?

It is beyond players and owners. Sports is so much a part of the American fabric that Apple Computer felt compelled to announce the introduction of a new line at Superbowl 1984. The announcement had less to do with the notion that thousands of sports fans would go out to buy computers than it had to do with casting the computer as part of the American fabric. And it all gets advertised at those games — the beer, the cars, the electronics goods. All advertised with women used as objects and not subjects, as folk that grin and skin and profile a product, sending out another signal.

For all the black male presence on the playing field, African Americans are largely absent in the ads that support the sports machine. I don't know that I want black women grinning and nodding like the white girls do, but I do know that the dominance in one field and absence in another speaks to the way sports has supported many of our nation's stereotypes. America's gladiator, America's entertainers, are impotent to influence their space and place around them. They can carry the ball and win the games, but they can't own the teams, write the bond measures that support the stadiums, or even, often, hawk the products (Michael Jordan notwithstanding).

San Francisco is weeping because Joe Montana is leaving, weeping to the tune of 48 point print. I'm hoping that this departure reminds us again of the way sports dominates and skews life in this country. I won't weep for Joe, but I'll cheer for Jesse as his boycotts struggle to make this point. Joe may weaken the heart that someone left in San Francisco, but Jesse reminds us that we should take a closer look at the sports institution.

King Features, April, 1993

MAGIC—TRAGIC, PRAGMATIC, BUT NO HERO

Excuse me if I don't join the crowds of people ready to induct Magic Johnson into sainthood. While I agree that it is a tragedy that the basketball star has been diagnosed HIV positive, and while I appreciate the candor with which Magic shared his diagnosis with the public, tragedy and candor do not a hero make. One might argue, indeed, that Magic's candor was unavoidable, given his absence from early season Laker games. Had he not told the world that he was HIV positive, some lab technician might have leaked it to a tabloid in exchange for some monetary consideration. By speaking up early, Magic Johnson may have salvaged commercial relationships that surely would have

99

been severed if his HIV infection was the subject of gossip and innuendo, not squarely faced fact.

I got turned off with the arrogance implicit in Magic Johnson's discussion of the way he contracted the HIV virus. "Anybody can get the HIV virus, even me," said Magic, implying that super immunity comes with sports superstardom. He said that every woman in LA wanted him and that he "did his best to accommodate them." Even after his tragic diagnosis, Magic Johnson hasn't learned to inject some humility into his conversation.

Perhaps he is no different than other athletes who see women as commodities, not individuals. Even as America sympathized with Magic Johnson and his family, former basketball player Wilt Chamberlain was on the talk show circuit crowing that he had slept with 20,000 women in his life. Clearly the man exaggerates – in order to have met his "count," he would have had to sleep with 1.7 women each day for the past 35 years. But Chamberlain's braggadocio, when combined with Magic Johnson's past willingness to "accommodate" suggest that these sports figures systematically devalue women.

Even in his announcement, Magic Johnson uttered no word of concern or compassion for the women he "accommodated." Yet studies show that a man is 20 times as likely to infect a woman with the HIV virus than a woman is to infect a man. If there are heroes in the struggle to stop the spread of the HIV virus, the heroes are women like DiAna DiAna, the Executive Director of the South Carolina AIDS Education Network, who passes out condoms and safe sex kits in her Columbia, S.C. beauty shop.

"When you look at the big picture, Magic Johnson did a good thing," said Kathleen Stoll, Director of the Washington, D.C. based National Center on Women and AIDS. "If his high visibility motivates young men to learn more about the HIV virus, that can only be good." She won't get any disagreement from me. But I cringe at the deification of a man whose sexual behavior has been, at best, irresponsible, and who has yet to acknowledge that he may have spread the virus to women he "accommodated." Magic says he will spread the "safe sex" message. But there ought to be another message that he spreads to the young men who idolize him. Women are people, not objects of conquest, notches on a belt. It ought not take an HIV diagnosis to change the way some men objectify women, but Magic would be a hero in my book if he used his diagnosis to make this point.

The excitement of the basketball court may be gone for Magic Johnson, but in his own words he has lived "the greatest life." Can the women who may have been infected say the same thing? Will they have the same resources to fight the HIV virus as Magic has? These women, and the hundreds of others who anonymously keep on keeping on despite their health status are the true heroes in the fight to stop the spread of this virus.

King Features, November, 1991

PUTTING SPORTS IN PERSPECTIVE

Twenty-seven year old Reggie Lewis, a star player for the Boston Celtics died in late July during a practice session at Brandeis University. Lewis collapsed three months before his death during a playoff game, was diagnosed with heart disease, and received conflicting medical advice about whether or not he should continue to play ball. Indeed, advice became so conflicting that during his April medical emergency, Reggie Lewis switched hospitals and was somewhat critical of Boston Celtics' doctors.

It is always a tragedy when a young person dies, the tragedy compounded when death didn't have to happen. The occasion of Reggie Lewis' death, though, is also an occasion to contemplate issues of sports, education, and society, especially as thousands of young black men head to campuses in weeks prepared, not to crack their books, but to "play some ball." Most of these young brothers aspire to be someone like Reggie Lewis, a starring player with a seven figure salary, the acclaim of millions, and a jet-setting lifestyle. Many would play, heart ailment or not, because they see the playing court as their ticket to a good life. Many would risk their lives and health, as Hank Gathers and Reggie Lewis did, because their love of the game and its rewards are so great.

Far be it from me to rewrite the work of folk like UC Berkeley Professor Harry Edwards or Indiana University Professor Gary Sailes. These sports sociologists have written, at length, about the game and its place and space on campus, both cautioning young men to view their chances of being sports stars in some sort of perspective. Edwards has noted that there are some four thousands "gladiators" out of a male population of more than a hundred million, so that even an exceptionally talented person has a one in two hundred thousand chance of making it big time. But that caution rolls like water off some ducks' backs – I know a man in his thirties who still shoots hoops two or three hours a day in the strange hope that someone will discover him and make a star out of him.

The point is not to dash the dreams of hopeful hoopsters but to challenge African American men to dream more broadly and more globally, to make the goal of inventing a cure for cancer or developing a community distribution system as lofty as the goal of making seven figures on the basketball court. It's been said time and again that if folk practiced reading and writing as much as they practiced hooping and jumping there would be a lot more African American men on Wall Street or in medical whites. It might be a trite point, but it's one that cannot be made often enough, and the tragic death of Reggie Lewis is one more occasion to make this point.

I have a special interest in making the point about sports, education, and society. Sports reek of an awful sexism that places men at the center, women at the cheering periphery. Despite the growing number of women who participate in the athletic enterprise, sports is generally a narrow male occasion. The deification of gladiators all too often includes the notion of no brakes, of pampered men who can take whatever they want and break any rules. Despite the regulation of the athletic enterprise, especially at the college level, the stereotype is all too often the reality, and at least some abuse of women students is associated with the "pack," i.e., team, mentality.

I'm not suggesting that sports are bad and ought to be eliminated, but I certainly think they ought to be put into some perspective and that the use of sports as our society's dominant metaphor needs to be eliminated. Too many of our clichés are borrowed from physical competition, too many rooted in a culture of winners and losers and doing whatever it takes. Too few of these sayings, "May the best man win," "Winning isn't everything – it's the only thing," aren't examined closely for the negative messages they send about the way we live.

And then there is the role model issue. Charles Barkley said it right when he said he is not a role model. But he blinked when he said he should not be required to be one. One of the few Biblical verses that I've committed to memory is the one that says something about much being expected of those who have been given much. Barkley can't be something he isn't – an outstanding citizen – when his only outstanding attribute seems to be the ability to dunk a ball into a hoop. But he can try, and that's the point. He is held up as a role model because he is African American and visible, because people want to be like him. I can't say I know why black men want to emulate Mr. Barkley, but clearly the disproportionate emphasis we place on sports is part of it.

Perspective. Balance. Powerful words. Important words to ponder as yet another black man bites the dust, not from a drive-by shooting, a drug deal gone bad, or one of those macho mano a mano "you looked at me too hard" kind of things. Reggie Lewis died because he had a bad heart but he kept playing ball, perhaps because his sport was not placed in perspective, so that it became more important than his life. As thousands of black men trudge off to school, not to open up books but to play games, I'd like to challenge them to consider the short life of Reggie Lewis, his stardom and his death, and what might have been. Sports skills are a small part of the measure of a man. Students who are also athletes, and those who coach and mentor them, need to remember that.

Black Issues In Higher Education, March, 1993

MIDNIGHT BALL:
MEN PLAY, WOMEN WATCH

Last week, the Ella Hill Hutch Community Center added another jewel to the crown of programs it offers the community. They kicked off their midnight basketball league amidst gala and excitement. Teams were sponsored by people like Judge Daniel Weinstien, City Attorney Louise Rennee, and restaurateur James Thigpen. The press was present, and the first games got much television coverage. And as much as I enjoyed myself, I had a sense of uneasiness as I watched and listened to the spiel about the midnight basketball league.

Here's the deal. In order to participate in the league, young men must attend workshops prior to the games. On Tuesday and Thursday nights, then, the schedule is workshop, then basketball, from 10 until 2. Those who don't participate in the workshops can't play ball. On the first night of play, workshop participants included Rev. Calvin Jones, Rev. Martin Grizelle, and Robert Christmas. So far, sounds good.

The midnight basketball concept originated in a DC suburb, and quickly got attention because it makes use of public resources while costing very little money. President Bush (not that his endorsement is compelling) named the program one of his "Points of Light," one of the volunteer efforts that can make a difference. Quickly emulated, there are leagues up and down the East Coast, but the first West coast teams are housed at Ella Hill Hutch.

As exciting as I find the concept, my uneasiness has to do with the way programs are targeted toward black male youth, with little offered for young black women. So men play ball, and women watch, men act, and women stand on the periphery. Yes, this is what the world is like, though some of these things are slowly changing. Ella Hill Hutch would put midnight ball on the cutting edge if it combined its programming for young men with programming for young women.

If young men can't play ball unless they attend seminars, why not offer seminars for the young women who will sit in the bleachers to cheer the teams on? Perhaps the Links, or other women's organizations, could take turns offering workshops. Now, I'm not picking on the Links, but this particular organization seems to be so cash-flush that they are an ideal candidate to roll up their sleeves and get involved.

Sports plays a role in our society – it perpetuates the idolatry of gladiators. Men who play ball are often seen as men who cannot do wrong, men who must be worshipped. Men who can grab at hordes of willing women. Men who, like Magic Johnson, tried to "accomodate" the women who wanted him, who like Mike Tyson think they can have any woman in their line of vision. This behavior doesn't take place on the playing field, but is a result of playing field idolatry. To the extent that sports is a metaphor for life, the games athletes play are symbolic of life lessons, and they are the philosopher-kings of our vapid society.. "It's not how you win or lose it's how you play the game." "Just do it." "Challenge your body" and all that. There is no such revered place in our society for women's achievement, no such lessons that are gleaned from the things women do for work and play. So the men are actors, women reactors or cheerleaders, men at center stage women on the periphery. The notion was reinforced for me when a DC football player, Gary Clark, waxed nostalgic about his youth. "The guys were playing sports and the girls were learning to be ladies," he told the *Washington Post*. And midnight ball seems to reinforce the same notion, men like peacocks, being gazed upon and admired by women.

Guns, gangs, and street violence have compelled community leaders to look at the black male youth and tackle the issues he faces. But many of these issues are women's issues too. The girls don't necessarily tote guns, but they felt the helplessness of urban situations and respond to them in ways that may be destructive. Some get pregnant, others drop out of school, and still others attach themselves to the men who are primary actors in urban violence. So when a feud between two groups in Oakland spilled over, it was three women sleeping in their beds who were shot, women who were victims of this overflowing of awful male aggression. Isn't there something that we should do to help these women make better choices? Shouldn't community programming do something to take women off the sidelines and into the center? Or are my brothers who put together a midnight basketball league, so used to having women revolve around them that they didn't see the way they are perpetuating myths and stereotypes?

In all fairness to the brothers at Ella Hill Hutch, it was announced that this program is "experimental." Perhaps as they fine tune their work, a focus toward young women will be included. Meanwhile. . .men are at the center, women on the periphery, and business goes on as usual.

Sun Reporter, March, 1992

BACK TO SCHOOL IN A MULTICULTURAL WAR ZONE

What has education got to do with it? The average earnings for a black woman with a graduate degree are about the same as the earnings of a white male college dropout. At the same time, a black woman graduate earns more than twice what a black woman who drops out of high school earns. Education is the ladder that pulls people out of poverty, but the rungs are spaced differently for whites than for blacks, for men than for women. And curriculums reflect the bias of uneven rungs, with the mythology of narrow history reflected in tests and in textbooks. Education is a ladder and a bridge, but it is also an industry.

ECONOMICS AND EDUCATION

What makes our economy putter along? The people who work in offices and factories, that's who. People who believe the hype, that the more they learn the more they earn. People who chase advancement as if it was a pot of gold, taking extra classes, shouldering new training, all in search of a better paycheck.

Watching people on the job won't tell you much about their education. That computer expert could be an electrical engineer or high school dropout who combined hacking skill with an inside track to get a job. That man sweeping the front of the store could be a high school student or an executive fallen on hard times. That secretary could be a college graduate – one in seven are – or someone who just completed secretarial school.

Economists believe that the more you learn, the more you earn. Human capital theory has driven public policy on education and training, spurring the development of vocational schools, encouraging college enrollment. But black college enrollment is dropping, both because of costs and because colleges are often a hostile environment for these youngsters.

Then too, a college degree isn't the union card it used to be. According to Barry Bluestone and Bennet Harrison, nearly half of all black women college graduates under 25 earned $12,500 in 1987. A third of all black men under 25 with college degrees earned the same amount. Far fewer white college graduates (just one in six white men, for example) have such low earnings.

What has education got to do with it? The average earnings for a black woman with a graduate degree are about the same as the earnings of a white male college drop-out. And whether we are comparing earnings in the executive suite or on the street, women still earn two-thirds of what men earn!

That isn't stopping those seeking education, enrolling in vocational school, college, or graduate school. But it ought to spur those who make public policy to strengthen the connection between education and employment, to eliminate bias in the workplace. How many students "do the right thing" only to face an economy that does the wrong thing by them?

What has education got to do with it? Ask Dan Quayle, whose middling grades and abuse of affirmative action catapulted him to the vice presidency. Ask the young people who, without resources, won't get the chance to be as pitiful as Dan Quayle academically. The more you learn,

the more you earn. That's economic theory or a broken promise, depending on your paychecks.

USA Today, 1989

SAVING TEACHERS FROM BURNOUT

A few months ago, I had coffee with a teacher, who spoke of her students as if they were monsters. She had her reasons — in two years she had been assaulted by junior high school youngsters, had her tires slashed and her purse stolen. I'd have been annoyed by her attitude, but for the fact that I knew her when she was idealistic enough to think she could teach any child. The teacher she once was differed sharply from the bitter and cynical woman she had become, a woman who viewed her students as the enemy.

How did she turn out that way? She works in one of the 28 urban school districts that provides education for three quarters of our nation's children. Her district faces budget cuts so often that three or four teachers in each school get layoff notices each year. All the notices aren't enforced, but in the dark days between notice and rehire, a teacher fears for her job and livelihood.

My teacher friend has seen good programs die from lack of funds. She has watched the school's parking lot turn into an urban looting zone, and seen a young child's eager eyes turn sour in just a few months. She has watched the political jockeying around education and found it to be more self-serving for school board members than enriching for her students. And, putting herself on the line, she has come to wonder if it is worth it.

The whisper of doubt becomes a roar when she speaks to her peers, writers, lawyers, and administrators who earn more than she does and face much less risk. In many ways, their salaries and attitudes eat at her sense of self, so much so that when she opens her sack lunch in the teachers lounge, she visualizes her friend lunching at the restaurant of the week.

Her view of their world may be distorted, but her working world has become a living nightmare. When the layoff notices come, she both hopes for one and dreads its arrival. What this teacher needs is a break! A sabbatical. Some time off. She needs to get off the treadmill of a class every hour, a meeting every afternoon, and stretch her brain a bit. She needs a new perspective on the neighborhood problems that frustrate her, the drugs, the crime, the violence. She needs to rediscover the open minds of her students, the motivating force within herself.

It is easier to say "children are our future" than it is to improve the lives of children we say we care about. So while both President Bush and the Democratic Party offer an educational agenda, teachers in Washington state are at the verge of striking and those in the bankrupt Richmond, California school district don't know whether their district can pay them to complete the semester. And these beleaguered teachers are the ones who will implement the new educational agenda!

What can we do? Why not offer these teachers sabbaticals every three, five, or seven years? Why not ask these teachers to go back to school to enhance their classroom skills? Why not help them develop new curriculum ideas, offer them new teaching options?

Most would answer "budget," but that's not the bottom line. If only one in ten teachers take sabbaticals each year, that would cost 10 percent of payroll, or about $10 billion per year nationally. That's a lot to ask schools to pay when money is tight. On the other hand, that was what we paid to spend just four hours in the Persian Gulf when we were bombing.

President Bush and Democrats have offered competing visions for our nation's educational future. They have offered a battle plan without looking at the anxious and burned out soldiers who will implement their plan. Teachers are the cornerstone of our educational system. Where is the plan that recognizes their needs and offers them relief from large classrooms, low pay, and burnout?

King Features, April, 1991

SAVE OUR LIBRARIES

You can't just throw money at urban problems, a friend of mine tells me. We are having the usual argument about money, values, and the government role. I think of his euphemism, "throwing money," every time I drive by the branch library in my neighborhood, a library that was once open seven days a week, then five, then three. Instead of reading inside the library, the children of the neighborhood swing on the banister outside the library, or sit on the ledge in front of the library.

The same is true at the main library downtown, where people line up outside to wait for the doors to open at noon. In a few weeks, doors won't open at all, at least one day a week. Everybody has to tighten their belt, our mayor says, while hiring 26 new staff people for his office. So our main library will be open six days, instead of seven.

San Francisco is not unique. Three quarters of the New York Public Library's 82 branches are closed three or more days a week. Chicago's public library lost nearly a thousand workers in the 80's, with staff dropping from 2,300 to 1,333. Volunteers are being sought to pick up the slack. Worchester, Massachusetts closed six of its seven branches at the end of 1990. In Bridgeport, Connecticut, the main library is open only 20 hours a week, and most branch libraries are open only one day a week.

When open, libraries are being challenged to do more with less money, and to cut adult literacy, bookmobile, and children's literacy services. Book budgets have been cut while the prices of books and journals have risen. The Philadelphia library canceled orders on 20,000 new books in 1991. The Belen, New Hampshire library made no new purchases in the 1990-91 fiscal year. When six new libraries open in Palm Beach, Florida, more than half the shelf space will be empty.

The forerunner of today's public library, the Philadelphia Library Company, was opened in 1731. The first American public library opened in Peterboro, New Hampshire in 1833. By the time the American Library Association was founded, in 1876, most major cities had free public libraries, supported primarily by city funds. Today, libraries survive through a combination of city, state, and federal funds, but all three sources are shrinking and libraries are closing, something that didn't even happen during the Depression.

The frightening thing about library closings is that they come at a time when there is a growing awareness of our nation's literacy problems. As many as 30 percent of all adults have literacy problems, as do a growing number of our young people. Many libraries had embraced the issue of adult literacy, and now are forced to abandon that mission and go back to the "basics" of keeping their doors open.

We also miss something less tangible when we close libraries. There is something magic and empowering about books, about reading. Even if you can't afford a tour of France, you can read about it. And while you may not be able to buy a bestseller or classic, a library makes that book available.

Whenever I see little girls swinging on library banisters instead of inside reading, I wonder what they are losing through lack of access. I remember the summer of my tenth year, when upon a challenge, I tried to read every book in the children's section of my neighborhood library. I didn't manage to read everything by summer's end, but I read enough to make books and reading a permanent part of my life. Now friends tease that I am addicted to the printed word, and I reply that there are probably less de-

sirable addictions.

It doesn't take magic to keep libraries open. It takes money, simply money. This is at least one case where throwing dollars at a problem will solve it.

King Features, June, 1992

EXCLUSION IN THE NAME OF THE LORD

Do colleges affiliated with churches do better than others in admitting students of color, especially African American students? The survey that appears in the November 1993 issue of this publication suggests not. African Americans are about 12 percent of our nation's population, and are generally not proportionally represented on the campuses of church-related institutions or other colleges. Overall, according to the American Council on Education, African American students represented about 8.2 percent of all students in 1990, significantly fewer than their representation in the total population. A quick eyeball of the statistics produced for Catholic (and other religious) colleges suggests that few do better than the national norm, and that most do worse.

Church-related institutions can say they do as well as anyone. Would they accept such logic if it were applied to their moral imperative, if they were forced to allege that their insider trading is as moral as anyone's, their record of integrity in athletics, or their history of sexual harassment? Doing as well as anyone else doesn't pass muster when a child tries to avoid homework by asserting that "nobody" does it, or break a curfew on the ground that "everyone" does. So it ought not be an acceptable argument for church-related schools that have refused to take leadership on matters of race and student enrollment. Of course, church-related schools do as well as anyone. Of course, racism is a fact of life in this country. Of course, institutions change pitifully slowly. Of course, church-related schools have good intentions. But, in the words of a blues singer, good intentions just aren't good enough.

After all, I'm sure there were nothing but good intentions when religion was used against Black folk (and other indigenous people) in white America. During slavery, jackleg preachers often exhorted slaves to "obey their master" using Biblical verse to justify awful oppression. The Catholic Church helped conquer the Americas on the basis that they were bringing "Christianity" to savages. People have used the Bible to justify everything from separating the races, to turning the other cheek, to (during this last horrible travesty of a Republican Convention) "taking our cities back from those boys," in the words of Catholic pundit Pat Buchanan. All in the name of good intentions. If such wrong, such outrage, can be done in the name of good, why can't church-related institutions do good for good's sake.

Why can't they justify their religious mandate and earn the many tax exemptions they get by exceeding the national record of Black (and other minority) enrollment? Why can't they take it upon themselves to create model campuses where race relations are concerned? In the same sense that religion is part of their mission, why isn't "doing the right thing?" Church related institutions have woefully failed to stand out in this matter; they've turned away from their religious mandate. They are excluding people of color in the name of the Lord.

I don't care whether this exclusion is active ("no blacks need apply") or passive ("we can't find any qualified blacks"); the result is still unacceptable. It sends a message that we can't do anything about low black enrollment in our nation's colleges and universities, and that religious institutions simply go along to get along instead of providing leadership on these matters. Colleges like SMU, Notre Dame, and Baylor University make national headlines because of their sports programs, but their student bodies are whiter than the overall population. The message – black students can play sports but not bust books. Is this hypocrisy justified anyplace in a church-related institution's mandate?

I make this point not as a "church-basher," but as an alumna of a Catholic college (Boston College, 1974). I think my alma mater shoots as far from the mark as any other institution. The Fall, 1992 issue of *Boston College Magazine* indicated that some 287 black students were enrolled at BC in 1992, just under 2 percent of the entire student body. The 287 students is only a handful more than were enrolled when I graduated. Indeed, the proportion of black students in the student body is lower in 1992 than at many points in the past.

BC has done better by other people of color – Asian American enrollment has nearly tripled in a decade, while Latino enrollment has almost doubled (and Black enrollment has increased by about 25 percent). The number of women in the student body has risen as well. On the surface, "diversity" has increased. But the bottom line is there aren't enough black students in the student population.

It doesn't take much for me to think back to the reasons the administration gave for low enrollment in the past. Black students had low SAT scores. They needed too much financial aid. The middle class students they wanted to enroll opted for other places, including historically black colleges. They just couldn't find enough qualified blacks. Fast forward 18 years and read the *Black Issues* interview with Father Ted Hesburgh. Despite his distinguished civil rights record, it sounds like more of the same excuses.

I know folks who say that little is gained by pointing fingers at those who, with good intentions, simply fall short of the mark. There are those with intentions less pure, with records less illustrious. But the only way that patterns of enrollment will be changed is if some institutions take it upon themselves to do not just "as well as," but measurably better than, other institutions of higher education. If church-related institutions aren't up to the challenge, they

ought to toss in the Bible instead of the towel, and admit that they don't mind excluding in the name of the Lord.

Black Issues in Higher Education, December, 1992

A NECESSARY AFFIRMATION

From the moment the Afro-American Studies faculty marched into the auditorium to the tune of Kumbaya, to the moment students strutted out to a jazz version of "We Shall Overcome," Berkeley's Black Graduation was a unique and moving experience. If it is possible to have Africa in the hallowed halls of elite education, then it was African. If it is possible to have individuality at a ceremony that recognized the accomplishments of more than 100 students, then it was individual. Ruby Dee, as guest speaker, shared glimmers of her many talents as she read from her book, *My One Good Nerve.* And I was immersed in the beauty and contradiction inherent in the ceremony.

You mean the Afro-American Studies Department graduation, a white friend said when I tried to tell her about it. She went on to explain to me (because I am so obviously ignorant and could not know) that every department at Berkeley has its own graduation. But the Afro-American Studies Department, with just a handful of majors, has been the safe haven for so many black Berkeley students, the place where they could learn about themselves. And the black graduation, I told the white girl, was just that, a ceremony for any graduating black Berkeley student who chose to participate. More than a hundred did, including a group of law school graduates, a new MBA, and an African brother who received the Ph.D. in public health.

I am getting too old, too impatient, to have long conversations with white people about why black people "need" certain things. These conversations take on the tone of "I been this way before," and mid-sentence I have to turn away to keep from blowing up. So after a half-hearted

116

attempt to explain the black graduation to this white woman, I told her that we should probably keep our conversations to subjects of mutual interest. And inside me the warm kernel planted from the Black Graduation burned like an ember on the fire.

The Black Graduation was necessary affirmation for the students, parents, and faculty that participated. Amidst music and song, we recognized and congratulated our own. Amidst music and song, with a guarded joy, we listened as statements that students wrote about themselves were read. Nearly everone thanked "mom and dad," and the sorority women whooped and the fraternity men barked. But beneath the joy there was a pathos. Too many black students talked about the hurdles they had to clear at Berkeley, and some referred directly to the racism they experienced.

Too many students "hoped to go on" to graduate or professional school, or "hoped to find employment" in a certain field. For a special day, they put a happy face on the fact that they have not yet been admitted, have not yet found the jobs they seek. And these are students from the best school in California, one of the best schools in the country. If they are still clearing hurdles, even amidst joy, what can the brother on the corner expect?

Even with the undercurrent that hope is a fragile bauble easily shattered against the jagged edges of racism, the Black Graduation was high and happy. It offered all of the participants a sense of renewal, a reason for motivation, a perspective for struggle. Events like Black Graduation are necessary affirmation for black students and their families who are not affirmed, but in fact denied, by white America.

Thanks to the Doonesbury cartoonist, Gary Trudeau, people all over the country are laughing about crazy Californians and the "Self-Esteem" Commission that was recently created. But it is even more amazing to me that so few people talk openly about race and self-esteem, about the way racism erodes self-esteem. And we black people

certainly can't expect the very white community that in-
stitutionally erodes our self-esteem to then turn around and
build it back up. After all, there is a war on black people.
The casualties are measured in terms of high unemployment and infant mortality rates, low graduation rates, high
incarceraton rates.

Black Graduation was a necessary affirmation, a moment of pause between battles in the war, a time for rest
and replenishment, a reminder of history, beauty, and dignity. This kind of affirmation needs to happen more often,
and we all need to participate in these ceremonies. And
even as we applaud our graduates and achievers, we need
to prepare them for the struggle that will surely continue.

Sun Reporter, May, 1989

THE WALLS WERE MADE OF DREAMS

"Have you ever lived in a nine room prison constructed
of your own hopes," wrote Leanita McClain in a communications she called her "Generic Suicide Note." And then
the sister killed herself. Young, black and a "superstar," at
least in white folks terms, she was also fated to live only 32
years, to write only a few columns that made people so
angry that they sent her boxes upon boxes of hate mail.
Her former husband has collected some of her essays into
a book called *A Foot in Each World*. The essays make interesting and highly recommended reading.

I had to laugh at her column about the Rev. Jesse Jackson, titled "Tree Shaker or Jelly Maker." She described the
good reverend as the former, and wondered aloud if he
had what it takes to be President. But months later, she
was more positive about Jesse's candidacy, and anxious to
put Jesse's "hymie" remark into the context that we black
folk have been on the receiving end of insults far too long.

I laughed and learned as I read her descriptions of
Chicago City Council meetings, about the way Harold
Washington and Eddie Vrdolyak have missed coming to

blows a time or two (or three or five). Her description of a friend's illegal abortion is heart-wrenching. Her suggestion that Marcus Garvey be pardoned was exhilarating. Her defense of "free speech" even when it is inflammatory shows that McClain walked a fine ideological line, alternately progressive and conservative.

When I saw Leanita McClain's book, I literally hungered to read. I identified with the sister who was born just a year before I was, who wrote about similar issues. I didn't read the book last week, I inhaled it, all the while wondering what Leanita McClain would be writing about now. What would she say about Gary Hart? About Contragate? About the Soviets suggesting that white Americans give us our own state? I didn't know McClain, but I think I miss her in an intangible way, miss seeing her work, her talents.

But her nine room prison made of hopes is much like the walls that many young black people face, walls made of dreams. Langston Hughes wrote, "And dare you dream, because when dreams die, life is a broken winged bird that cannot fly." A Boston poet once wrote "It is the death of a crippled dream that brings me here." Both writers used the concept of mutilated dreams, took that concept and made it as visual, as real, as cutting as the shattering of glass.

A dream should take you out, it should not wall you in. But walls, like prisons, can be built with dreams when dreams are dashed, crippled, and broken. And this happens in the black community day after day, when young black men and women are denied opportunity because racism is alive and well in white America. I'm not saying that racism killed Leanita McClain. She overdosed on pills. But the dynamics of racism and the way they affected her had an impact on the fact that she was successful, not happy. Racism, race hate, touched Leanita McClain and made her want to kill herself, to die in a prison with walls made of dreams. That same racism touches others of us, makes us angry enough to struggle against racism.

But as black students all over this country graduate this month and next, they will approach the world with cloud-like dreams of who they are and what they want to be, fluffy dreams that may have nothing to do with race, something to do with careers. Many of them will leave warm environments and move to places hostile. Or they will leave hostile environments and move to places even more hostile. Their dreams may be crippled by white racism, may be battered by doors that keep closing in their faces. But black folks have limped by with crippled dreams as long as any of us can remember, which may be why Mary Frances Berry titled her book on black history *Long Memory*. The black musicians who worked in the post office because they had to earn a living had crippled dreams, yet they were warriors. The black women who scrubbed floors to send their children to school had broken dreams, but they were pioneers.

Those black folks who live in prisons where bricks were made of dreams need to read McClain to understand that bricks can be used to fence us in, or we can throw them, break glass,and struggle out. When young black students step out, placing a foot in each world like Leanita McClain did, we need to stand firmly behind them so that even when they are standing on a limb, the support we offer is there to break the fall.

Sun Reporter, June, 1988

MULTIPLE CHOICE STUPIDITY

What do standardized tests measure? The ability to do multiple choice-think, to answer complex questions monosyllabically, to respond to options in literature, math and science with answers like "all of the above." But multiple choice-think isn't the only skill one needs to succeed in college, and standardized tests are a weak predictor of a student's probability of college success. Educational psychologist Asa Hilliard says that standardized tests add precious little predictive power to high school grades, and that college admissions officers are better off relying on those grades than on SAT and ACT tests.

How come? Standardized tests are largely written by white men, for white men. Even the Educational Testing Service concedes their cultural bias. According to Leslie Wolfe, of the Center for Women Policy Studies, women who earn straight "A" grades in high school score lower on SAT tests than men with the same grades. They are as likely as these men, if not more so, to do well in college and to complete their educations. Black and Hispanic students similarly earn lower scores than white men, but low scores on flawed tests mean very little. Black and Hispanic law students, for example, earned grades as high as white counterparts who scored 100 points higher on Law School Admissions Tests (LSATs).

When the possibility of teaching and tutoring intervention is considered, standardized test results mean even less. Students who consciously address deficiencies in their educational preparation have generally had successful college careers. At the University of Georgia, for example, special admissions students with low standardized test scores who participated in tutorial programs did as well or better in core courses than general admissions students.

Why, then, do universities rely on standardized tests to make their admissions decisions? Partly because it saves them money and time, allowing them to screen thousands of applicants quickly and cheaply. Partly because it is easier to write "different" students off than to take chances on their success. And tragically, because they have forgotten that the purpose of higher education is to increase understanding and communication, not diminish it. Colleges should open doors, not slam them in the faces of students whose options may shrink to "none of the above" because tests are flawed.

USA Today, January, 1989

BLACK BOY SCHOOLS AND THE
BLACK GIRLS THEY IGNORE

They have been proposed in New York and Milwaukee, and public schools just for black boys will open in Detroit this fall unless a lawsuit by the ACLU and NOW Legal Defense Fund is successful. Why should black boys have their own schools? Those who support them say black men are "endangered" and cite statistics on dropout status and arrest rates to back themselves up. They say that too many black boys lack positive male role models, and raised by their mothers they are all too vulnerable to negative influences, like gangs. They say that the public school curriculum ignores black achievement and gnaws away at self-esteem and that an *Afrocentric* curriculum taught by black men is necessary to rebuild this esteem for black boys. And they say these schools address some of these problems.

But every problem that black boys face is also faced by black girls. Girls are rarely arrested but they, too, drop out and get caught up in all of the urban negative — teen pregnancy, dead end careers, and sometimes worse. Like black boys, many black girls would benefit from male attention and positive male role models. Like boys, they are vulnerable to gangs and others in the absence of those models. And girls, like boys, read books that denigrate African Americans, those histories that only mention a black presence in the context of slavery, Booker T. Washington, or Dr. Martin Luther King. Black girls, like black boys, would greatly benefit from an improvement in the quality of urban education. These girls are sent a stunning negative message when they observe a shift in resources from all students to male students. They are being told, implicitly, that their *educations* are less important than black male educations.

Proponents of all black boy schools, like Chicago author Juwanza Kunjufu, would not only segregate students. Kunjufu, alleging that "black women cannot teach black men," would also make teaching environments almost entirely male. Yet if Kunjufu is right, if black women can't teach black men, then the illiteracy rate among African-Americans would be even higher than it is now, as black women teachers have historically been the back bone of urban school systems.

Those who say black boys need their own schools are crying "crisis." Their argument does not stand up unless we believe that the black man is "endangered." To protect against "endangered species" status, these boys bond under the leadership of African American male teachers. But these separate schools seem simply to reinforce the notion of "endangerment," stigmatizing black male youngsters and separating them from the general school population. And it sends these boys the message that something is so wrong with girls and women that they are incapable of learning in their presence!

The existence of all black boy schools suggests that black boys are special, but black girls are not. And this is a message girls may carry through womanhood. If black boys/men are so special, must black women support them financially when they cannot find work? Should she put up with his violent or abusive behavior because he is so special? Should she cling to traditional roles to please this "special" man? Should she make her needs secondary to his?

Because of each student's different capabilities, there is no one model of education that serves every child. Some learn best in a highly disciplined parochial or military school, others in loosely structured programs for the gifted and talented. Under the umbrella of education, there may well be room for Afrocentric academies targeted toward black male youth. But these academies may cause more problems than they solve unless the educational needs of black girls are also addressed.

King Features, August, 1991

BETWEEN CENSORSHIP AND CONTROL

Censorship. When I hear the word, I think of McCarthyism and the brutal treatment of thousands of American intellectuals who were branded as "Communist sympathizers." I think of Paul Robeson and W.E.B. DuBois and the ways they were silenced, muted by witch-hunters. I am reminded of Lillian Hellman's wonderful statement, "I will not cut my conscience to fit this year's fashions." I am glad that her statement will be remembered on May 21, when writers who are victims of political persecution will receive awards from the Fund for Free Expressions, with proceeds from the estates of Hellman and Dashiell Hammet.

The writers who will be honored have lived through horrors. Vietnamese writer Duyen Anh was placed in a "re-education" camp. After his release, during a 1988 visit to the United States, he was attacked by right-wing Vietnamese and is still partly paralyzed. Guatemalan Byron Ortiz has received numerous death threats and had his papers closed by the government because of his views. South African writer Veliswa Mhlawuli worked for a community based newspaper, *Grassroots*, until she was shot in 1988. She lost her eye in the attack, but was detained by the South African government for more than six months despite her condition.

Three women in the United States will share a Hammet/Hellman award. Chrystos, a Native American writer; Audre Lorde, the black lesbian poet and professor; and Minnie Bruce Pratt, another lesbian poet/professor; received National Endowment for the Arts awards in 1989. North Carolina Senator Jesse Helms targeted them as "obscene" writers because of their lesbianism, and they were subject to nearly a year of harassment.

Harassment. Now there's a word. As I read through the descriptions of writers who will receive the Hammet/Hellman award, I thought of the way conservatives have attempted to redefine "censorship." They've described those they disagree with as "the thought police" and "fundamentalist," and suggested that concern about the widespread use of racial epithets is tantamount to censorship.

Harvard Professor Stephen Thernstrom has been talking about this. He stopped teaching his course "The Peopling of America" after he got criticism about the way he taught the class. He used the colonialist term "Oriental" to refer to Asians, and chose to use the term "Indian," though students said they preferred to be called "Native American." The students who criticized Thernstrom did not force him to stop teaching his class. He made that choice. Before students raised questions, he was a tenured professor at Harvard. After students raised questions, he retained that status. Contrast his situation with that of Veliswa Mhlawuli. Her views got her shot, not criticized. She may never write again. Contrast Thernstrom's situation with that of Audre Lorde or Minnie Bruce Pratt. He has the national media camping at Harvard to hear about his brush with the speech police. Lorde and Pratt were stuck in the eye of a storm for a year, and have had few opportunities to comment on their harassment.

The difference between writers who are being honored by the Hammet/Hellman awards and those who have whined about political correctness is control. Those who have been beaten, harassed, and prosecuted for their views have no control and were voices of dissent in their countries. Those who would silence the "politically correct" are in control, but see diverse and questioning voices as a threat to their control.

The "politically correct" don't have the power to silence anyone, merely the opportunity to raise questions. Is it so difficult to understand the difference between criticism and control, the difference between the questions students asked Professor Thernstrom and the accusations lobbed at Chrystos and Audre Lorde?

King Features, May, 1991

NOT CENSORSHIP, JUST CIVILITY

Remember the term "ivory tower"? That's how campuses were once portrayed, as lofty bastions of thought and study. Despite the obvious racial correlation, I never thought "ivory" meant narrow, white and male. But resistance to the presence of women and people of color on the part of the white male campus majority has made me wonder what "ivory" means.

The latest chapter in resistance is the evocation of the First Amendment to justify all kinds of hate speech and action on campus. Those who urge caution to protect First Amendment rights seem to defend the hurling of slurs in public space; a hurling is as real as an assault. So in the name of the First Amendment, I heard pundits defend the right of a student to call black women "water buffalo," a slur that has historical roots in the defeminization of black women. In the name of the First Amendment, students who have hung black folk in effigy, who have demolished replicas of South African shanties, have been defended. I guess when the tower gets a bit less ivory, it also gets a bit less civil.

Just like you can't shout "fire" in a crowded theater, you ought not be able to shout racial epithets on a civil campus. It is disingenuous to invoke "free speech" when freedom isn't free, when a campus is something more than a corner, a bar room, or an alley. Will the same folk fighting to dismiss campus speech codes also fight to dismiss behavioral codes, to champion the cause of students who attend class inebriated, perhaps?

While regulating speech is like tiptoeing on land mines, campuses are doing the right thing in attempting to create collegial environments. That means that in common spaces, like classrooms and public buildings, hate speech ought to be no more tolerated than other forms of anti-social behavior. It's not censorship; it's simple civility.

USA Today, August, 1993

CHAPTER SIX

WE ARE NOT YOUR BOTTOM LINE:
AFRICAN AMERICANS AND OTHERS AT THE PERIPHERY

By the year 2010, a third of our nation will be black and brown, and some projections say more brown than black. And somehow, as the demographics change, African Americans have become everyone's basis of comparison. The benefits of being "first minority" carry less weight than the burden of economic inequality, and the successes of others in the economy are often used to suggest African American societal inequality. Such analysis assumes that race, immigrant status, and sexual orientation all result in the same kind of discrimination, suggests a uniform oppression and uniform obstacles to overcome.

WE ARE NOT YOUR BOTTOM LINE

We live in a competitive and a comparative society, so it seems natural that writers of one group would use the experiences of another to illustrate a point. But whether writers are Hispanic, female, Jewish, disabled, or gay, they are bound by an ability to use the black experience as a bottom line. Why? Is it carelessness, thoughtlessness, or

127

intellectual laziness? Has the black experience been so vivid that it stands out in everyone's mind? From where I sit as an African American, I am often angered and resentful of the comparisons made, mainly because they place blacks in discussions where we don't belong, and often make unwarranted implicit assumptions about black progress.

For example, when busybodies questioned the appropriateness of Los Angeles anchorwoman Bree Walker's pregnancy because her disability condition might be passed along to her child, disability rights activist Nancy Becker Kennedy commented, "I couldn't be more shocked that this was even a topic of discussion. What's next, a discussion of whether black people should reproduce?" If Ms. Kennedy wanted to raise eyebrows, she might have asked whether *whites* should reproduce. But this woman was seeking the most dramatic indignance to illustrate her point, and she didn't have to look far. She treated African Americans as a lower bound, and inserted us in a discussion that had nothing to do with race.

She's not the only one who sees African Americans as a lower bound. Following an August study that the Children's Defense Fund released on Latino child poverty, a commentator mentioned that these children experienced more poverty than *even black* children. It is so hard to believe that any children could be worse off than black children?

These comparisons are bad enough in numerical discussions, but more jarring in the historical analysis of people who ought to know better. In a recent column about patriarchy *(LA Times,* September 6, 1991*)*, "feminist" Suzanne Gordon made one of these gratuitous comparisons: "The search for a positive patriarchy is as insulting and threatening to women as a nostalgic celebration of life in the Jim Crow South would be to blacks." Here's the rub. People celebrate life in the Jim Crow South all the time, in traditional Southern organizations that forgot who won the civil war. You don't have to look too hard to find Rebel flags in parts of the South; until recently the University of Mississippi had "Old Reb" as their mascot. Searching for a way to illustrate patriarchy's effect on women, Suzanne Gordon had only one analogy — that of the segregated South. The problem is that she behaves as if *de facto* segregation is part of our past, while golf courses, private clubs, and the United States Senate remain segregated.

Letty Cottin Pogrebin makes a similar comparison in her book, *Deborah, Golda and Me: Being Female and Jewish in America* (New York: Crown Publishers, 1991). In talking about the way Jews feel about Christmas, Pogrebin asks, "Why should Jews be required to spend six weeks a year immersed in Christian imagery? No one would ask black people to tolerate whole cities festooned with Confederate flags and pictures of the Battle of Bull Run and paeans to Generals Robert E. Lee and Stonewall Jackson. We understand that a South that flaunts the Confederate flag is disregarding the sensitivities and perspectives of black Americans. Why is it so hard to understand how a nation that flaunts Christmas does not fully belong to the Jews?"

Pogrebin fails to note that the Confederate flag flies in some cities, sensitivity be damned. The signs "white" and "colored" no longer hang in restaurants, but crosses still burn when some blocks are integrated, and Jesse Helm's use of the "white hands" commercial in his Senate campaign against Harvey Gannt was Confederate flag-waving if I ever saw it. Cannot Pogrebin think of any other way to make the point about Jews and Christmas than to use Black people as the bottom line of comparison?

There is some irony here. While conservative blacks like Shelby Steele are suggesting that African Americans should stop using our slave past as a bargaining chip in the present, every other kind of activist in the world, when pushed to explain the nature of wrong, uses the black experience as the basis of comparison. The people of Operation Rescue, people who probably scorned Dr. Martin

Luther King during his lifetime, did not miss a beat before likening their movement to the civil rights movement. Animal rights activists will walk over homeless people on the streets to sing "We Shall Overcome" for minks.

Some of these people have no use for Black people except to refer to them as the worst case at a pity party. They shamelessly trade on the historical treatment of Black people, but have no intention of acknowledging (or working to redress) that historical treatment. For them Black people are a rhetorical prop used to support their weak comparisons.

Harvard Professor Alan Dershowitz's book *Chutzpah* is full of such comparisons. After discussing the pressures on professional Jews to assimilate, Dershowitz writes that "Blacks are expected to speak and react strongly about any manifestation of anti black attitudes, as well they should. We (Jews), too, should feel proud to vigorously defend Jewish rights." Dershowitz seems ignorant of the pressures that black professionals feel to assimilate, the extent to which some pick their words and battles carefully lest they be accused of "whining about racism."

While some comparisons place blacks on the bottom, in implying that blacks have the enormous power to transform institutions like Harvard, Dershowitz falsely places black people on top. He says he wants Harvard to "put its considerable power and prestige behind Jewish values and aspirations the way it had done, for example, in regard to black and third world concerns." What power and prestige do Blacks at Harvard have? Professor Derek Bell struck Harvard Law School for a year over its racist and sexist hiring policies. His action, which cost him his full salary, changed nothing at the law school. So much for "power and prestige." If Dershowitz is concerned about having more Jewish honorary degree recipients at Harvard, that's one thing. But to tie that to black "power and prestige," given reality, is deliberately divisive.

The same kinds of comparisons leap out of every issue of *Hispanic Magazine.* The September issue has an article that compares the combined budgets of the Mexican American Legal Defense and Education Fund and the National Council of La Raza, at $8.7 million, with the "whopping" NAACP budget of $12 million (about 35 percent more). Author Roger Hernandez does not bother to control for membership or history, nor does he acknowledge the large legal debt that organizations like MALDEF owe the NAACP Legal Defense and Education Fund. His point, simply, is that Black organizations have money that Hispanic organizations do not have, as if foundations are making a choice between funding blacks and funding Hispanics, as if there are no other competing causes. Once again, black people become the universal litmus test.

These comparisons suggest that people look to the treatment of blacks as a bellwether of what is acceptable treatment of other minorities in America. If you raise a question about the disabled, what, then, about blacks? If the Confederate flags come down, what about the Christmas trees? If blacks get foundation grants, what about Hispanics? What I find offensive about these comparisons is the fact that some who make them could care less about the rights of African American people. They feel that if blacks are treated fairly, they must be treated even *more* fairly because no population group should be worse off than blacks.

The African American experience should not be used as everyone's point of comparison unless it is also everyone's focus for justice. If writers like Alan Dershowitz, Letty Cottin Pogrebin, Suzanne Gordon, Nancy Becker Kennedy and Roger Hernandez can't help us move ahead, they need to stop trying to leave us behind with rhetoric that seems resentful of our slow progress, and insistent on keeping at the bottom of any ladder of power and influence.

Los Angeles Times, October, 1991

BLACKS AND GAYS — IT'S NOT THE SAME

On the way to the White House, President-elect Clinton pledged to lift a ban on gay people in the military. In the weeks since the election, he has not backed off the pledge, though he has spent time talking to military leaders about their opinion on what will happen if he lifts the ban. Many see this talk as a retreat from Clinton's promise, but others see it as nothing more than Clinton as usual, the President-elect's customary path to a decision.

I agree that Clinton should keep his promise and lift the ban on gays in the military. Gays and lesbians serve anyway, often with distinction. To say there should be no gays in the military simply forces people to hide in closets constructed by intolerance. Lifting the ban stops the intolerance and acknowledges the potential contribution of all who wish to serve in the Armed Forces.

As firmly as I feel about gays in the military, I am equally firm that gays should stop using Harry Truman's order to integrate the Armed Forces as a rationale for the lifting of the ban against gays. The situation that faced (and still faces) African Americans, and the situation that faces gays are hardly identical. African Americans served prior to Mr. Truman's order — they simply served as segregated troops, often relegated to menial tasks, to cooking, cleaning, and maintenance, not fighting. African Americans were often excluded from officer training, or as officers were restricted to commanding black troops only. Mary Berry described the relationship of African Americans to the military as "the paradox of loyalty," of black folk's fighting for the right to fight. Even after winning the fight, men in uniform were often lynched when they returned to civilian life. Truman's order didn't stop the racism or the lynchings, but it signaled the beginning of the end of these in the military.

The history of gays and lesbians in American life is hardly parallel to that of African Americans. Gays and lesbians were not slaves. They were not lynched. They have not served the military as segregated troops burdened by enforced inequality. Gays and lesbians don't earn unequal pay. True, gays and lesbians often face discrimination in housing and employment, but white gays and lesbians do not have the historical weight of racial discrimination on their shoulders. President Truman's executive order was cloaked in the moral and legal authority of the Thirteenth, Fourteenth, and Fifteenth Amendments, and was aimed at shattering institutional patterns of segregations that created rigid barriers against the full participation of African Americans in a national institution.

General Colin Powell bristled, recently, when a news reporter began to lecture him about the status of gays in the military. "I don't need to be reminded of the history of discrimination in this country," he said. Amen, General, I hollered at the television screen. How dare gays lecture African Americans on what it is like to be excluded, all the while attempting to cloak themselves in the morality of our struggle? How dare they claim our hard-won gains, without acknowledging how much more must be done until racism in this country is eradicated? Why don't we hear their voices raised against the awful utterances of Cincinnati Reds owner Marge Schotts, against the persistence of racial inequity in the labor market. Instead, they've taken the tools we have fashioned for our advancement, like affirmative action, and sought to push their own agendas, often to the exclusion of ours.

If gays in the military spoke up so that their numbers could be counted, perhaps those who make public policy will understand how many soldiers they are talking about, how well integrated these soldiers are into the military, and how high-ranking some of these gay soldiers are. The difference between blacks and gays is that African Americans have never had the choice to speak up or be silent about our presence in an institution. And gays have never come to the table with the same institutional history as blacks.

No group of people should experience discrimination in our society. No group should be told they need not apply for any job in any institution. The ban against gays in the military should be lifted. But the case for lifting the ban cannot be made by comparing the status of gays with that of African Americans.

King Features, December, 1992

WHAT ABOUT RELIGIOUS DIVERSITY?

You can take the girl out of Catholic school, but you can't take the Catholic school out of the woman. In the twenty some years since I graduated from a Catholic elementary school in San Francisco, I've drifted far from the church. The major reason for my drift has been my feminism, the anger and exclusion I feel at the patriarchy, at the preachers talking "man of God" as if women do not exist.

Drift as I may, the Lent and Easter season are important to me, especially because of the symbolism of death and rebirth, of resurrection and redemption, the universal symbolisms that define so much of life. I will go to Easter services with very mixed feelings, and I will repeat the words, with many Christians, "Christ has died, Christ is risen, Christ is born again." I will inhale the incense and sway to the music and leave the church generally uplifted. But I will also leave with a state of ill ease at the overwhelming influence of Christianity in public life, and of the way it excludes so many, those Jews, those Muslim, those atheists who cannot relate to our observance of Lent, Easter, Christmas, and other Christian observances.

It is true that more than 80 percent of all Americans are Christian — 56 percent are Protestant, and 25 percent are Catholic like me. But then 11 percent have no religious preference, 2 percent are Jewish, and 6 percent are of another religion. Fewer than half of us attend church regularly, but 65 percent say we are members of church or synagogue. Those of us who are members, who genuflect at the altar of Christianity, are able to impose their religions on the lives of everyone else. The non-Christian minority — nearly 20 percent — are rarely considered when issues of religion are imposed in public life. I know dozens of people who have Good Friday off from work.

But few have time off for Passover, and those who wish it off have to declare it a "personal day." I think religion ought to be everybody's personal business, not a matter of public concern, of public observance.

More and more, though, it is a public thing. President Clinton prays openly, his voice sometimes cracking at the mention of God. Baseball and baseball players dedicate their games to the Lord, and make a great show of thanking God after their wins. Business leaders get on their knees too, praying for profit or for a break. And some members of Congress come together for prayer breakfasts, seeking biblical solace for the dirty work they do.

And yet one wonders if we read the same Bible, if the worker praying for fair pay kneels to the same God as the Lord the profitseeker (who would cut pay) supplicates. One wonders if this public prayer is less about the Lord than it is about public shorthand, a declaration that "I'm okay." One wonders if those who dedicate games, profits, and bill passage to the Lord are connecting to religion as some form of arrogance, some way of saying "my way or no way."

The Republicans said it some months ago, when in their post-election disarray they described this nation as a "Christian" nation. Their myopia for 20 percent of the population was troubling to this African American who belongs to a group that is perhaps 12 percent strong. Indeed, it is membership in a minority group that evokes my concern for the non-Christian, for our nation's cultural domination of them. In many ways, it is a similar cultural domination that African Americans have experienced when we are excluded from curricula, from public imagery, from discourse.

Our nation has not made nearly the headway it ought to on the matter of demographic diversity, of the fact that our nation is fast headed to, in New York Mayor David Dinkin's words, "a glorious mosaic" of color and culture. During this Easter season, I am reminded that we have moved as slowly on issues of religious diversity as we have on other diversity issues.

King Features, April, 1993

DON'T ASK, DO TELL

Matthew's office is, like most, decorated with photos of family and friends. There he is, hugging a precious child that I must assume is a son, cousin or nephew. There he is, standing behind an older man, perhaps his father, arms linked with a woman who looks enough like him to be a sister or aunt. There he is, with the CEO of his company, their arms clasped and both men smiling. Behind them stand a group of men and women, all also cheered by the occasion. One of the women is the CEO's spouse, and she is perched at his elbow, a fluttering bird of companionship. One of the men is Matthew's lover. He has his hand on Matthew's shoulder, and his grin is as big as anyones, but he is standing aback, behind. Don't ask, don't tell.

I am thinking about the issue of gays in the military, thinking about the silly compromise position our nation has found itself in, the kinds of denial we are being forced to cosign, this absurdity "don't ask, don't tell." Don't ask, don't tell suggests that personal lives and work lives can be so completely separated that there is no overlap, that what we do at work and what we do at home have no bearing on each other. That's a joke, as a glimpse at any office will tell you. People whose work lives are more than eight hours a day find their personal lives sloppily overflowing into the workplace in ways that human resource departments are just beginning to get a handle on. If child care falls through, some employees have been known to bring their children to work. If a meeting runs late, a clerical assistant may be asked to call home to let family know of the delay. At the Christmas parties and the birthday parties and the company celebrations, there are the invites, "bring the family." Should the invitations stop because colleagues aren't sure who the family is?

Don't ask, don't tell. For some it is benign, for others it is a muzzle. Does it mean that pictures of friends and lovers should be swept off a desk because lovers, significant others are of the same sex? Does it mean that speech has to be censored so that "we" is always "he and she?" Does it mean conforming to an unspoken norm, the norm that is heterosexual?

Gays in the military? Why not, I have said. Gays have always been part of the military. We can work it out, I said. It is not that big of an issue. But it is a big issue – it has taken six months for our Armed Services people to come up with compromising language. And in the process of coming up with language, lots of ugly stereotypes have been discussed. People have paired the Bible with their biases to justify the rhetoric used to exclude gays and lesbians. But I'd be less than honest if I didn't note that the issue of gays in the military is way down on my list. When African American unemployment rates are double those of whites, I am motivated to action. When black incomes are about 65 percent the level of white incomes, I am called upon for action. When women like Lani Guinier and Jocelyn Elders are bashed by bully conservatives, I am ready to call my Senators and Congressional representatives, ready to get busy. I am less ready to jump for gays in the military, and find my willingness eroded by the way that gays and lesbians have tried to make their cause our cause, to pretend they have a piece of the civil rights struggle, that their oppression is kissing cousin to African American oppression.

At the same time, something rankles about the notion of "don't ask, don't tell." What rankles is the notion that people have to cut and paste their lives to conform with four narrow words, words that give them less right to display photos on their desk, to use family words in a work context, to let their lives spill out of the office without holding them back. And that which rankles is the sense of unfairness, the sense that a policy called "don't ask, don't tell" will cause more problems than it solves. My friend Matthew had as much right to his lover at his arm as his CEO did. Don't ask, don't tell is not tenable military policy — it is compromising nonsense.

King Features, July, 1993

HARD WORK AND THE IMMIGRANTS

"My family came here in 1976 with very little money," says the woman. She speaks without a trace of an accent, and if she hadn't prefaced her comment with a qualifier, I'd have guessed she was the second or third generation offspring of immigrant parents. But her family has been here for less than a generation, and already they have attained the trappings of American success. She is telling me her life story, the struggle and the triumph, because she thinks too many African Americans resent the economic success some immigrants find in this country.

Immigrant success has always been thrown up in our black faces. If the Asians can make it here, we are told, why can't you? They come and work hard, we are told, as if black people are strangers to hard work. They come here because their life chances are better than they are in their own countries.

But even as the immigrants come, the doors open more widely for some than for others. While Haitians risk life and limb to get here, even though many will be turned around and turned away, thousands of people from other ethnic groups are admitted to this country each day. Eastern Europeans, Asians and others are all settling as the Haitians are being told they are not political refugees. Exactly what is a political refugee, anyway, in the "new world order?"

People come to this country seeking the elusive freedom that some call the American dream. They don't just flock here for political asylum or for economic advancement — they come to be "free." They come seeking an elusive dream that may work for some of them, but their dream is a nightmare for millions of African Americans. In seeking the dream, immigrants often come attempting to assimilate all that is American. Including American racism.

African Americans experience that racism, not just from whites, but very often from people who can barely speak English. Folk who haven't been here long enough to get a driver's license have been taught somewhere, somehow, that they are better than black people. Novelist Toni Morrison writes that one of the first words some new immigrants learn is a racial epithet, one they have no hesitation trying out.

One of twelve people counted in the 1990 census was born in another country. The foreign-born population increased by more than 8 million in the last decade. Some have called the 80's "the decade of the immigrant" and lauded our country's ability to absorb new people. The problem is that our country can absorb new people without making room for other people, namely African American people.

And so, though I'm not proud of it, I wonder whether an African American youth lost out on a job when I see a hard-working immigrant working in a service job treating me with minimal courtesy, or less. When friends suggest I show more compassion, I wonder how much compassion they have for the inner city youngster who wants work. I wonder why broken English is so much more acceptable than "black" English, and whether enduring ethnic stereotypes slam doors for some while opening them for others.

I wouldn't close the borders, as some suggest, or go as far as California Governor Pete Wilson to blame economic sluggishness on rising immigration. I'm not even especially proud that I sometimes play a zero sum game in my head. I'd rather not think of a shrinking pie with more people fighting over it, but of a pie large enough to feed us all.

Still, that's the rhetoric. The reality is starker, sharper, and more heated. Just like you can't build a luxury condominium next door to a housing project, you can't regale black people with stories of immigrant hard work without provoking an angry response. Where does that leave us when it is clear that the immigrant population is not shrinking, but growing?

King Features, May, 1992

NIGHTMARE, DREAM OR IN BETWEEN

> *" The problem of the twentieth century will be the problem of the color line."*
> *—W.E.B. DuBois*

> *"There is no history, only fictions of varying degrees of plausibility"*
> *— Voltaire*

Race. You can't get with it, can't get away from it. Even when it has nothing to do with everything. Everything to do with nothing. Some days it is an exhiliration, on other days a suffocation. In any case, the fact that I am African American is both part of my reality and part of my identity.

"But people are people," the man at the deli says. We nod at each other and exchange banter whenever I go in to stock up for a party. He mentions that he has seen me somewhere, talking about something "black". He tells me that people are people as he hands me my cold cuts and I smile because I'd rather avoid political discourse at this moment. "Some people's realities are different than others," I offer in cryptic response. A transaction has been completed, confrontation avoided. But it is not always this way.

"Black b—ch", the crudely written letter says. It comes in a red envelope, on white, lined paper, and for a clumsy paragraph it lambastes me for my "perverted" views. It comes with the territory of being a columnist, and I don't so much mind being called something that rhymes with witch, but I'm not sure why my race has been added to the epithet. For me, it lessens the sting of the intended insult, instead of sharpening it.

With Spike Lee's film, Jungle Fever making the front cover of news magazines, with debate on the Civil Rights Act dominating policy discussion this spring, with the "new politics" of race making cover news in the *Atlantic Monthly* (May, 1991), and *Newsweek* (May 6, 1991), race is one of our nation's most heatedly discussed topics. The debate — which embraces policy, politics, education, poverty, unemployment, class, the media, and crime — has even generated international attention, with a recent editorial of *The Economist* (March 30, 1991) focusing on "America's wasted blacks".

Heated discussions take place against a backdrop of racial change. Once African American people were protrayed as moral giants, we often turned the other cheek and chanted "We Shall Overcome". Now, the media depicts us as moral midgets, as those who use drugs, live on welfare, commit crime. The depiction is a lie and a distortion — the majority of welfare recipients, drug addicts, and criminals are white. But the depiction plays into every racist myth that exists, and the evening news often manipulates opinion as clumsily and effectively as films like "Birth of A Nation" once did.

The issue is how we make the transition from a society that was completely segregated to one that is at least somewhat integrated. The issue is how people stop judging people based on skin color. The issue, also, is how to develop effective tools to tear down racial barriers. And the issue is whether something should be done to redress past wrongs.

But it is hard to discuss these issues against a backdrop of a racism that is alive and well in the United States. A January study showed that 75 percent of all whites thought that African American people **prefer** welfare to work; 65 percent described us as lazy or violent. Those perceptions all too often distort black economic chances. A May report by the Urban Institute showed that when matched pairs of black and white young men applied for jobs, blacks received differentially negative treatment at least 20 percent of the time. They were not asked to apply for work, when whites were, were not offered jobs, when whites were, or were offered jobs at lower rates of pay.

Of course things are different from the days, a generation ago, when openly posted signs said "No Negroes Need Apply". Things are different from the days when black people had to sit on the back of the bus, no questions asked. Now, blacks are as likely as whites to be driving the bus, and the question of seating is often a question of money. Discrimination is often more subtle than it was a generation ago, but it is often as palpable, as strong, as frightening.

Much of this discrimination is reinforced by the fictions that we call history, the notion that Columbus discovered America (while Native Americans sat around waiting to be discovered), the notion that Abraham Lincoln "freed" slaves. Every shred of our history screams with white male supremacy, but the fruit of the sixties is a generation of people who were emboldened to raise questions. Much of the agitation around racial (gender, ethnic) issues comes when questions collide with tradition. For all too obvious reasons, there are those who like the world just the way it was, thank you, and who see no reason to change it at all.

Some of these are the people who celebrated the anniversary of Ellis Island. They saw no irony, as immigrants, in the fact that many were unwilling and unwitting immigrants who didn't come to this country voluntarily. These folks, the descendants of slaves, were redlined out of that celebration, in the same way that they were excluded from the industrial revolution that provided so many immigrants with economic opportunity. But protests of the Ellis Island celebration were seen as mean-spirited attacks on history and tradition.

That is what Ronald Reagan's presidency was about, in many ways, a return to the values and customs, the history and tradition of the 1950's, when men went off to work, and women stayed home to raise children, when gays and lesbians stayed in the closet, and black people kept their mouths shut. Reagan could no more turn the clock back than he could remember why he told Ollie North to sell arms to the Contras, and though his presidency chilled some protest, emboldened some conservatives, and caused the dismantling of some social programs, it did not stop the questions, some of which focus on the way society works today, some of which focus on the way it worked in the past.

Those asking questions, especially when they are women or people of color, are often made to feel as if they are in an awkward position. We have just reluctantly been asked to sit at the edge of the table, and for many that was a major concession. But here we are asking how the meal was cooked, as if we had as much a stake in the food as anyone else. Our hosts may plan to feed us nothing but the crumbs, but here we are, ungrateful souls, asking for the composition of those crumbs. The white men who feel they have done enough by passing a Civil Rights Bill in 1964 feel pinched by those who suggest they should pass

143

another one in 1991. "Just what do you people want," they ask perplexedly. The answer – the same things you want. We don't want to be treated like guests at the table, but instead like full partners in the corporation that makes decisions while they sit gathered around the table.

But given our changing economic situation, it is becoming more and more difficult for any of us to get the things we want. In 1980, 24.5 percent of all workers earned less than $12,000. By 1990, that number had increased to 31.5 percent (The State of Working America, 1991). Working class men with high school educations are watching their jobs disappear before their very eyes, and the visible signs of even modest black success cannot help but fan the flames of their resentment. A skinhead is, ultimately, nothing more than a working class white youth without a job, a youth who has been misinformed and manipulated into thinking that he would have a job were it not for the black presence. His fears have been cynically fanned by President Bush whose use of Willie Horton to win the 1988 election was evidence of both his racism and his lack of leadership.

All the mail I get from readers doesn't contain epithets. Some letters contains the simple suggestion that if I don't like things here, I can go back to . . . Africa, Russia, or someplace else. If my readers would send round-trip tickets, I'd be glad to visit those places. But after a two or three week vacation, I'd be back, rested and refreshed enough to continue to fight both for my place at the table and for the right to have input into the menu. During the Vietnam war era, there were bumper stickers that boasted the sentiment, "love it or leave it". My motto for the United States is "improve it or lose it".

How can we justify the beating of Rodney King? How can we justify the deliberate underdevelopment of inner cities (which got 70 percent less federal money in the past ten years)? How can we justify our nation's failure to develop employment and training policy? How can we justify corporate salaries that are 110 times worker salaries? How can we justify a continuation of bias that sullies the American dream?

Here we are in a "new world order" grappling with the same old problems. The United States is no longer the big country on the block — we get stiff competition from Germany and Japan, and both countries spend more than we do on developing human resources. It is frightening to think that urban education has been abandoned by the federal government because urban education all too often means minority education.

David Dinkins calls New York City a "glorious mosaic", the term a metaphor for the many cultures that define that city. For some, that mosaic is the American dream. For others, whose realities are still defined, still constrained by the color of their skin, it is a harrowing nightmare.

Boston College Magazine, Fall 1991

THE WOLF AND THE DENTIST:
GOVERNMENT, REGULATIONS AND SOCIAL POLICY

Free markets are like wolves. Without regard to issues of consequence and distribution, markets run prices down, just as without regard to injury, predatory wolves run their victims down, chew them up, and spit them out. But like markets, wolves aren't bad if they are managed a bit, especially in cases like the market for heroin, education, child care. In some cases, wolves should be taken to the dentist to have their teeth blunted a bit. What dentist? A Reagan-Bush dentist actually sharpened the wolf's teeth, a Clinton dentist put a slight retainer on the wolf, while dentists in previous administrations, especially in the eras more receptive to passage of public policy, may have filed or capped the wolf's teeth or even pulled them out! In no arena is the issue of government's role more critical than in the health care arena. With cost careening out of control, government may be the only force that can slam on the brakes.

WHEN REGULATION HELPS

If President Bush or Vice President Quayle accuses the Democratic ticket of being "tax and spend" candidates one more time, I think I'll scream. They must believe that repetition makes it right, and that if they keep whining tax and spend, the American people will flock to them at the polls. Not. Their other mantra is "big government." These two — they'd like to take government out of our lives at a time when our economic competitors are trouncing us because government is actively involved, in both Germany and Japan, in economic planning.

Bush has said that we should "let the market work" time and time again. But one of the features of unregulated, undirected market competition is that it produces economic excess, private gains for a few and poverty for many. We've seen this in the past decade, when corporate restructuring cost the American taxpayer more than $90 billion in revenue, reducing the corporate tax bite by some 60 percent. The result — a growing deficit, a President who keeps pushing further tax breaks for the rich, a heavy tax burden for the American middle class, and growing poverty.

What can government do? In the past, it has ameliorated hardship for the masses by providing relief in the form of legislation. In 1906 - 1913, a spate of anti-monopoly and consumer protection legislation was passed. The 1906 Food and Drug Act regulated the manufacture of food in response to widespread abuses as documented by Upton Sinclair in *The Jungle*. (If you eat hot dogs, don't read this book, or you may never eat them again!) The 1907 National Child Labor Act regulated the employment of children and the abuse of children in the workforce. Prior to the passage of this act, children were only protected under legislation that prohibited cruelty to animals. In 1913, the Revenue Act was passed, creating the income tax.

Another spate of legislation designed to assist the

masses in a hostile economy were passed in the 1930's on the initiative of Franklin Delano Roosevelt. The National Labor Relations Act, protecting the union right to bargain collectively, and the Minimum Wage Act and Social Security Act were passed during this period. Our system of income maintenance was also created then. When white people were the only ones who received public assistance, the word "welfare" carried a lot less stigma than it does now.

In the late 1950's and early 1960's, legislation was again passed to adjust the way that markets worked. The National Defense Education Act, creating the National Defense Student Loan, was passed in response to our fear that the Soviet Union was producing better educated students than we were. By making the money to attend college available, we made it possible for more people to go to school. The Vocational Education Act was passed in 1962, the Equal Pay Act in 1963, and the Civil Rights Act in 1964.

Just because legislation is passed doesn't mean that it is enforced. Unions still have a hard time getting certified in some workplaces, and the economy has not been especially amenable to strike activity. Drastic cuts in the budgets of labor regulatory agencies, such as the Occupational Safety and Health Administration, have made it possible for unscrupulous employers to continue to maintain horrid workplace conditions. But the legislation on the books sets a standard. It attempts to alter, for the good, the workings of the market.

If Bush and Quayle had their way, they'd probably repeal much of the legislation I mentioned. But much of this legislation changed our society for the better. The President denies tough economic times, smugly noting that we are the envy of the world. But labor market conditions and rising poverty suggest that it is time, again, to develop a package of legislation that will help workers secure fair pay, provide better training opportunities, and provide for national health care. It's not a matter of "big government" doing the "tax and spend" thing. It's a matter of government nudging markets in the right direction to alleviate hardship for the many Americans who have been permanently damaged by 12 years of economic neglect. This kind of government intervention has worked before and it can work again, if those at the top have the will for change.

King Features, October, 1992

SHOULD WE PASS PROTECTIONIST LEGISLATION?

Why should we pass protectionist legislation? Do we gain anything by imposing tariffs and quotas on those countries that import goods to the USA? Proponents think that when we hike the prices of imported goods, consumers will buy lower-priced domestic goods. Tain't necessarily so. The evidence suggests that when consumers think foreign-produced goods are of a better quality they'll pay the additional cost for foreign goods. Protectionist legislation, then, has the effect of causing price hikes for consumers.

Poor consumers are the hardest hit by tariffs. Telephones, television sets, tape recorders, radios, and other small electronic goods are only affordable to the poor because of the low prices of imports. Increase these prices by 15 or 20 percent and some consumers are taxed out of the market! Likewise, while it is great to "buy American," lots of those who commute to low-wage jobs can afford little more than an under-$5,000 imported car.

The urge to pass protectionist legislation perhaps stems from the economic ground the USA is losing in the international arena. The Japanese are more efficient in some areas of electronic equipment manufacturing, but we've also lost ground in auto and steel manufacturing. Protectionist legislation won't restore lost ground, better developed industrial policies will. Instead of trying to penalize our competitors abroad, our Congress needs to be concerned with strengthening industry at home.

One critical aspect of strengthening industry at home is developing domestic human resources. We've done a woeful job at this, cutting educational spending, making health care resources less available, and reducing government spending on job training. Our tax system encourages the export of employment opportunities by transnational corporations. If we remove jobs from the domestic labor market and raise prices at home, we make it harder and harder for those at the bottom to survive.

Protectionism assumes that everything is all right with USA industrial policy, everything, that is, except those pesky competitors of ours who manage to import goods more cheaply than we can produce them at home. But there is little wonder that our industrial complex is faltering in the face of Japanese competition – Japan spends 2 percent of its R&D budget on military applications, but our country spends almost a third of its R&D budget that way.

Instead of pointing fingers abroad and passing laws that hurt consumers at home, we need to look long and hard at USA industrial policies and take steps toward cleaning up our act and making production more efficient in the USA.

USA Today, April, 1989

GUN CONTROL LEGISLATION IS LONG OVERDUE

There is a terrible irony in the slaughter of Dr. David Gunn by a member of a "pro-life" organization. Michael Griffith apparently felt so strongly about life that he was willing to take a life to make his point. His weapon was likely a .38 caliber revolver that was found on the scene. Would Dr. Gunn still be with us if handguns weren't so easy to come by?

In some counties, it is as easy to buy a gun as it is to buy groceries. From .22 caliber pistols to AK47 semi-automatic assault rifles, guns are readily available. The lack of gun control laws is responsible, in part, for the size of the arsenal that the Branch Davidians have stockpiled in Waco, Texas. Three federal agents have been killed, and even more have been wounded because guns are so available.

According to a group called Handgun Control, Inc., only 7 people were killed by handguns in Great Britain in 1988. Nineteen were killed by guns in Switzerland, 25 in Israel, 13 in Australia, 8 in Canada, and nearly 9,000 in the United States. Yet, there is organized resistance to Virginia Governor Doug Wilder's plan that people be allowed to buy only one gun a month. Now, people can buy as many guns as they want for personal use.

Handguns are the tip of the iceberg. Plenty of civilians in the United States own assault weapons. In January, 1989, Patrick Purdy took his AK47 to a Stockton, California elementary schoolyard. He shot 106 rounds in 2 minutes, killing 5 children and wounding 29 others. His gun was imported from the People's Republic of China.

Whenever the question of gun control comes up, an outcry comes from those who say they have the right to bear arms. Virginia Governor Douglas Wilder has proposed a gun control measure that would limit handgun purchases to one a month. He made this proposal once before, but the National Rifle Association killed the measure. They are gearing up to fight gun purchase limits again, but their opposition is short-sighted. Virginia is a major source of guns on the East Coast. In Washington, DC, where the homicide rate is among the highest in the nation, most guns come from adjacent Virginia.

This handgun violence has a racial dimension. Black victims of violent crimes are twice as likely to be confronted with handguns as white victims of violent crimes, and gunshots among young black men caused more than 80 percent of the deaths in a period between 1984 and 1987.

Children are not immune to the violence that comes from guns. The American Academy of Pediatrics says that gunshot wounds among children in urban areas increased 300 percent from 1986 to 1988 and continue to rise. Firearms were the fourth leading cause of accidental death among children aged 14 and under. But some children's deaths aren't accidental. In some cities, youngsters carry guns to school for protection.

The National Rifle Association consistently opposes gun control legislation, and they have a few members of Congress in the pocket. But unnecessary fatalities, like the drive-by shootings that kill innocent bystanders, or the murder of Dr. Gunn, reminds us that these tragedies are preventable. If our response to Dr. Gunn's murder is not some form of gun control, then we invite tragedies like his murder to happen again and again.

Sun Reporter, March 1993

WHOSE BILL OF RIGHTS

I am one of those card carrying members of the ACLU who is sometimes tempted to tear up her card. First Amendment rights? Free speech? My civil libertarian allies have forgotten about the right to a life free of physical harassment and threats. And black people's rights are violated, their safety threatened when crosses are burned on their property. Jews are threatened, frightened, when swastikas are emblazoned on public space.

This is more than trespass, more than expression. This is the arrogant attempt to use history to intimidate. After all, a burning cross was once a certain prelude to the murder and intimidation of black people. Now, the punks who resort to this symbolism may be unwilling or unable to murder, but perfectly capable to using history to terrorize. If the Supreme Court says it's okay to burn crosses, next they'll say that the crowd gathering for a lynching is merely exercising their right of free assembly. At least one some-body on that court is young enough and Southern enough to recall the stench of burning flesh, connected enough to this travesty to realize that freedom isn't free.

My grandmother used to tell me that I had a free right to swing my arm as long and hard as I wanted, as long as that arm didn't hit somebody else's nose. I wonder what she is thinking as she watches lawyers argue that it is okay for racists to terrorize their neighbors with cross burnings, that no matter how far from poverty a black family escapes, a lunatic with a burning cross has the right to confront them with a blazing reminder of the way it used to be.

This is not about free speech, this is about racial in-timidation, and the court has to say whether they support this terror or oppose it. If they say that it is okay to burn a cross, to flaunt a swastika, they are saying that the Bill of Rights is a document that protects only white Christian Americans.

USA Today, December, 1991

DRUG WAR?

Our nation's drug problem is nothing to sniff at, but Washington politicians elevate it to mammoth stature with the terminology they use to fight drug abuse. We found ourselves in the middle of a "drug war," which was to be managed by a "drug czar." The proceeds from these bond sales will be used to build more prisons and hire more drug enforcement officers.

Drug war bonds dredge up images of the little chil-dren buying war bonds with pennies, nickels, and dimes during World War II. They allow the "average American" to buy into a warped view of crime and punishment, to blame too many of our nation's ills on the use of drugs, and to reinforce that blame through investment in these bonds. Is drug use and abuse a symptom or a cause of our troubled society? Are we treating it in the same way we treat other symptoms? When will we issue booze war bonds? How about illiteracy bonds? Or does our concern about drugs in our society take on a dimension that makes some more willing to declare a drug war than an unemployment war?

Drug war bonds are a gimmick that would be silly if the proponents weren't so serious. These bonds are a way to hide government debt behind a good cause without reference to the deficit. But face it — borrowing is borrowing. If these bonds float, they'll divert money from other uses, including savings bonds, treasury bills, stock purchases and other investments. If these bonds are a success, they'll push up interest rates in other sectors of the money market. More than that, they'll generate investment by exploiting people's fear of crime, but offer a measly 4 percent return.

The proposal to float drug war bonds is similar to the proposal to fund a $200 billion bailout to the savings and loan industry without charging those funds against the current deficit. Both proposals would keep down the reported deficit while spending money that must eventually be repaid. These fiscal sleights of hand are neither justified by the emergency that motivates the S&L bailout, nor by the emotion that would generate drug war bonds.

Somebody learned at the feet of a master — the Reagan Administration's solution to drug problems was "Just Say No," while this administration has the gimmick "Just Buy Bonds." Both our budget and drug-related issues should be taken more seriously.

USA Today, March, 1989

LIFE IN SPACE?

Is there intelligent life in space? And should taxpayers pay millions of dollars to find out? The fact that we are asking these questions a quarter century into our space program really makes one wonder if there is intelligent life at our White House, in our Congress, and among those taxpayers who are willing to sign blank checks for space research.

Our infatuation with space programs is revealed in the launch of the space shuttle Atlantis. Carrying plutonium, this launch could cause an explosion, radioactivity, and a major threat to our environment. NASA estimates a 1 percent probability of an accident; citizens oppose the Galileo mission because of its danger. Yet we persist in planning this launch.

Just like space programs threaten our environment, the high cost of space exploration is a major threat to our budgetary stability. There are a range of social programs that might better benefit from the use of funds than some futile search for intelligent life that has managed to elude 25 years of space exploration.

How can our President convene an education summit, yet siphon so much money from education to our space program? How can we grapple with issues of labor shortage, yet spend money on space, not employment and training? How can we acknowledge the 37 million Americans who have no health insurance, yet fail to spend our funds on health care programs?

There may well be some scientific benefit of space research, but must we harp on this benefit while exempting space programs from economies that every other program in our federal budget should be subjected to. We cannot throw millions at space research with abandon while cautioning those who run domestic programs to watch their pennies. We have no choice but to place this space spending in perspective. Putting our foot down on spending to search for intelligent life is a step in the right direction.

Some legislators and taxpayers are adamant in seeking life in space, perhaps because they have been watching too many "Star Trek" reruns. But we can't let fifties

nostalgia and science fiction gone awry set the budget priorities for our nation. The money some would spend seeking intelligent life in space could be better spent nurturing intelligent life at home!

USA Today, June, 1989

TOXIC WASTE IS BUSINESS AS USUAL

When a rail tank car's safety valve ruptured Monday in Richmond, California, thousands of gallons of sulfuric acid were spewed into the atmosphere, forming a toxic cloud and causing thousands to seek medical treatment. Toxic spills like that are not exceptional in Contra Costa County – just six weeks ago a mixture of gasses were released from a relief valve at the Tosco refinery in that area, sending several people to the hospital with burning eyes and shortness of breath. A year ago, a hose burst while workers were repairing a Texaco oil pipeline, and one worker was killed while another was injured. Last May, highways were closed for several hours when a cooling tube ruptured at Pacific Refineries, releasing a cloud of oil mist. Three years ago, an oil processing unit at Chevron exploded, injuring nine people and forcing the evacuation of nearby school children.

What's wrong with this picture? The plants that leak toxic gasses are located near residential areas, a stone's throw away from housing projects, elementary schools, and shopping centers. They are contiguous to commuter highways whose shutdown has implications for hundreds of businesses in the Bay Area. If the record of toxic spills is explored there seems to be a callousness, if not a willful carelessness in handling dangerous chemicals. Indeed, the General Chemical Corporation refinery responsible for Monday's spill has been fined hundreds of thousands of dollars by state regulatory agencies for health and safety violations, as well as violations of hazardous waste laws.

Monday's spill is likely to garner a scant $25,000 fine, a slap on the wrist so mild as to nearly condone Monday's accident.

The toxic spill is awful enough, but the horrors compound when one realizes that the largest polluters in Contra Costa County are located in areas where the populations are mostly African American, Latino, or Laotian, and where residents are poor. Henry Clark, Chairman of the West County Toxics Coalition, describes the spatial pattern as "environmental racism," because he notes polluters would not be allowed to locate in residential areas populated by the more affluent, because the more affluent have enough clout to force polluters to clean up their act.

"People of color bear the brunt of the nation's pollution problem," wrote Rev. Ben Chavis when he led the United Church of Christ's Commission for Racial Justice. Now Executive Director of the NAACP, Chavis remains interested in ways that racial discrimination affects environmental policy making. The interest is critical – from uranium mining on Navaho lands, to farm worker communities where people are routinely exposed to pesticides, to Warren County, North Carolina, where a PCB landfill was located because people perceived that citizens there were powerless to resist the danger, to Contra Costa County, California, where elected officials actually voted to locate public housing in very close proximity to a refinery.

Those who worship at the altar of free markets put this problem in the context of land prices, and suggest that the poor are, indeed, free to move away from areas where pollution is rampant. Free market types reject the term "environmental racism," preferring to see the location pattern as "Markets as usual," and to speak of the jobs that refineries generate. Interestingly, those most exposed to pollutants by residential proximity are least likely to work for the refineries.

Although refineries and toxic dumps are located near

predominately poor, predominately African American communities, wind knows no walls. The thousands of people affected by the General Chemical Corporation spill were not all African American, not all poor. Many of them were yuppie commuters, pushed past the toxins and the cities by housing prices, but tied to the highway by the jobs they can't flee as fast as they flee urban areas. Like the people whose homes shrink in the shadows of refineries, they too had burning lungs, stinging skin, watery eyes. They, too, had to queue up for medical assistance. They, too, felt nauseous for a day or so after breathing the foul gas. And they, too, ought to feel insulted at the slap-on-the-wrist fine levied on the General Chemical Corporation.

Eight thousand people sought medical treatment in the wake of Monday's toxic spill. How many people have to be hurt before our nation's regulators take stronger steps to prevent industrial accidents?

Sun Reporter, September, 1993

MAKING HEALTH CARE A CHOICE

Outside abortion clinics and inside the Supreme Court building in Washington, DC, women are fighting for their right to choose. At the Buffalo abortion clinic, pro-choice advocates have been forced to take to the streets to defend themselves against so-called pro-life advocates who would block paths to their clinics. Inside the chambers of the Supreme Court, lawyers argue about Pennsylvania's law that would make a woman's choice contingent on the permission of her parents or husband, on her submission to a waiting period.

Both of these fights draw heat, light, and press, but the bigger fight about a woman's right to choose was lost a long time ago. Poor women have no right to choose; Medicare will not pay for their abortions. Women who lack mobility have no right to choose, either. The absence of clinics, combined with the rigors of travel, mean that they do not have access to abortion. As the issue of abortion has been politicized, fewer and fewer medical students are trained in the procedure. As rabid right-to-lifers rally around clinics, fewer doctors are willing to put their personal lives at stake as they offer women the right to choose their reproductive fates.

Roe v. Wade said that states could not restrict a woman's access to abortion. But when congressional candidates run ads with photos of fetuses, moral persuasion is a greater preventer. A woman with money will never lack a medical procedure that she wants. She can shop for it, find it, fly to it. But the woman whose mobility is constrained by lack of money and information is often stuck without any choice at all. One of the lawyers who argued against the Pennsylvania law that requires notification and a waiting period said it could return women to the back alley. I shuddered because too many women's reality is already the back alley, the home remedy, the prayers. Too many women cross their fingers in hope or bow their heads in fear for their circumstances after they learn that they are pregnant. Too many women have written the abortion option off because they see it as unavailable to them.

The greater crisis in this abortion brouhaha is the failure of our national health care system to provide services for 37 million Americans, including many women whose pregnancies are the result of reproductive ignorance. People are suffering because they can't get abortions, but some are also distressed because they can't get checkups, shots, vitamins, contraceptives. It begs a cliché to say that pro-lifers should really be "pro-life," that is in favor of a quality of life that makes it easy to live and breathe in the world, and then perhaps to bring a child into the world. But the crisis in medical service delivery draws less heat, light, and press than the right to choose abortion. There aren't enough protesters to scream, gird their bodies, and stand outside public health clinics that can't take another

160

patient. Those who are willingly jailed because they wanted to block an abortion clinic won't picket a White House with a glass ceiling on compassion and its ability to respond to our national health care crisis.

Neither the right nor the left is fighting for the bigger health care issues. Outside Buffalo clinics, inside Supreme Court chambers, women are fighting for a right that is more abstract than real, given the availability of abortion in this country. The pity is that so many of us are riveted by the abstraction than the reality.

I think a woman's right to choose abortion is as important as her right to breathe air. But I believe that no woman chooses abortion as easily as she chooses breath. Breathing is an effortless process; abortion is a tortured one that requires pause and writhing, pain and balancing. Fewer women would choose abortion if better health care were available.

Why can't women generate as much support for national health care proposals as some can galvanize for "right to life."

King Features, April, 1992

COMPREHENSIVE HEALTH RIGHTS: THE ONLY WAY TO GO

"I didn't see many black women at the abortion march," a white woman tells me, tentatively. She doesn't want to make much of a point of it, she says, but she can't understand why the April 9th march looked to be about 95 percent white to her. "It happened in DC, a city that is mostly black," she said in a puzzled tone. "Don't black women care?" (For the record, we do. An *Essence Magazine* poll indicated that two-thirds of all black women support abortion rights).

Local papers have asked a related question, not about abortion, but about AIDS. Recent coverage seems to imply that black people are just coming to grips with the AIDS crisis, with a headline "Blacks Face Up to AIDS" (*Examiner*, April 16, 1991) suggesting that the black community once buried its head in the sand where this disease was concerned. Yet the very papers that run these headlines once failed to cover AIDS issues in the black community. Two years ago, a local black reporter attended and covered a national AIDS conference at his own expense and published his coverage in the *Sun Reporter* because his own paper could not see the impact that AIDS had on the black community. Have Black people buried their heads in the sand about AIDS, or have health policymakers buried their heads in the sand about black health status?

Free needles have grabbed the headlines lately, with do-gooders claiming that passing out these needles will stop the spread of AIDS, and with black leaders wondering if the free needle movement doesn't mean sudden death for so many black addicts. Free needles, but not free health care? This is the crux of the issue.

No one health issue can be viewed in a vacuum. Many in the black community have restricted access to health care and are at higher risk for a range of health symptoms. With life expectancies that are as much as a decade lower than white life expectancies, issues of black health care cannot be reduced to one or two issues. Black people need comprehensive health care, not just access to abortions, or care for people with AIDS. This comprehensive health care starts with pre-natal nutrition, continues to include new baby care, dental care, preventive medicine, and access to contraception. Comprehensive health care would include education about safe sex and AIDS prevention, abortion counseling and availability, but it would also strengthen mental health resources, and address the health issues for the elderly.

(Clearly, comprehensive health care has taken a step backward in San Francisco, where the recent impact of budget deficits has been to eliminate services at sites such as the Westside Community Mental Health Center).

While it makes sense for segments of the population to fight for one form of health care or another, it makes more sense for all of us to coalesce around the issue of comprehensive health coverage, access to preventive medicine, to health education, to research and development. If this coalition doesn't come together, there is danger that "outside consultants" will determine the priorities of some communities. Already, in Alameda County and in Oregon, consultants have been asked to determine public health priorities. We, the people, need to know how they make decisions and whether their values are reflective of ours.

Even more than that, be it abortion or AIDS, the health care access question is, bottom line, an economic one. Women who can afford plane tickets will get abortions out of state or out of the country. Those who can't afford to escape the scourge of inadequate health care will have illegal and unsafe abortions in back alleys. AIDS victims who have the economic means will fly from country to country seeking cures for their disease, and drugs to alleviate their pain. Others will become destitute before they qualify for public health assistance.

Economic differences in health care distribution mirror economic differences in other sectors of society. Some schools have a computer for every student, while others are lucky to have one for every classroom. Some neighborhoods have their share of municipal services, while others struggle to hold their own. Some neighborhoods are chock full of banks and supermarkets while, in others, residents drive blocks for service.

In some instances these differences have minor but immediate consequences. In other cases, like education, the consequences are longer term. When some people don't have access to health care, society's failure becomes a matter of life and death.

The only way to deal with abortion, AIDS, and needle exchange is to deal with them in the context of comprehensive health care. Instinctively, the African American community has raised this issue, by responding to short term health care issues with the refrain, "but what about this other problem."

In other words, we can march for abortion, and agitate for more funds for AIDS education, care, and prevention. But we need to march to change the way health services are delivered, to deal with the whole system, not just some of the parts. Even as we pressure our Congress to respond to specific health needs, we need also ask them to develop legislation that provides comprehensive health care.

Sun Reporter, June, 1991

PREVENTABLE DEATHS: AIDS AND THE HEALTH CRISIS

Less than a year ago, a close friend, one of my play cousins, died of AIDS. Like everyone who has lost a friend to the epidemic, I was stunned, numbed by the physical deterioration that preceded the death. It was shocking, infuriating to see a man who had once been drop dead fine fade to a bag of bones, to see his skin that once shined like sun turn to ash. It was frustrating to contemplate the wonderful talent wasted by such an early death. I felt helpless, less than useless, because there was nothing I could do. Like millions around the country, I wanted to see our nation's scientists develop a cure for AIDS, and for public health professionals to do all they can to prevent the spread of the disease.

Yet I was angered when the ACT-UP group shouted down HHS Secretary Louis Sullivan. Part of me realized that the protest against Sullivan was part protest against the Reagan-Bush Administration's disregard for the AIDS crisis, protest that the President chose to spend time with reactionary Jesse Helms rather than come to San Francisco to address those assembled at the International AIDS conference. My anger went deeper than my realization, though. I thought the protest tacky and tasteless, and resented, more than the horns and shouts, the fact that people saw fit to throw paper airplanes and other things at Sullivan.

I wondered, as they threw those things, if ACT-UP thought at all about Sullivan's career and the way our nation's health crisis affects his community, the Black community. Before joining the Bush Administration, Sullivan was dean at the Morehouse Medical School, working to eliminate the critical shortage of Black doctors. Before that, as a physician, he served the black poor, a group whose health risk is high and rising.

Life expectancy in Harlem, they say, is lower than that in Bangladesh. On average, black men live a decade less than white men do, paying into a Social Security system they never collect from because of early death. Much of the difference in black-white life expectancies is due to stress, much of it racial stress. The number of prominent black men to bite the dust at age 60 is high and rising, and that's a crisis.

Health crisis. Thirty-seven million Americans have no health insurance. Some of those are people with AIDS, or people who have been diagnosed HIV positive, but many are people who would be wiped out if they were diagnosed with any illness. Our Congress won't provide the money to fund a national health insurance program, and from where I sit this is our nation's highest health priority — to make sure that everyone has access to health care.

Not only must scientists find a cure for AIDS, but there are a range of cancers that we need to know more about. Breast cancer is a major killer of women, but the National Institutes of Health rarely study women's health status, so this disease remains a killer. Early detection often means prevention, but this is a message that is not often publicized in our communities.

We could lower our infant mortality rate, but our government doesn't want to. We just cut the WIC program that provided food for women, infants, and children, a program that helped women deliver strong and healthy babies as opposed to weak and fragile ones. The dollars cut from WIC affects more than 300,000 infants. Our president says we can't afford the program.

If anybody was listening to Louis Sullivan, they would have heard him say that we had to come together around health issues. He talked about AIDS in a context of all health issues, and that's the context in which I think it needs to be discussed. After all, the spread of AIDS in the black community is likely to follow the health status of the black community in general. Those already underserved will be more susceptible to a virus than those who are well-served by health systems, who eat right and get regular medical attention.

ACT-UP surely had a right to make its point — the Bush Administration has lagged with regard to money for AIDS research and treatment. But if they took a minute to listen to Louis Sullivan, they might have found themselves listening to a man who walked their walk.

We are all diminished by unnecessary death, whether from AIDS, from malnutrition, or from something else that could have been prevented.

Sun Reporter, June, 1990

BREAKING THE SILENCE: BLACKS AND AIDS

Sometimes I can't even bear to call their names, the black folks I know who've died of AIDS. The statement of their syllables cuts me like a knife, especially when I realize that the victims I have known have been young, vivacious, funny people who had no business going so early.

But if we fail to call their names, fail to acknowledge the cause of their deaths, then we keep the silence about

AIDS. And keeping the silence means losing access to resources, as many of the delegates at last week's conference on AIDS and minorities learned. Though those present in Atlanta chided the Federal Center for Disease Control on responding slowly to the incidence of AIDS in the black community, the government won't respond unless we make them, lobbying as passionately for funds for AIDS prevention as we lobby for money for anything else.

But too many of us see "AIDS victims" as a faceless mass of people dying of a sexually transmitted disease, and that image does those dead little justice. They were someone's brothers, sons, or fathers; they were husbands, wives and lovers. They worked with their hands or their minds and left products for us to remember them by, like Willie Smith's clothes or Michael Bennet's plays. They touched us and they left that touch, soft or hard, an indelible mark on our souls.

AIDS victims are not all gay men. Some are infants, children, and women. Some have been straight, having caught the disease through blood transfusions, not sex. And the incidence of AIDS is higher in the black community than it is in the general population, and especially higher among black women than it is among all women. In fact, the majority of women who are stricken with AIDS are black.

Yes, blacks get AIDS. Yet our community has kept the silence about victims of AIDS in our community. At a recent meeting with a group of ministers, I cringed when one referred to AIDS as a symptom of some "moral breakdown" and wondered how he thought that infants had strayed from the moral straight and narrow. Outrageous descriptions don't mute the horror of the disease, or the sadness I feel when I think of the victims, once vibrant, and now I can't even call their names.

If our community has ignored the AIDS plague, the larger community has moved AIDS education and prevention resources away from the black community. Attorney

Norm Nickens, currently working at the Human Rights Commission, has had to ride herd on the AIDS Foundation and others to make sure that a fair share of funds earmarked for outreach and education are targeted to our community. Health Commissioner Naomi Gray has scrutinized Health Department programs, standing firm on the need for minority participation. But these advocates too frequently stand alone.

The local media is even more remiss in the way they depict the victims of AIDS. Although reportage on the disease has been comprehensive at some levels, it has ignored the effect of AIDS on blacks. And while *Chronicle* reporter Randy Shilts was sent all over the country to report on AIDS programs in Houston and other cities, his reporting pointedly ignored programming that targeted minorities.

Our community has not been completely silent. In recent months, a spate of conferences have been held to talk about blacks and AIDS, conferences in Boston, Washington, DC, New York, and Atlanta. The NAACP has issued a statement calling for more money for AIDS research, and SCLC women have held meetings to inform black women on the risks of AIDS. The developments in the black community are interesting, important, and invisible for the pages of the mainstream press. But *Chronicle* reporter Perry Lang has covered an Atlanta conference on AIDS for the *San Francisco Sun Reporter*, not his own. I heard that Perry traveled to the conference at his own expense after his *Chronicle* bosses declined to send him to Atlanta. I wonder why.

Gritty gossip and pithy politics. Sunny days and serious jazz music. A houseful of people and buzzing conversation. I have memories of my friends who died from AIDS, memories poignant and precious, and sometimes so pungent that I am moved to tears in minutes. Memories so bittersweet that some days I can't call their names. And yet, we have to break the silence, own these folk, men, women, and children, as an important part of our community. And when we break our silence, we should break it

by thanking Perry Lange for his initiative, by shouting at those who would shut us out of the AIDS crisis.

With AIDS, as with unemployment and infant mortality, the statistics have an amazing symmetry: twice as likely to be disadvantaged, half as likely to succeed. Black men are twice as likely to get AIDS as white men, and black women more than ten times more likely to get AIDS than white women. Unless we break the silence on this grim reality, our ignorance about AIDS will cripple our community.

Sun Reporter, March, 1989

SHAKING THE HAND THAT KILLS

Street fairs are always exhilarating experiences, especially when the food is spicy, the music pulsating, the interaction electric. In the middle of one of these street fairs, when I am almost high on my surroundings, a brightly colored flyer takes the wind out of my sails. In the listing of the many groups who provided sponsorship for the street fair, a tobacco company is mentioned.

The street fair or tobacco company doesn't matter. Advertising for cigarettes is pervasive in our society. The billboards pollute our public space; the ads spill out of our magazines. The women are always as long and lean as the cigarettes they carelessly dangle from their fingers. They are almost always provocatively dressed. And they are pushing poison.

About 46 million Americans smoked in 1992, down from 50 million smokers in 1988. But women and African Americans are smoking more than they did five years ago, while white male smoking rates have dropped. I don't know why more women and African Americans are smoking, but I'd guess that the $3.9 billion the tobacco industry spends on advertising and promotion has something to do with it.

For the record, the promotion includes sponsorship of several worthy causes, including the United Negro College Fund and women's tennis and sports events. But as the United Negro College Fund asserts that "a mind is a terrible thing to waste," what do they think about a body? More than 1,000 African Americans lose their lives to tobacco each week; in total, more than 500,000 Americans are killed by tobacco each year.

Free market types will say that the choice to smoke is just that, a choice. But that choice is influenced by advertising. Tobacco companies say they are just advertising to inform people of their choices and brand names, but the fastest growing segment of new smokers are women under the age of 23. These young women devour the fashion magazines that prominently feature cigarette advertising. A quarter of the readers of *Glamour* Magazine are girls under 18; $6.3 million of cigarette ads appeared in that magazine in 1985. A recent issue of *Cosmopolitan* Magazine had more than a dozen tobacco and alcohol ads. Theoretically, the editorial side and the advertising side are separate, but the fashion photos in the cigarette ads are nearly indistinguishable from the fashion photos on the pages of the magazines. And the words—lean, slim, trim—communicate the "never too thin" message that women are constantly bludgeoned with. Few women's magazines have done hard-hitting articles on health that talk about the pitfalls of smoking. How can they? That's like biting the hand that feeds them.

In the African American community, tobacco company sponsorship of civil rights organizations and community events is like caressing the hand that kills us. These legal drugs, tobacco and alcohol kill ten times more people than illegal drugs. Last week, Lee Brown was sworn in as American's "drug czar" and the fifth African American member of the Clinton Cabinet. Where is the "smoke czar?"

The women's magazines that tout a feminist message ought to think about the messages they are sending to

women and consider declining tobacco ads or at least, occasionally, running articles that counter the message that tobacco is good. The civil rights organizations that talk about freedom and justice ought to think twice before they shake the hand that will ultimately kill more African Americans than crack cocaine. While cities like Los Angeles pass ordinances to ban smoking in restaurants and airlines prevent smoking on planes, there are lots of people who are trying to have things both ways when it comes to tobacco. Smoke kills. No doubt about it. And now it is killing women and African Americans in increasing numbers. All the street fairs in the world, all the scholarships, all the magazines, simply can't make up for that.

King Features, July, 1993

THE THIRD WORLD AND THE NEW WORLD ORDER

What new world order? When the G-7 countries met in July of 1993, there was nothing more than the same old stuff... five white men, a Canadian (white) woman, and a Japanese man who represented less than half of the world's population presumed to discuss the direction of the world. What happened to Africa? Latin America? The Caribbean? In many ways G-7 meetings are a new world order version of old world imperialism.

THE THIRD WORLD AND THE NEW WORLD ORDER

All eyes are on the political entity once called the Soviet Union as it makes its transition from Communism to capitalism. Russia took its first steps to a "free market" by eliminating price subsidies for consumer goods. Some see these steps as the final nails in socialism's coffin. To let the pundits tell it, capitalism triumphs in the "new world order" with the newly formed Commonwealth of Independent States as a junior, but important, world power.

It is early to celebrate socialism's demise, but not too

early to ask what will happen to developing countries under the "new world order." Russian President Boris Yeltsin seems to be pandering to George Bush, Japan, and the Western European powers of the G-7 and their version of capitalism, so it is unlikely Third World countries can count on the former superpower for help. The G-7 countries that are best off, Germany and Japan, have little recent history of involvement in Third World economic development. The traditional imperialists, the US and Great Britain, will probably continue to offer international aid, but only to those countries that conform to their notions of politics and economics. There is no alternate source of funds for these countries – the Soviet Union no longer exists, and its replacement is in such economic trouble that it cannot possibly justify asking for Western help on one hand, while distributing international aid on the other. Now, more than ever, it is clear that "new world order" ignores Africa and Latin America. Only those countries that have a strategic importance to the G-7 can expect a push along the development path.

Even those countries can expect, at best, a nudge and not a push. When Grenada attempted to develop tourism, the Soviet Union, Cuba, and others provided the money and technical assistance to build an airstrip so that larger planes could land and more tourists could come to the small island. The United States then invaded the tiny country, charging that the airstrip was a threat to military security and the socialist New Jewel government was overthrown. Later, it offered the new, non-socialist government less than one hundred thousand dollars in aid. That's quite a contrast, an airstrip and an opportunity for economic development versus loose change. But unless our priorities shift, loose change may now be all countries like Grenada, Tanzania, and Cuba, once recipients of Soviet help, can expect.

The Soviet Union's collapse will have ripple effects in developing countries whose already precarious economies may totter and fall because of aid they no longer receive.

174

Will any of the G-7 countries fill the void left by the Soviet Union and assist these countries on their path to development? Or is the "new world order" a meaningless concept for those countries that are not world powers?

USA Today, January, 1992

SECOND THOUGHTS ON SOMALIA

You can't look at the photographs of skeletal children, skin stretched across protruding bones, without thinking that someone ought to do something. From the vantage point of those photographs, the deployment of United States troops to Somalia to assist with food distribution is right on time. But even as troops land, we must raise questions about this humanitarian mission. And we must look at United States involvement in the current chaos in Somalia.

I don't think we will ever know what atrocities our government has committed in the name of "strategic position," but certainly the arming of the Somalis was one. There had been Soviet involvement with the Somalian military in the 1970's, and contact between the United States and the Somalian government in the 1980's. We become a large source of military and economic support of Somalia, and our base in Berbera helped secure our "strategic position" in the Persian Gulf. Somalian warlords are well armed with weapons that came from both the United States and the Soviet Union. According to TransAfrica's Randall Robinson, "When Said Barre (Somalia's previous dictator) was overthrown in 1991, he was long a client of the United States with American weapons to use against his own people. By then we might have stepped in and seen to it that the country democratized, but we did nothing."

If the United States would intervene in Kuwait, we ought to intervene in Somalia. Probably, we ought to have been there sooner, as early as 1991 when Barre was overthrown. I have no problem with our current presence in Somalia, but I have problems with the timing of our intervention. Did it take 300,000 deaths to motivate President Bush? Is the timing of the intervention somehow designed to shore up the image of his failed presidency? Certainly the President has gone from a dispirited loser to a decisive leader, engaged in the activity of rescuing Somalia. His action on this crisis reminds us of the international role which he enjoyed most throughout his tenure as President.

I also have problems with the passive role of the United Nations in this matter and am dismayed at that organization's lack of effectiveness. Their indecision forces the United States into the role of "world leader" even as world economic shifts suggest that the role of superpower must be shared.

In many ways our presence in Somalia is nothing more than chickens coming home to roost, and we need to think about that as we watch the Marines land on the shores of Mogadishu. Many of us are patting ourselves on the back. We feel good about the fact that we are able to help starving Somalians get badly needed food. As we pat ourselves on the back, we ought not forget the role we played in creating the starvation in Somalia, and in remembering that role, we ought to ask what happens after the food is delivered. Finally, we need to ask if we have created Somalia-like situations elsewhere in the world, like in Central and South America.

Where else has our sense of strategic position generated internal conflict, war, and possibly starvation? When will we be called upon to intervene again? Will we be willing to do so? The Somalian situation must motivate discussion about criteria for intervention elsewhere and about the role of the United Nations. We must also be willing, because of this situation, to own up to the damage we have done in the name of strategic position.

King Features, December, 1992

WHAT THE UNITED STATES COULD LEARN FROM SOUTH AFRICA

As South African President F.W. deKlerk sits with black African leader Nelson Mandela, African National Congress chief negotiator Cyril Ramaphosa, South African Communist Party head Chris Hani, and others, it is clear that constitutional negotiations are underway and that there will be no turning back. The process of dismantling apartheid, installing a system of one person, one vote, and ensuring the full civil, economic and political rights of every Black South African will be a painstaking one, and one in which South Africa can learn much from the United States. They can learn, for example, the difference between de jure and de facto discrimination, and they can learn of the many ways that power and privilege can be grandfathered into the law. But I am watching the South African negotiations with a tinge of envy, because I see something that American whites could learn from white South Africans like F.W. deKlerk.

I don't know whether deKlerk wanted to free Mandela, or whether he wants to negotiate with the African National Congress, but I know that he is bowing to the inevitable, and negotiating, like it or not. And I know that when slavery came to an end, there were never negotiations like this. Sure, the Thirteenth, Fourteenth and Fifteenth Amendments were passed, but racist laws stayed on the books well into this century. It took more than a hundred years after Emancipation to pass a Civil Rights Act, and just a generation after the act was passed, the vultures are trying to dismantle it. Never, in the history of American race relations, has there been a direct discussion, a formal meeting, a notion of forward movement. African Americans have never been treated as equals sitting around the table with those in power and authority. Even the March on Washington of 1963 was tampered with by Presidential forces who tried to tone down the speeches that were given and influence the list of those who could speak.

America has never confronted its racial problem directly. Instead there has been the blind faith that our system of "fairness" would work everything out.

It hasn't. The statistics are alarming, disparate, and penetrate every walk of life. Black babies are twice as likely to die as infants; black youth are twice as likely to be unemployed as adults. Black middle class adults are three times as likely to be denied a mortgage, even when income levels are the same. Black families are two and a half times as likely to be poor as white families, and are less likely to own a home, a car, or financial assets. Laws deal with some of these problems, but not all of them. And then there is de facto discrimination.

I don't think negotiations would solve any of this, but I do think open talks about race and disparity might, and I do think the United States could learn from the way South African whites have felt compelled to negotiate with South African blacks, as equals. They don't do this out of benevolence, but partly because they realize that the destinies of all South Africans are intertwined, that blacks and whites will sink or swim together.

This directness and sense of mutuality is missing in this country, and instead, we have bought into the politics of separation. When David Duke hollers "welfare cheat," the nation thinks black. When President Bush cries "Willie Horton," the nation thinks black. And they don't think equal, either; they think inferior. They think, exasperated. They sigh, "How much longer do we have to worry about race."

We never worried about race in this country; we just hoped problems of race would disappear. They won't unless, as in South Africa, blacks and whites sit down and do some negotiating.

King Features, December, 1991

178

SARAJEVO AND SOUTH AFRICA: BLOOD FLOWS

Sarajevo was once the capital of Yugoslavia. Now it isn't clear that there is a Yugoslavia. That country is torn by war, one of the casualties of Eastern European political shifts. That country has attracted the attention of the international community, with a visit by France's Prime Minister Francois Mitterand, and promised peacekeeping troops from the United Nations.

This is not another Vietnam, the foreign policy jocks protest. But didn't Vietnam start out sort of this way? First it's peacekeeping, next it's warmongering, and mostly it is a vacuum cleaner, sucking up the resources of uninvolved countries. I know, I know, we live in an interdependent world. But that argument carries the most weight in this country when those involved in conflict are European. There aren't any US troops in South Africa, or in Haiti for that matter.

Indeed, the Haitian refugees have been turned away, the rationale for their rejection framed by the very cousins of those we are helping in Sarajevo. Their conflict, somehow, has more legitimacy than a Haitian conflict. Their pain is somehow more real. Their blood somehow bleeds more red.

Which makes me wonder why white folk are unnerved by Sister Souljah. US actions toward Sarajevo undergird Souljah's point about black and white life and death. Just like the drive-by shooters, the US is happy to tolerate the loss of black life 52 weeks of the year. Her question, why not tolerate the loss of white life? Their answer, because they can't. So while youngsters in South Central Los Angeles still haven't roused the lousy and the lazy with their violent wake-up call, a month's worth of conflict in Sarajevo is worthy of this country's attention. People who risk their lives to flimsy rafts as they escape Haiti are overshadowed by the smoke and mirrors visit of Boris Yeltsin. Thanks to Yeltsin, indeed, Congress passed an urban aid bill that was

179

a shadow of its former self. Thanks to Yeltsin because his presence made the contrast. He was asking for $24 billion abroad, while the folk at home wanted a scant $2 billion. The President has minimized domestic issues, but he could not ignore them, when a globe trotting bagman like Yeltsin had come to pick up the megabucks.

Along with the world, I mourn the loss of life in Sarajevo. But in this small, quiet space called my African American brain, I wonder why that loss of life is so much more important than the loss of black lives. I think, indeed, of Frederick Douglas and his words on the Fourth of July 140 years ago, when in his speech, *The Meaning of July Fourth for the Negro,* he said, "You shed tears over fallen Hungary, and make the sad story of her wrongs the theme of your poets, statesmen and orators, till your gallant sons are ready to fly arms to vindicate her cause against the oppressor, but, in regard to the ten thousand wrongs of the American slave, you would enforce the strictest silence and would hail him as an enemy of the nation who dares to make those wrongs the subject of public discourse. You are all on fire at the mention of liberty for France or for Ireland, but are as cold as an iceberg at the thought of liberty for the enslaved of America."

There are no more slaves in America, but the double consciousness remains. We would rush to Sarajevo but not South Africa, open our borders to Russian Jews but not the Haitian dispossessed. We see some revolutions as "gallant" and meaningful, but others are unimportant.

Blood flows in Sarajevo, but it flows in South Africa, in Haiti, too. And though all this blood flows red, somebody at 1600 Pennsylvania Avenue has lost sight of that. He sees those losing blood as black, or white, and responds to their cause on the basis of the color of skin, not blood. Indeed, when blood flows in political struggles, the color of skin seems correlated to the intensity of our country's response. Abroad and at home.

Sun Reporter, December, 1991

WORLD HUNGER:
WHY CAN'T WE DO MORE?

The child is almost always black or brown, with match stick legs and arms and a distended belly. She is usually from a developing country, from Haiti or Ethiopia, Central America or Southern Africa, although she has an increasing chance of being a home-girl, a hungry child in the United States. The hunger has happened because of war or famine, drought or poverty, and the image is flashed before us twice nightly on television news as awareness of the crisis emerges.

It doesn't matter what the country is, or why the child is hungry, or what year it is, since world hunger crises don't seem to go away. We are moved by the pitiful pictures of mothers too skinny to nurse their own babies. We give. We ask our government to give. And we sizzle with anger at cycles of hunger. Why can't we do more? Why are our dollars banal band-aids to solve short-term problems? Why can't we deal with some of the structural reasons for hunger?

We stockpile wheat, waste cheese, and used to pay farmers not to grow things. Now our government is squeezing small US farmers off their lands. We spend billions on MX missiles and B1 bombers, but just a fraction of that preventing hunger. Our president, who once decreed catsup a vegetable, has distilled domestic hunger to a "knowledge" problem, saying that anybody who is hungry doesn't know where to get help. With such an enlightened approach to domestic hunger, it is no wonder that so little has been done about world hunger.

Throwing money after hunger will feed people in the short run, but it will never solve the institutional problem of world hunger. So much of the drought, freezing, and storms that cause hunger are the result of the intensity of summer and winter, and a long-term climate change. We need to do more about soil regeneration and reforestation, to deal with realities of the changing glacial condi-

tion, and its impact on world hunger.

As children who learned about world hunger through our membership in the "clean plate" club, we were told to eat all our food because children in one country or another were starving. Children are still starving, and we are reminded by the blurred image of another thin and hungry child on a TV screen, in a magazine.

Writing a check to the latest relief fund may feed someone tomorrow, but it doesn't erase the haunting image of hungry children. We are the richest country in the world and we could stop the cycle of world hunger if we committed the price of an MX missile to hunger research. If not us, who? If not now, when? Time is running out. The problem is getting closer to home.

USA Today, December, 1989

UNDER AFRICAN SKIES: ACCRA IMPRESSIONS

> *What is Africa to me*
> *Copper sun or scarlet sea,*
> *Jungle star or jungle track,*
> *Strong bronzed men or regal black*
> *Women from whose loins I sprang*
> *When the birds of Eden sang?*
> *One three centuries removed*
> *From the scenes his father loved,*
> *Spicy grove, cinnamon tree,*
> *What is Africa to me?*
> *— Countee Cullen*

Countee Cullen's "Heritage" is a lush, lengthy poem, rich with imagery and symbolism, a commentary on Christianity and colonialism, a rhythmic pulsating scat of tribute and tragedy.

> *Quaint outlandish heathen gods*

Black men fashion out of rods,
Clay and brittle bits of stone,
In a likeness like their own
My conversion came high-priced;
I belong to Jesus Christ
Preacher of humility
Heathen gods are nought to me.

I carried Cullen's poem with me the first time I traveled to the continent, in 1974, when I attended the Sixth Pan African Congress in Dar-es-Salaam, Tanzania. Nearly two decades later, with some of the same players present, I journeyed to Accra, Ghana for the National Council of Black Studies 17th Annual Conference. This time, I didn't carry Cullen's poem in my pocket, but the indelible pulse of his verse pulled me into his orbit from time to time. African Americans bring some nostalgia, some yearning, to our visits to the motherland, some notion that because our space and place in the United States is often tense, taut, uneasy, there may be a better fit someplace on the continent. But it takes a trip to Africa to be reminded just how American we are, how influenced we have been by our time here, how privileged and polluted we are in comparison to our African brothers and sisters. Privileged — we have been exposed to all the technology, all the "modernization." Polluted — we are African and American, both. We embody the best and worst of all our heritage. We are capitalist and communalist, as much a set of contradictions as the 50 countries in Africa, the countries some scholars would reduce to stereotype with their shorthand, "Afrocentrism."

First we called it Afro-American Studies, then Black Studies, now African American studies. It takes coming here to understand the linkage, the change in terminology, the reason for it. African and American, here. Some find that fits, and relocate, as did W.E.B. DuBois, and the dozens of people that I met from the African American Society of Ghana. Some juggle the fit, visit and feel at home without being home, as I did. Some look askance at the fit and distance themselves, which is a chapter of African/African American history that needs to be explored.

But it doesn't look like a chapter of history. It looks like any developing country. Flat. Dusty. Crowded. Harried. No matter that there is a new language to speak to inconvenience. "Please, my sister," the woman says, slapping the palms of her two hands into each other. "It will come any time from now," says another clipped black woman, trying to defuse my impatience. Accra is like Kingston or Bahia or Lagos. And yet it is different.

The difference begins with a visit to the graveside of Kwame Nkrumah. A stone's throw from the dust and fuss, it is one of the most serene places I have been to in my life. There is the statue, masterful, a reminder of the man who led Ghana into independence, the first independence an African state won on the continent. There is the mausoleum, the notion that this great man's graveside is accessible to those who have been his students, at best. And then there are the manicured lawns, the pool, the sense that this is the absolute heart of Africa.

For African Americans, there is another heart, because W.E.B. DuBois is buried here. He, too, is interred in a stately mausoleum at the DuBois Center, in a gazebo that makes you want to sit and read something like, *From Dusk to Dawn*, or old issues of *Crisis*. Ruth Love told us of having met DuBois in the early 1960s, as he walked along a road, his car trailing along. They struck up conversation and he invited her home, where she was a guest for a few days. As she spoke of him, I had a vision from his pictures, a stately man with a proper walking stick, a man who died hours before the first March on Washington in 1963. Thirty years have passed since we marched, thirty years since DuBois died. Where have we been, black folk, in thirty years? If I had never pondered those questions before, I asked them of myself in Accra.

In the talks that I did, I spoke of the structural rela-

tionship between the developing countries and those, like
the United States, that presume to make world policy. In
preparing to talk, I pored over World Bank documents,
and analyses of the policies of other international monetary
groups. I learned how much has been repaid on loans, and
how developed countries extract their pound of flesh from
Africa. And I wondered what it would take for us to push
for debt forgiveness, and what it would mean for the path
of development of countries like Ghana.

In absence of debt forgiveness, African countries sell
raw materials at depressed prices, and squeeze their citizens with a currency that continues to devalue. They throw
their economies up for grabs to outside investors. They
have no choice, but their lack of choice causes political,
economic, and environmental instability. And we, the
United States, the international monetary agencies, are
partly to blame for that.

The National Council on Black Studies pulled together
a stellar group that included African and African American
scholars, activists, and policymakers on the continent and
in the Diaspora. Randall Robinson stirred us with his
thoughts about human rights. Ruth Love hit home with
her thoughts about education. A group of economists from
Rochester, New York explored ways African Americans
can be involved in natural gas development. Scholars explored linguistics, child development, psychology, and
feminism. Like every conference, this could have been an
eye-opener or a bore. It moved me because of the place,
space, and thought.

My trip was not all economics and academia. I took a
day to go to the Gold Coast and see the castles where those
who were shipped as slaves were held. It didn't sit well
with me, to walk into dark dank places, where there was
nothing, no light, no irrigation. Friends said they went and
cried or screamed before leaving. I was simply numbed
and jarred, touched by something indelible and haunting,
silenced by something bigger than me. Upon leaving the

second set of dungeons, I walked out into air and space and decided that whatever else the tour held, it held nothing for me. How many enclosures can you see?

I was in Accra for three more days after visiting the Gold Coast and Elmina, after seeing black folk live in fishing villages as primitive as anything I could imagine. Although there were many more highlights, it was the Gold Coast that penetrated my soul and left me stunned. It was something I found difficult to discuss, something I found urgent to distance myself from. And although I understand the basis for the restoration of the Elmina Castle, I must take issue with those international agencies that want to prop up this reminder of the slave era, a reminder I would prefer to see crumble as surely as I'd like to see racism crumble.

In any case, it took me nearly a week to decompress from the whirlwind week I spent in Accra, Ghana, nearly a week to place my experience back in the context of my life. I went to attend a conference, to talk about Africa and the US Economy. But in the process of going to part of the "motherland," I experienced an expanding personal and professional journey, a journey that compared to the sojourn I took nearly two decades ago when I traveled to Tanzania. This trip stripped me of pretensions and lies and forced me to look honestly at the status of African people in the world. It reminded me of the words of those philosophers greater than me, people like Frederick Douglas who said that "power concedes nothing without a demand," or W.E.B. DuBois who said "the problem of the twentieth century will be the problem of the color line." It reminded me that African women's voices are not heard because they have not been recorded.

I went to Ghana, not with the wide-eyed romanticism of a black person going to Mecca, but with the pragmatic vision of a scholar that saw black blood and green dollars on the walls of the Gold Coast Castles where our foremothers and fathers were held until they shipped us here. I went, not expecting an outpouring of emotion, but looking for people who looked something like me. I went to Ghana, not only in search of kente and colorful clothing, but also in search of understanding. And in many ways, I found it all, and more.

Africa? A book one thumbs
Listlessly, till slumber comes
Unremembered are her bats
Circling through the night, her cats
Crouching in the river reeds,
Stalking gentle flesh that feeds
By the river brink; no more
Does the bugle-throated roar
Cry that monarch claws have leapt
From the scabbard where they slept
Silver snakes that once a year
Doff the lovely coats you wear
Seek no covert in your fear
Lest a mortal eye should see;
What's your nakedness to me?

Countee Cullen's rhythm and reality are his African space, not mine. What nakedness? The nakedness that forced me to the Gold Coast and then into a Ghanaian brother or sister's eyes. What nakedness? The nakedness that makes me African/American, in the DuBois words, two souls in one divided body. What nakedness, what myths, what power to influence?

What is Africa to me, wrote a poet whose answer was so layered that it weaves bats, cats, Christ, and twice-turned cheeks. For contemporary African Americans, the question is less complicated, and at the same time more. And my impressions, formed under Accra skies this August, represent just one part of this Rubick's cube.

Sun Reporter, August, 1993

AFRICAN DEBT AND
THE NEW WORLD ORDER

Accra, Ghana might be any city in a developing country, its small concentration of tall buildings quickly leveling to a dusty flatness, the red dirt reminiscent of Georgia or someplace in the American South, the stately women with parcels on their heads reflective of women in Jamaica, Brazil, or someplace else. But scratch the surface of Ghana, and there is much more. This is a country that has a growth rate — at more than five percent — double that of the United States. This is a country that has made the transition from dictatorship to democratic election. And more than that, Ghana is a country that some once called the cradle of Pan-Africanism, the burial ground of Kwame Nkrumah and African American scholar W.E.B. DuBois. It was the first of the African countries to win independence in 1957.

I am just back from Accra, just back from a sojourn with the National Council of Black Studies, back and bubbling with insights and enthusiasm about my trip. But any thoughts I have are dwarfed by the words of Harlem Renaissance poet, Countee Cullen, who raised questions that many ask today. "What is Africa to me," he wrote, "Copper sun or scarlet sea, jungle star or jungle track, strong bronzed men or regal black." Cullen wrote his lush poem in the 1920's, his words rich with imagery and symbolism, a commentary on Christianity and colonialism, a rhythmic scat of tribute and tragedy. In the context that the world press covers Africa, his words have turned into dust in our collective throats, the African image one of famine, like Somalia; political instability, like Nigeria; or apartheid, like South Africa. Little is written, little said, of those attempts at stable political and economic life on the continent of Africa, in countries like Ghana.

The economic realities that drive developing economies are stark and frightening. The World Bank and International Monetary Fund have provided loans, but on terms that are nearly untenable. In the 1982-1990 period, Sub-

Saharan Africans received $214 billion in loans, grants and development aid. Africans paid $217 billion in debt service during the same period, $3 billion more than they received. This region is not a region of deadbeats, but a region locked into a no-win loan situation. A less level playing field created a situation, in the United States, for the consolidation of the savings and loan industry. In Africa, however, international lending authorities have held to the hard line that debt must be repaid.

In the aftermath of World War II, some $14 billion in US funds (or $70 billion in current dollars) were spent rebuilding Europe. African countries have paid more than three times that sum in the past decade on debt service alone. Why haven't those groups agitating for civil rights in South Africa argued for economic rights in other Sub-Saharan African countries? The G-7 countries have been critical of political instability in parts of African, but are seemingly unable to make the connection between economic instability and its political results.

The results hit home, too. Developing countries are less likely to import when they are straddled with massive foreign debt. Some estimate that more than a million jobs in the United States have been eliminated because African and Latin American countries are importing less. There is a Ghanaian proverb, "My cloth is tied to your cloth." It reinforces this notion of connection, the notion that the G-7 countries and international monetary authorities need to consider debt forgiveness.

The United States invested in a Marshall plan because the ramifications of perpetual European dependence were untenable with our own development. We relied on the United Kingdom, France, and Germany to absorb our exports and to be our partners. Now there are other reliances – on the former Soviet Union, on the former East Germany, on places like Bosnia. Africa might get lost in the new world shuffle unless there is pressure otherwise. If the G-7 countries, courting fiscal distress, can make grants to the former

Soviet Union, why can't they help African development along by promoting debt forgiveness?

King Features, August, 1993

THE POWER OF THE PEOPLE

When I learned of the coup in the Soviet Union, my thoughts turned first to President George Bush. Hearing of the house arrest of Mikhail Gorbachev, a man he has worked with and became close to, I wondered if President Bush saw any parallels between his presidency and Gorbachev's. Gorbachev has ushered in sweeping reforms to bring "freedom and democracy" to the Soviet Union. Through the combination of his Supreme Court appointments, his economic policy, his failure to deal with unemployment and other domestic issues, President Bush has sought to separate the American people from their freedoms.

While Gorbachev has tried to empower the little people in the Soviet Union, President Bush has catered to the fat cats here. Why else does he keep harping on a capital gains tax cut? Why has he turned a blind eye to the financial industries – savings and loans, commercial banks, and insurance companies – and their rumbles of ruin. Why did he snub the US Conference of Mayors so he could play golf with Ronald Reagan? When he learned that Mikhail Gorbachev and his wife were being held under house arrest, I wonder if President Bush wondered what it would feel like to be in Gorby's shoes.

After the 72 hour roller-coaster ride of the coup's success and failure, President Bush made an ironic statement about the "power of the people" that made it clear that he does not reflect on the damage his Presidency has done to the American people. While the Soviet people were empowered to resist a right-wing coup, the American people have been rendered powerless and dissatisfied by the Reagan-Bush decade. While the Soviet people look forward to the possibility of voting, the majority of eligible American voters stay away from the voting booth.

According to pollsters, President Bush enjoys enormous popularity. The same pollsters say that 67 percent of all Americans disapprove of the President's handling of the economy. As large a number says that the country is on the wrong course. Democrats have been unsuccessful in translating poor economic performance as chinks in this popular president's armor. They might begin by exploiting the irony in the phrase he used to praise the Soviets, "the power of the people."

The American people are worse off than we were a decade ago. We have more national and personal debt, and a horizon clouded by job uncertainty and insecurity. We have been so barraged by social problems — hunger, homelessness, joblessness — that many have retreated to their cocoons rather than deal with these pressing issues. We cannot deliver health care to all of our citizens, and have been late and slow to respond to epidemics like the AIDS epidemic. We abuse our environment, then the White House suggests ways to streamline the litigation that gets polluters to stop. More of us are frightened and alienated than ever before, with 57 percent of the American people afraid to leave their homes at night because of crime. When President Bush says "the power of the people," he is more likely to mean the power to lock criminals up than the power to get to the bottom of our problem.

Nobody will storm Kennebunkport for George and Barbara, despite the mess he has made of this country. That's just not the American way. Still, when this President speaks of the "power of the people" in the Soviet Union, he must be aware that his words ring hollow at home. Three million unemployed people who can't get benefits past 26 weeks, or the hundreds of thousands who know no due process under the law, must get a bitter

chuckle when President Bush speaks of the people's power even as he stifles it.

King Features, August, 1992

WATCH AND LEARN: PERSPECTIVES ON THE MIDDLE EAST

The military version of "read my lips" seems to be "watch and learn." At least that's what President Bush told the press when they barraged him with questions about our country's response to Iran's invasion of Kuwait.

Watch and learn. In the days after Iraq's action, the United Nations Security Council imposed military and trade sanctions against Iraq. The flow on two Iraqi pipelines was cut off, and the US sent troops to Saudi Arabia, supposedly to prevent Iraq from moving into that country.

Yes, we can watch, but when will we learn? We invaded Grenada in 1983, as much on a whim as because of any perceived security threat. We sent 7,000 troops to an island that was smaller than 110 square miles, bombed a mental hospital, and gave out thousands of Medals of Honor for the effort. We ran to Panama on a humbug, sending a cast of thousands to find one man, Manuel Noriega. And now, we are swarming all over Saudi Arabia, the lessons of the decade past barely learned.

There was a time when the United States could throw its military weight around with the same ease that a President invited the public to read his lips. That was when we dominated the world economically, something that we have not done for years. Now we've got to line up behind the Japanese and the United Germanys when it comes to economic dominance. Like the Soviet Union, we are learning the hard way that there is a negative correlation between military prowess and social program sufficiency.

The President says we intervened in the Middle East

because our national interests were jeopardized. Why should our national interests dominate world politics? Iraq invaded Kuwait because there's an income distribution problem in the Middle East. Some countries have more oil, and are pumping it more rapidly, than countries who have less and are pumping slower. Iraq's per capita income is dwarfed by that of Kuwait. Saddam Hussien got mad enough to do something about it, and the United States has intervened on the side of Kuwait because we're concerned about our national interests.

"Read my lips." "Watch and learn." It is amazing how easily clichés flow in the name of leadership. Suddenly balancing the budget is a moot point. Suddenly, weapons once declared obsolete and ineffective are being dusted off and planned for use in the Middle East. The President's men are falling in line in a manner that almost makes one ask whether there is a relationship between George Bush and Saddam Hussien, much like there was a relationship between our Chief Commander and Panama's Manuel Noreiga.

The oil companies have reacted to trouble in the Middle East by jacking oil prices up like crazy. The talk of panic, along with gimmicks like KGO's gas giveaway, remind me of 1973, the first time we had trouble exploiting another country's oil resources. In a number of states, drivers with license plates ending in odd numbers could buy gas on odd numbered days, and drivers with license plates ending in even numbers could buy on even days. As serious as the situation was, it gave rise to all kinds of market opportunities and warped humor, as people hired their services out to stand in line for other cars, and youngsters made a few extra bucks hawking coffee on gasoline lines.

During the summer of 1972, I worked at the Black Economic Research Center, a New York based organization that developed and implemented a program of research on black economic status. BERC's director, Robert Browne, was contacted during the 1973 crisis by Arabs who offered to help get gas to black communities if we had the distribution network. We didn't have it then; we don't have it now. As much as anything else, this current flap makes a powerful point about the lack of economic clout in Black America.

Watch and learn. Or just look at a map. Much of what is called "the Middle East" is dead up in the continent of Africa. Much of the land over which troops will march is populated by African people. These are people who can't get a nickel of assistance from the State Department without promising to give back their country's sovereignty. And, though Africa is barely mentioned in the context of Iraq and Kuwait, it is a factor in the current crisis.

Early this week, there was an estimate that as many as 200,000 US troops will be stationed in the Middle East by fall. How many of them will be young black and brown men, folk who are in the military because doors were closed to them in the labor market or in universities? How far will we go to take control of a natural resource that really doesn't belong to us. Would we rather spill a barrel of blood than lose control over a drop of oil? In the words of George Bush, watch and learn.

Sun Reporter, September, 1990

STOP THE GAMES

The horrible reality of our war with Iraq is physically remote to most of us. We go to work as if nothing has changed, lead our lives as if we are hardly affected. Traffic is not down at shopping malls or movie houses. Many of us are living through this war as if it is business as usual.

Wake up! We bombed Baghdad with more firepower than was used in Hiroshima. Iraqi forces bombed Tel Aviv. At home, thousands who oppose the war have gathered to show their displeasure, blocking bridges and burning flags. Hundreds have been arrested. This is a sad and somber time, hardly a time for business as usual, for football, basketball and hockey as usual! If only to remind us how serious this war is, this weekend's games should have been postponed.

While Israelis wear gas masks and Iraqis sift through Baghdad's rubble, we can assume that our cities are safe. We have the luxury of business as usual, but we ought not have the arrogance. War has not come to our shores, but many are tied closely to events in the Persian Gulf as those who are there. A sister, a cousin, a husband's life may hang in the balance. And the NFL wants to play games!

A few in sports have had the wisdom to pause. Hockey's Wayne Gretzky called for cancellation of today's All-Star Game. The University of North Carolina's Chancellor Paul Hardin canceled a basketball game Wednesday. But they are the exception. The NFL playoffs will go on as scheduled, as well as the All-Star hockey game. Some say we need the diversion to take our minds off war, but I say we have kept our minds off war so long we've backed our way into a conflict that might last months or years and is costing us a billion dollars a day.

At least the networks have not bowed to the demand for sports as usual. Games will be televised subject to events in the Persian Gulf. They ought not be televised at all! How can anyone think of touchdowns and scored goals when bomb drops and ground maneuvers dominate the news? How can players concentrate on catching a pass when friends and relatives stationed in Saudi Arabia are catching bullets and worse.

We'd cancel these games if a bomb hit our shores, suspend them for the death of a world leader. Something greater than a person died when we bombed Baghdad and began hostilities with Iraq. The notion of a peaceful solution to the Persian Gulf conflict was annihilated. Those in sports ought to be willing to mourn that death and to rec-

ognize the astronomical price we will pay for this war by stopping the business as usual, postponing the fun and games.

USA Today, January, 1991

ATROCITIES ALL AROUND

What do you call it when five hundred civilians, huddled in a bomb shelter, lose their lives? How would you describe thousands of deaths because water sources have been contaminated by bombing? How would you describe hospitals bursting with wounded people, with doctors unable to exercise sanitary precautions because there is no water or electricity? I call them war crimes, atrocities that violate the Hague and Nuremberg accords. These are war crimes committed by the United States, not by Iraq.

My colleagues across the page are correct — Saddam Hussein has blood on his hands. But in this conflict, there is more than enough blood to go around, and some of it flows right to 1600 Pennsylvania Avenue. Let's stop it with the double standards! If bomb-dropping, civilian-harming behavior is atrocious when Israeli citizens are affected, what makes it any less atrocious when Iraqi citizens are affected? Have we valued some lives over others as we fight, sup- posedly "for democracy?" If so, what kind of democracy are we fighting for?

Why have we rushed to increase the hostilities in this fight, even as the Soviets seem to be nudging Iraq toward a peaceful conclusion to this conflict? Why have we em- barked on a ground war, even as Iraq has, for the first time, offered the possibility of withdrawal from Kuwait? In im- posing deadlines and ultimatums, President Bush is behav- ing like a landlord serving an eviction notice on a recalci- trant tenant, demanding withdrawal from Kuwait by high noon Saturday and not a minute later? Given that high handed arrogance, is there any wonder that Saddam Hussein has dug in his heels and taken the ground war gambit? The tragedy is that neither world leader has stopped to consider the heavy burden the people pay because of his war.

The United States bears the greater responsibility in this conflict. Our military budget is four times as large as Iraq's total gross national product. Our per capita income is eight time as large as Iraq's. We clearly have the military edge in this conflict and we have wielded that edge in a blustering way, rushing to bomb, rushing to ground war. We are rushing so blindly that we have failed to obey the international laws we refer to so blithely or to consider the civilians that bear a heavy burden in this war.

There is no shortage of atrocities in the Persian Gulf conflict. But the man who has called Saddam Hussein a demon is not exactly the prince of peace. Both George Bush and Saddam Hussein share culpability in the thousands of civilian casualties. If we take prisoners for these "war crimes" then give George and Saddam adjoining cells.

USA Today, March, 1991

CHAPTER NINE

AFRICAN AMERICAN HISTORY:
MORE THAN A TEXTBOOK THING

Why is February, the calendar's shortest month, also African American History Month? And why do some schools think that this is the only month in which issues concerning African Americans can be discussed? Why do they dust off the same old books and discuss the same few icons in textbook terms. African American history can be found in textbooks, but also in the words of groits that sit on corners, hold forth in barber and beauty shops, or carry those sites like a mantle on their elderly shoulders. Packed into the corners of our attics or in the brains of our great-grandparents, we all have immediate and personal access to African American history.

WIDENING THE LENS ON BLACK HISTORY

During Black History Month, our lens is turned toward the achievements and accomplishments of African American people. In many ways, the angle of the lens has widened from focus on ubiquitous historical figures like Martin Luther King, Jr., Malcolm X, Mary McCloud Bethune, W.E.B. DuBois, and others to include those lesser known who made equally clear contributions. Indeed the deaths of people like sports scholar and activist Arthur Ashe, musician Dizzy Gillespie, jurist Thurgood Marshall, and economist Phyllis Wallace reminds us of the diverse contributions that black folk have made to American life. The lens has widened further, still, with the publication of books by former Black Panther Party leaders Elaine Brown and David Hilliard. Brown offers a formerly taboo view of the Panther Story — a woman's perspective — in *A Taste of Power*. Hilliard, in *This Side of Glory,* reminds us of both the Panthers' moment of power and its denouement. When books like these are released during Black History Month, we've come a long way from the swaying, "We Shall Overcome," pious, noble, and myopic version of our history.

Now the lens must widen enough to include the globe. Like most African American discourse, Black History Month has an unfortunate domestic cast and focus. Somehow we forget our connection to Africa, to the Diaspora, so that even as we describe ourselves as African American, the only "African" in our consciousness is brightly colored clothing and red, black, and green flags. This point came home to me not long ago when a Liberian sister asked me why African Americans had been so silent about the US' role in Liberia, a country she described as the "first ally" because it was the only African country willing to house a US military base. She said that US tax dollars — black American tax dollars — were being used to prop up a corrupt government in Liberia. As she talked, I realized how little I knew about the situation in Liberia. Her words were both an accusation and a plea to black Americans. You know about Somalia and South Africa she said, not Liberia.

Forced to respond, I tried to remind the sister that African Americans have been so burdened by domestic public policy issues that international issues have been at the periphery. I told her that many of us have mixed feelings about our ties to Africa, especially to Liberia, a country the US supported because it might offer a repatriation opportunity for freed slaves. I hope I was convincing, but to me my words were a hollow echo of a narrow lens on Black History Month. It also reminded me that, except for TransAfrica, African American perspectives are largely absent in the determination of our county's foreign policy.

Broadening the lens on Black History month forces a focus both on Africa and the Diaspora. I was reminded of that on a recent trip to Brazil, the country where slavery was condoned longer than in any other country in the Western Hemisphere. Most Afro-Brazilians are able to trace their family history back to the countries of West Africa, thanks to an oral history that is passed from generation to generation. In parts of Northeastern Brazil, the Yoruba language can still be heard. Brazil has the second largest concentration of black people in the world, second only to the country of Nigeria. And though Brazilians are of mixed heritage — African, Portuguese, European, and native—the African presence and heritage is almost everywhere present.

Condomble is a Bahian version of widespread African religious rites, where Catholic saints are icons in African religious rituals. Our heritage is also present in the stylized kick-dance, capoiera, where men, crouched low and wide, duck each other's blows in simulation of the protests of manacled slaves. And I imagined that black women's sororities had roots in the Order of the Boa Morte, a sorority of black women who are direct descendants of African slaves. The white-turbaned, black robed women of the Boa Morte are headquartered on Cachoeira Island, about 100 km from Salvador, Bahia.

Though Brazil is an interesting and historical site, sociopolitical issues there are similar to those that confront people of African descent all over the world. There is poverty, discrimination (at one hotel, a dark-skinned maid told me she would not be able to work in the gym, which paid more, because of her skin color), and a terrible situation for children, many of whom can be found begging in the street after midnight, many of whom are randomly killed. Human rights violations? Of course. But if African Ameri-

201

cans don't lift their voices in protest, if we continued to be strangled by our domestic concerns, don't count on anyone else to pay attention.

Between Liberia and Brazil, Africa and the Diaspora, there are many ways to focus on broader aspects of Black History Month (and on a black perspective on foreign policy). It seems to me that all it takes is a shift in the kaleidoscope, a widening of the lens, a notion that people of African descent in the United States came from someplace and are connected to some other people.

Black Issues in Higher Education, February, 1993

GIVE ME MY MILE

If you give them an inch, my grandmother used to say, they will take a mile. Usually these proverbs would be uttered as she stood over a stove with a pot of something steaming. Or at least with steam rising, that was when the point made its greatest impression. Give 'em an inch and they'll take a mile, she'd say, and I'd just shake my head.

It started as Negro History Week, then it became Black History Mile. The inch we needed was the collective recognition that we had a history to celebrate. As African Americans, we haven't gone the mile yet, haven't quite taken control of our images, nor made it clear that it is not just a month, but all year, that we want.

In other words, it doesn't make any sense to have newspapers brimming over with positive black celebrations this month, only to revert to racist coverage next month. It doesn't make any sense for us to gather in music and song and celebration to deal with black filmmakers and artists and writers, only next month to go back to news of black pathology.

Face it, in any month but February, front page black news has something to do with drugs, pregnancy, dropout rates, incarceration, as if we are the only people to fall peril to those ills. You'll never read about black people buying homes or cars, going to school or work, volunteering or running for office, or just living a regular life at any other time.

Pick up a paper. Turn to the "People" section. Why don't they just break down and call it the "white people" section, since those are the only people whose happenings seem to draw ink. Why doesn't the *Chronicle* or *Examiner* send its society reporter to cover the events at the United Negro College Fund telethon or the NAACP life membership dinner? Perhaps they assume that the general reader isn't interested in such. Why, then, should they assume that we want to know when Muffy and Puffy get out their ball gowns to attend a benefit for the ballet or the symphony?

The business pages are just as bad. Once in a while, a postage stamp-size portrait of some brother or sister will show up on the second page. But when is the last time somebody profiled one of our black entrepreneurs? When have we seen Andrew Johnpierre, James Jefferson, Frances Covington, Gwen Mazer, Vanessa Winegan, Fred Jordan, or any one of a few dozen others profiled?

I'm not asking for February stories. I'm suggesting that black news is year round news. Give them an inch and they'll take a mile, said my grandmother. I think we have given the white press more than an inch in allowing biased coverage of our community. And I mean we gave the inch! How many of us write letters to the editor? How ever many it is, more of us pay our quarters and swallow the news!

I want my mile! I want good coverage of the black community year-round. It happens occasionally, but it needs to happen more often. When somebody does an article about people buying homes, some of those people should be black. When they write about people who are afraid to travel because of terrorism, some of the people should be black. When they write about the youngsters from the Bay Area going to college, some of those young-sters should be black. Black faces should not only be rec-ognized when people are writing about welfare, drugs, crime.

And it's not just the media. It is society that has closed its eyes to diversity, presumed, in the words of legal scholar Derek Bell, that there is an operating principle causing white supremacy. He writes, "We underestimate when we do not entirely ignore the fact that there is a deeply held belief in white superiority that serves as a key regulative force in an otherwise fragile and dangerously divided soci-ety. Indeed, it is difficult to think of another characteristic of societal functioning that has retained its viability and its value to social stability from the very beginning of the American experience down to the present day. Slavery and segregation are gone, but most whites continue to expect the society to recognize an unspoken but no less vested property right in their whiteness." Those property chits are cashed in when the "People" section of the newspaper looks like the "White People" section.

For me February is the shortest and the cruelest month, a month of poignancy and possibility. For every program that is organized in this Black History Month, there are a dozen that could be organized during other parts of the year. For every show recognized this month, there are a dozen whose praises are unsung. For every footnote of the past that is savored in February light, there is a paragraph that is unpublished. Black History Month is not enough!

Sun Reporter, February, 1991

BLACK AMERICA'S UNTOLD STORY

If someone were to come to this country from outer space and turn on a television, they would be exposed to a distorted set of images of black people. To let the tube tell it, with a few notable exceptions (like *The Cosby Show* and *A Different World*), black girls get pregnant early and black boys use crack. The news screams with headlines of shootings and stabbings, but is notably silent about black achievement outside the area of athletics. "Soft" feature news frequently features a woman who has opened a business, a teenager with high test scores. Rarely, if ever, does the feature focus on an African American.

We are damned by the very statistics we use to motivate social change. The black unemployment rate is twice the white rate; black poverty is three times the level of white poverty; black families are disproportionately represented on the welfare rolls. But black people aren't the majority of all welfare recipients, the majority of the unemployed, or the majority of the poverty population. The "typical" welfare woman, quiet as it's kept, is white. But let the news cameras go to do a story on welfare, and watch the woman featured be a black one.

The flip side of these statistics is a quiet story of black American success. If 12 percent of the black population is officially unemployed, that means that 88 percent of those who look for work have found it. If 10 percent of the black population uses crack, that means that 90 percent of us do not. If one third of all black families are poor, then two thirds are not. It seems obvious, but the obvious is all too rarely stated. Despite institutional racism, and against all odds, millions of black people are doing okay.

They may not be "outstanding" and that is the other piece of the trick bag. When African American success is discussed, the first people who come to mind are those who make a million dollars, earn an advanced degree, or are elected to political office. But there is another kind of black success. It comes when a single mother raises two or three children and sends them to college. It happens when a black man goes to the same boring job each day, puts up with the racism, and brings home a check home to feed his family. It happens when a black youth walks on by his drug using friends and slides into his desk at the beginning of a school day, homework done. It happens when a black man spends his free time working with the homeless and hungry. It happens when a black organization raises money for scholarships, when (truth be told) most of the work was done by the one person who doesn't want and won't get recognition.

Nobody talks about this quiet success, about the drama inherent in these stories of "making it," not with aplomb but with quiet perseverance. No news cameras highlight this aspect of black America's untold story, and yet this untold story is at the foundation of black life.

The same is true of our history. Usually we focus on slavery and the civil rights years, ignoring the century between them. We focus on the first and the only, the big names and the bright lights. We rarely ask how we got over, from slavery to civil rights, what contributions, what quiet acts and efforts, made it possible for African Americans to survive. Who baked cakes and fried chicken to build hundreds of black churches? Who scrubbed clothes and gathered pennies to send black youngsters to college? Who worked as a porter and sent money home? Who sharecropped? Who organized trade unions, against all odds? Who took to the road to preach and teach about lynching? Who started banks and whose deposits sustained them? All of this is part of black America's untold story.

February is Black History Month, and all month we will celebrate, commemorate black achievement, black excellence, black success. We will sing and dance and speak and hope our children's chests will puff out with well-deserved pride. In a moment before or after some of the festivities, we should all take time to reflect on stories untold, but no less important.

Sun Reporter, February, 1989

THE CHOICE: THEN AND NOW

Sam Yette's book, *The Choice*, was the black student's bible of the early 1970's. The book was published at the tail end of the 60's exuberance, just after a pin pricked the full balloon of black self-affirmation, but years before that affirmation turned again to self-hate and loathing, before the full balloon had shriveled into shreds of rubber. The book was published just after promises were made, but well before we understood that these promises would be broken. Yette said the choice was between accommodation and extinction, and though his message was ominous it had such a ring of truth to it that it was compelling.

When we read *The Choice*, with its predictions of genocide, the erosion of due process, and the expansion of the police state, with its predictions of an economic attack on black people, we were frightened and yet energized. In a different time, the 1970's, black students refused to accept the possibilities of either extinction or accommodation. We thought we could fight!

We fought in small ways and big ones. After reading *The Choice*, a group of us swore to prepare ourselves for what we thought was immediate battle. We ate beans out of cans, walked instead of using elevators, carried cash instead of putting our money in "white people's" banks. We were convinced that there would be an attack, that it would be dramatic, that we would die. We wanted to die hearing the words of Claude McKay, "If we must die, let it not be like hogs, haunted and penned to this inglorious spot."

Some of us did die. Some dramatically. Some quietly and inside. The brother who came back from the Nam, went to Boston College, went mad in his junior year when he was told he wasn't "law school material." The sister who was so frightened by her dreams that she married and had six children in short order and now fights her personal poverty with the same passion that she used to fight institutional racism.

Some didn't die; we just accommodated. As ideologies have shifted, it is interesting that some black people have maintained their positions, while others have shifted with the wind. Some don't want to use the word black anymore, preferring "minority." Some people won't say "black," pushing policies for poor people as if race and poverty are the same thing. We accommodated. We swallowed at least some of the bile we may have sputtered out fifteen years ago, because we wanted the degrees, the jobs, the promotions, the money. Consider the black developers who sell their communities down the drain, or the black faculty who have affirmative action jobs but little to do with black students. Some of these people wear their price tag around their wrist (some "marked down" for quicker sale), while others prefer the traditional form of sale, the auction. Some don't think they are for sale, just for rent, but you know you can rent with an option to buy. Some see accommodation as a question of survival, and for many, it is!

There may be no way around some form of accommodation, and so we must applaud the folk who walk the tightrope between extinction and accommodation. Selective fighters, they swallow bile when they must, saving up the strength, perhaps, for the fights that require the passion of those who don't fear death or consequences.

Sam Yette's book has been rereleased. Though he could easily write a sequel, he hasn't changed a word of the original manuscript. Without changes, the manuscript is still a clear picture of power and institutions in white America, a challenge to black leadership, a "must read" for every black person who can. There is a new foreword, by novelist John Oliver Killens. There is a new preface, which undergirds the prophecy Yette made sixteen years ago. There is a new and exciting development. Yette has published the second edition of the book himself, under the imprint Cottage Books. Yette has published the book himself, partly because black people aren't as "in" as we used to be for white publishers, and partly because he believes in black self-reliance.

I used to read *The Choice* every six months, but then I fell out of the habit, chilled by the message. It reminded me too much of those daring days when some black people were ready to fight to avoid extinction. It pained me to contrast that daring with the cautions, tentative steps we take now, asking not demanding. Now we wear blinders to avoid anger. We walk around, and away, to avoid fighting a system that attacks our rights. And yet, as our economy becomes more bifurcated, the choice is never clearer. Black people are an endangered species. We will die, in McKay's words, "hunted and penned" unless we choose to change things. The reissuing of Sam Yette's book is a reminder of our choices.

Sun Reporter, April, 1991

BLACK WOMEN'S IMAGES IN WOMEN'S HISTORY MONTH

> *She does not know her beauty*
> *She thinks her brown body has no glory*
> *If she could dance naked under palm trees*
> *And see her image in the river*
> *She would know*
> *But there are no palm trees on the street*
> *And dishwater gives back no images.*
> *— Waring Cuney, 1926*

Waring Cuney wrote his poem, "No Images," in the same year that Carter G. Woodson established the Negro History Week that has expanded to African American History Month. Woodson's action is a tribute to African American people; Cuney's poem is a tribute to black women's beauty. But at almost every Black History Month commemoration that I attended, men were front and center, women at the periphery, in terms of the portraits on the walls, the quotations on the programs, the ancestors invoked.

If African American people were serious about black women's contributions to our history, we'd claim Women's History Month as our own. And we'd celebrate Black women's history, our ideology, our struggles, our feminism, and our contributions as joyfully as we celebrated in February. Our churches and our community organizations and our corporate groups that came together in February could do it, one more time in March, and for black women. Because if the whole truth is told, those organizations would not exist were it not for black women's efforts. Our churches and civic groups thrive because of black women's volunteer labor. Some estimate that 70 percent of all black volunteers are women.

We black women tend to be the last to sing our own praises. Many of us are modest, but some of us are silenced by the myth of "black man as endangered species." I reject the terminology and the notion that the black man should be revered above others in the black community. Think about what that notion, "endangered species" implies — that black men are a separate and distinct species from the rest of humankind. It's a throwback to the 19th century eugenics movement, an attempt to so clearly sever black men from the rest of humanity that they are beyond the reach of public policy. In addition, the notion of black man as endangered species is especially oppressive to black women. It suggests that our men are some rare prize, something to be protected like the baldheaded eagle and the red spotted owl. It suggests that they are as rare as a national monument, something to be polished, cared for and maintained. The language of black men as endangered species turns black men into some passive object, and women into caretakers. And it minimizes black women's contributions.

But the other language that minimizes black women's contributions is the language that places us as all powerful "supersister," able to hold two jobs and care for three kids with a single set of respiratory organs. It is mythologized that black women have "broad shoulders," that we can take anything, take care of anything. But that myth is as dehumanizing as the myth of the endangered man because it denies us, in Roberta Flack's words, "our problem, our amphetamines, and our curse." We can take it if we lose our job, if our kids get strung out on crack, if we have problems in our relationships, if we live in the midst of urban crime. We can take it if our pocketbook is snatched, if the stock market crashes, if we are sexually harassed. And the myth of broad shoulders is why so many of us cringed and looked away when Professor Anita Hill spoke of her treatment by now Associate Supreme Court Justice Clarence Thomas. "No big thing," we whispered. "Why now?" we wondered. We have to get past the notion that black women have to swallow pain, or that we do our community a service by swallowing the pain that is put on us by black men.

In black communities and white, the gender wars are old news. Men and women see the world so differently that our gender-based linguistics have become an academic enterprise. What is interesting about this enterprise is the willingness of many to probe our language, myths, and assumptions about gender. In the interest of building a strong community, African Americans must do much of this probing, raising questions that make some of us squirm. For example, is there conflict between womanism and "Afrocentric values?" What are "Afrocentric values" anyway? And what part of our African tradition are we talking about – that which is matrilineal, or that which is patrilineal that which glorified the warrior Nzinga or that which found liberation through the Masai?

We cannot afford to allow a new black patriarchy to emerge in the name of "Afrocentric values." Nor can we afford to forget the heritage of those black women warriors who helped move along the liberation agenda –

women like Sojourner Truth and Ida B. Wells, Dr. Sadie T.M. Alexander and Mary McCloud Bethune, Dorothy I. Height, and contemporary heroes like Maxine Waters, Eleanor Holmes Norton, Mae Jemison and Queen Latifah.

If black folks cared about black women, we'd make March as much our month as February (actually if we really cared, we'd make every month Black History Month). After all, in the words of Sojourner Truth, "Ain't I A Woman?"

Black Issues in Higher Education, March, 1993

COMMEMORATE COLUMBUS

"In fourteen hundred ninety two, Columbus sailed the ocean blue." The ditty is indelibly imprinted on my mind some thirty years after I learned it, the ditty and the names of the "great explorer's" ships, the Pinta, the Nina, and the Santa Maria. I had to wait until college to learn the real deal on Columbus: that he was traveling on behalf of the imperialist Spanish monarchy locked in a race with other European powers to search for and colonize the "new world," that blood was shed on Columbus's arrival, both through warfare directed at the inhabitants of the Americas, and through a slew of deadly European diseases. Now, we are on the verge of the quincentennial of Columbus's arrival here, and the real deal makes the ditty look naive and stupid. No wonder a group called Rock Against Racism has produced a series of "Columbus Got Lost!" concerts that will benefit Native American health clinics and counseling centers.

Columbus probably did get lost, but given the realities of Europe's economic situation in the fifteenth and sixteenth centuries, had Columbus missed the Western Hemisphere, some other sea captain sponsored by a European monarch would have made a landing close enough to assert a "discovery." This is what we need to commemorate, as much as we commemorate Columbus on October 14 – the materialistic and acquisitive drive that allows someone to snatch someone else's home and call it a "discovery" (or a reservation or a homeland). It is a drive that, if unchecked, can end in nothing but war and destruction. Such land-snatching acquisitiveness is responsible for the face-off between Arabs and Israelis in the Middle East, but also the tension between developers and urban preservationists in inner cities.

Given all that, should we celebrate Columbus Day? I say "yes." If we use Columbus Day as a time to reflect on the values that defined our early society, those values that still shape and warp us, then a Columbus Day celebration is in order. Americans being who we are, we can't reflect without the giddiness of parades, and with advertising disguised as "corporate support." Still, to the extent that Native Americans and others are excluded from these gala moments, parades serve to remind us how deeply rooted inequality is in our society.

Let's celebrate the sea captain who turned left when he might have turned right; his error changed the course of history. If reflection is an inherent part of celebration, then we can examine, and perhaps learn to harness, those forces – imperialism, capitalism, greed, misplaced religious zeal – that propelled Columbus on his journey five centuries ago.

USA Today, October, 1991

VALUES AND VILLAINS, FAMILY AND OTHERWISE

When did the word values come to mean repression? How did the Christian Coalition come to imply that they had values and the rest of us are heathens? How did progressives allow them to declare the world a hostile place that they had to "take back" from the boyz in the hood? What irony! Submerged in values rhetoric, those who use values in a divisive way suggest that some people are to be more highly valued than others. Not that all is well in the African American community, or on the left. But to me, the word "values" speaks to who we are, how we live, what we say, what makes us tick, what makes us pause, and the way we obey the first commandment : "Do unto others...."

PLEDGING THE FLAG

For as far back as I can remember, I have had trouble pledging allegiance to the flag of the United State of America. There is an idealism in the works that sharply contradicts the reality that I know, a reality that income, employment, and poverty statistics show all too well. The average full-time black worker earned $329 per week in 1990, compared to $427 for the average white worker. Even when people worked in the same jobs, there were measurable earnings differences. One nation, with two employment systems, two health care systems, two justice systems. The thought that senators who oppose my civil rights pledge allegiance to "one nation under God, indivisible with liberty and justice for all," makes me wonder about the allegiance I am pledging. The thought that the police officers who almost beat Rodney King to death cross their hearts with their hands and pledge "justice for all" is enough to turn allegiance into ashes in my mouth.

If you don't like it here, why don't you leave? People ask me that all the time, reminding me that there is more liberty here than in some totalitarian country. They may have a point, but I'm not going anywhere – my ancestors built this country as much as anyone else's did, even though they didn't get paid for it. I don't believe in the adage love it or leave it. I think the words are improve it or lose it. In order to improve it, must I pledge allegiance to it? I hope not, because I have lots of trouble mouthing the words of hypocrisy.

There are lots of ways I get out of pledging the flag. Usually, I either simply fail to stand, or fail to cross my hand over my heart, or fail to mouth the words of allegiance that I find as much a curse as a pledge. But sometimes it seems churlish to make an issue of the flag. At a recent fifth grade promoting ceremony, I felt compelled to place hand over heart and to attempt to mouth the "pledge," mainly because the joy of the day was more important than my feelings about the flag. I went through the motions, mouthing the words, but mentally editing as I went along.

"I acknowledge the flag of the United Racists States of America and to the repression for which it stands, two or three bifurcated nations, two economies, two health care systems, two nations under God, divisible by color, class, gender and access, with liberty for some and justice for even fewer."

Even as I edited my words, I watched the fifth graders

who stood and recited the pledge with enthusiasm. They were black and white and yellow and brown, a rainbow of open faces that had not yet been blemished by cynicism or bitterness. In their dresses and ribbons, suits and shined shoes, as they recited the pledge of allegiance, they were good citizens for the moment, conformists. As I watched them, I remembered my fifth grade self, pigtailed and uniformed and following the rules.

In the fifth grade, I pledged the flag. By the ninth grade, I wanted to burn it. As an adult, I find the words one of our nation's big lies. And the reason we are a nation of liars is because we elect people who preserve power and privilege instead of providing "liberty and justice" for all. What liberty is there for 37 million Americans who are excluded from health insurance coverage? What justice is there for those minorities and women whose civil rights have been turned into a political football? What access is there in states that close libraries and open jails? What kind of nation will fifth graders inherit when they reach adulthood in a decade, and will they pledge the flag as willingly then as they do now?

King Features, June, 1991

ANGRY

I don't mind raising hell. I thrive on it. I think of hell-raising as a useful endeavor. Of course, everybody doesn't have a stomach for raising hell. It requires you to get angry, to go out on a limb, to scream and shout, to shake trees and boggle minds, to move people from a comfort zone to a place where they are willing to consider changes. In order to raise hell, you've got to be an angry person. And that I am. Angry. Angry and proud. Upon hearing myself described by a white feminist as "one of those hostile black women," I beamed with pleasure because she got exactly what I was putting out: an anger and assertiveness that would not allow her simplest remark —

217

on women, feminism or anything else – to go unchallenged. Her description gave me even more pleasure when I remembered that critics once described James Baldwin as an "angry black man." If I can walk in company like that, I told myself, that's good company to keep.

Anger, writes author Carol Tavris, is a sign of something amiss, something wrong. In her book, *Anger: The Misunderstood Emotion*, Tavris writes of women and anger, of targeted anger and of anger used as a tool or weapon. She concludes that anger is okay, but urges women to look carefully at their anger and understand where it comes from and where it is focused.

Her book is one of a series of books that examines this intense emotion. In the days of "do your own thing," people were encouraged to shout, scream and get angry to express their feelings. This kind of self-expression was said to be healthy, preferable to holding it in and letting feelings fester. Then other experts begin to study anger and raise questions about its unharnessed use. Letting it all out, some said, hurt feelings, left residual resentments and created hostility.

I agree with Tavris: Anger is a sign of something gone wrong. Every hell-raiser knows that. What alert black woman living in this racist society doesn't have a right to be angry? Walk down any city street and see strong and healthy black men out of work. Who doesn't feel a burst of anger? Flip through the pages of our federal budget and look at the tax dollars spent on MX missiles and B-1 bombers, not food or books. Isn't that cause for anger? Think about Michael Griffith chased to his death by white men in Howard Beach. Anger. The US Supreme Court trying, again, to snatch our hard-won civil rights by challenging affirmative-action set-asides by asking for "proof" of discrimination in the recent *Richmond vs. Croson* ruling. Anger. Or what about the thousands of black women who crave marriage and families and the forces that conspire to keep them from having them? Anger. And that Bill Moyers special, *The Vanishing Family: Crisis in Black America*, and the arrogance implicit in his wishful thinking? Anger. Or workfare programs, some of which look like a new kind of slavery, being implemented in city after city? Anger — a reaction to something very wrong.

But there are a lot of wrongs in this unjust world, and as I get older and wiser I consider the advice of people who say "Pick your battles." I can't raise hell all the time; if I did, I'd be a raving, raging fool. So I step back from time to time and ask myself these questions: Why this anger? What does it mean? What do I want to do about it? Reflecting on my anger lets me fine-tune it, revise it, enjoy it, use it as a powerful, motivating tool.

My anger has fueled many a protest, been part of many a movement. My crisp letters, composed in the middle of the night, have caused many an institution to consider change. I got angry about San Francisco's investment in companies doing business in South Africa and wrote a successful initiative to remove pension funds from such businesses. I got angry that Robert H. Bork could be nominated to the Supreme Court, and so prepared dozens of letters for colleagues to send protesting that choice. Thousands of angry people like me, from all over the country, stopped that appointment. I was angry about the Feminization of Power campaign because it excluded the interests of women of color; I wrote an article that was printed in newspapers across the country. I got angry about a woman being denied food stamps, so I helped her get them back.

Black women have a hell-raising tradition. Many of us share the social anger that I feel, and lots of us do things about it — organize for change, write letters to editors, make phone calls, or march in protests. Often our anger is triggered by racism or sexism, but many of us choose to "take no stuff" in our personal lives as well: We speak up when things go wrong instead of swallowing our words to keep the peace. But "take no stuff" women often get labeled "bitches," "hostile" or "Sapphires," and people who are

219

turned off by rage or raised voices parody our legitimate anger as extreme. Many women, not wanting to be "Sapphires," shy away from anger as something unfeminine.

But who defined anger as unfeminine? We can trace black women's angry, hell-raising responses through the centuries. Angry Harriet Tubman responded to something wrong by leading hundreds of slaves through the Underground Railroad. Angry Sojourner Truth raised her voice and asked "And ain't I a woman." Angry Ida B. Wells documented lynchings and agitated for change. Angry women from Delta Sigma Theta sorority marched down Pennsylvania Avenue in 1919 in support of women's suffrage. Angry Mary McLeod Bethune founded the National Council of Negro Women. Angry Rosa Parks said she wouldn't move to the back of the bus. Anger is not a dirty word; it is a justified and understandable response.

I'd be less than honest if I described my anger solely as the social kind. Sometimes my angry antennae settle on issues far less global than war and peace, race and rage, welfare and workfare. Yet my personal response to things gone wrong is often as strong as my political one: A friend fails to repay a loan as promised, and I respond with crushing and chilling anger. A man I am seeing fails to show up for a date, and I chew him up and spit him out with stinging words. A neighbor blocks my garage, preventing me from backing my car out; I call her everything but a child of God with wings. I am told that these displays of anger are inappropriate for the incidents that occur. Part of me agrees, but another part of me says I am just drawing lines around my personal rights the same way I do around my political and civil rights.

Perhaps I could learn to "lighten up" from time to time, but I respond angrily to people who say they want social change but are unwilling to change the way they treat others. Often at the cost of harmony, I bristle vocally at contradictions. I find it infuriating that a man who works for a civil rights organization will not pay his child support. That a woman working for an equal rights advocacy group will pay her household help less than minimum wage and claim it's economics. That a group of black women will gather to talk about aging and dignity but not treat other sisters in their community with respect.

The minutiae, the little stuff that seems too petty to get angry about, is often an indicator of something bigger. The man who always asks a woman to pour coffee at a meeting can be ignored or he can be called on it, even though he may say it was "unintentional" and do it again. (Of course, "unintentional" discrimination is the kind that has resulted in fewer than 3 percent of all middle managers having black faces.) And then there are those liberal white people who say they are on "our side" with issues, but behave as if Jim Crow is alive and well. For example, an aide to a progressive congressman clearly has her head in the right place on issues, but tells me she can't be bothered with the black press (too small) and makes a point of confusing two black women who write for the same paper (a mistake, or shades of a racist past?). Or that modern day Miss Ann who goes to the head of a book line at a "peace and justice" rally because *she* is in a hurry.

There is not much one can do about minutiae except point them out and risk being called disruptive, belligerent, hostile, difficult and angry. I'll admit a fourth of that, the angry part. I get angry that you still have to go along to get along (if black people always went along, we'd probably still be picking cotton). Angry enough to distance myself from friends who say I overreact, mind other people's business, and take a "hard line" with "good people" who have just made one or two mistakes.

Sometimes I joke that I am so angry that I get up in the morning fighting, but the ability to "pick my battles" is coming to me slowly. I'm learning to cover my trigger points so the gun doesn't always go off. The lesson hit home one Saturday when I sat in a restaurant with friends eating a long, leisurely lunch. Despite the fact that the place wasn't crowded, our waitress kept trying to hustle us out, plopping down the check just as we were asking for another pot of tea and walking by asking "Anything else?" every two minutes. I was shocked, then angered, when I heard her complain loudly that she wished "those black women" would hurry up and leave. My first inclination was to ask for her supervisor. My second was to picket the place. But my friends sipped their tea with such serenity that I understood that we made our point as much by sitting there as by making an angry scene. I shrugged off my cloak of anger, slipped it around the back of my chair, and turned inward, asking myself a series of questions.

Do we angry people have to carry our cloak everywhere? Does our anger prevent us from enjoying our lives? Are we people who must be watched askance because our friends and colleagues don't know what will set us off? When does our anger serve us and when does it do us wrong? When is it "acceptable" and when does it go too far? When should we let our anger go so we can keep our balance?

The way we women show our anger is as personal and unique as everything else about us. Some women wear anger like a special hat, later packing it back into tissue paper until another occasion arises. Others wear it like a stole, shrugging it off only occasionally when the weather makes it oppressive. Some feel anger, then hide it, like money under a mattress or a lace camisole beneath a severely tailored suit. Others exult in their anger like frisky ducks splashing the water for all it's worth. But we should understand that anger, neither bad nor unfeminine, is part of our legacy. It can be shouted or screamed, or even whispered or swallowed, but it is part of us. And when we stop feeling that there is something wrong with our society, we will have divorced ourselves from our heritage.

The third cup of tea my friends and I sipped that Saturday was as delicious as the first; it blended with our kinship and my insights to make me feel content. I was glad that we sat at our table until we were ready to go, glad I didn't shatter our tranquillity with a lecture to management. We departed in our own sweet time, leaving a small tip and a handwritten note that said, "The tip would have been larger if the service had been better." And we laughed on our way out, not so much at the incident as at the good time we had.

These reflections about anger don't have a resolution; anger never ends for a hell-raiser. As quickly as I learn to probe my anger, I learn to appreciate it. But as I read and think about my hell-raising ways and about the lives of other angry people, I have begun to place my anger in some perspective – it doesn't define me, but it is a very essential part of who I am. And so when people ask me what I do, I tell them that I "write, talk and raise hell." In light of my history, I can't suppress the pleasure I feel when I'm described as a "strong and angry" black woman.

Essence Magazine, May, 1989

AMERICANS AND CHILDREN: PUBLIC AMBIVALENCE

I was about to become disgusted with all of the publicity around Baby M, when I realized that the wrinkled, bald-headed one-year-old is a symbol of so much that is wrong with the way Americans deal with children. The upper middle class people like the Sterns treat them like consumption goods. They are well off enough to buy a baby, the purchase cheaper than that of a Benz and more narcissistic since the Benz is of German origin, but Baby M has at least some of their own blood. No doubt little Sara/Melissa will be clad in designer diapers, shod in miniature Reeboks, trotted through a series of dance, music, beauty, and art appreciation lessons, and pushed through all the "right" schools from kindergarten to Yale.

Had the Whiteheads, the losing family, been awarded the child, she'd probably get her clothes from Sears and not Saks, and end up in a community college not a prestigious private institution. The judge, wanting to spare the child from a troubled working class existence, said he awarded her to the family that could create the better "environment" for her, and we all know what environment is a buzzword for.

Meanwhile, hundreds of thousands of children can't find homes at all, and will hardly have the choice between Sears and Saks. Those children who are not adopted by age 6 or 8 are likely not to be adopted, and many instead make the rounds from foster home to foster home marking time until they are on their own, at 18. Not many judges are worried about the environment of these children, not many of them play Solomon in attempting to award them between warring factions. Why bother, since nobody wants them!

Nobody much worries about the new homeless children, those who don't even have access to the bare amenities of foster homes, but who instead move from pillar to post with the parents who have lost jobs and homes. Not too many people worry about migrant children whose parents are farm workers. These children have minimal access to educational systems, to adequate nutrition, to the whole set of services that they need to help them grow into productive adults.

Our society's contempt for children doesn't stop at those who are homeless. Families that lack the resources of the Sterns have to worry about the education that their children have available, especially as educational systems have been threatened badly by state and national cuts in educational budgets. In California, we subsidize the least needy, providing the greatest subsidies to those who attend the University of California system, and the least subsidies to those who attend the community colleges. Without education, what can we expect from these children in the future? And there is not a horde of Sterns to rescue them from the "poor" upbringing they may be receiving because they can't afford private education.

The arrogance of the judge who ruled in the Stern-Whitehead case is reflected daily in a society where parents are told what they "should" do for their children. Even as society lays down a set of "shoulds," it makes it impossible for the "shoulds" to be attained. I am reminded of the woman whose child was shot by a Los Angeles policeman as the child sat watching a cop and robber show on television, and the police thought the TV sounds were those of real guns. The woman was accused of child neglect because she left her son alone, but on a $4 an hour job she couldn't afford child care. Or there is the story of the struggling couple who had their infant child sleeping in a drawer until they could afford a crib. They, too, were charged with child neglect. But the same people who will point fingers of neglect at families who are doing their best can't see the true neglect — society's neglect of people, of futures, of life chances.

But it is safe to neglect children. They don't vote. They don't lobby. They don't write letters to the editor. That's why people like Marian Wright Edelman at the Children's Defense Fund, Margaret Brodkin at Coleman Advocates for Children and Youth have shouldered the fight for children's rights. As compelling as their fight is, though, it will be all the more compelling when the rights of children are connected and related to the rights of the adults who are the parents of poor children.

All of this takes us well past the court fight in New Jersey, the two embattled families and the little girl they both say they want. And this, indeed, is the irony. Reporters, policy experts, feminists and lawyers have all flocked to the Baby M case like sharks flock to blood, all eager to enter the fray to talk about the fight over one little girl. And while they are riveted by this small child's fate, they have implicitly thumbed their noses at all of the American children who have been rejected and neglected by public policy.

Sun Reporter, September, 1988

RHETORIC AND FAMILY VALUES

Why have "family values" become a political football in this election year? Does the Republican emphasis on these values suggest that solely they have families, while Democrats live in unorganized and random chaos, devoid of both "family" and "values?" With unemployment rates skyrocketing, and our international economic position deteriorating, why have these nebulous "family values" earned such a prominent place in the Presidential campaign?

In trying to answer these questions, I keep thinking back to the White House Conference on Families, scheduled by President Carter to be held in 1980. From its very announcement, the conference was controversial. President Carter had appointed a divorced black woman to chair the conference. Critics charged that it was inappropriate for a divorced woman to head a conference on families. Then, as state meetings were held, there was dissention over how the word "family" should be defined. Gay and lesbian families, extended families, and any that broke the husband-wife mold, were considered less than "family." In some states, two or three meetings were held simply to define what was meant by family.

Then there was dissent about "family issues." Some conference participants wanted to discuss abortion, but others didn't. Some thought child care and health care should be matters of concern; others wanted to talk "morals." Some thought family issues were related to economic issues; others thought that families were families for richer or poorer.

In the long run a White House Conference was held, but dissent delayed it for a year. The divorced woman who was initially nominated to chair the conference was replaced by a former Congressman from Tennessee who apparently headed a nuclear family. What might have been a clarifying experience turned into yet another conference that focused more on talk than action.

226

I think some people use the term "family values" to speak about ideal conditions. Most women who head households would rather not, but men don't come with warranties. When spouses die, leave, or don't come through, the women who head households have two choices – maintain a family or abandon their children to foster care. I'd argue that the person who stays behind to raise children when a relationship dissolves shows more adherence to family values than the people who look down their noses at her.

Some speak of hard work and industry when they speak of family values, but they speak as if unemployment happens by choice, not chance. Picking the wrong job or industry to work in might speak of a lack of judgment, but not of values. And staying home to raise children might make sense from every perspective but the economic one.

President Bush and his cronies have mentioned a "moral meltdown" in referring to crime, but the crime they decry happens on the streets, not in corporate boardrooms. In the long run, corporate crime will cost more than burglary and robbery, but the criminals who wear three piece suits are rarely portrayed as lacking "family values."

In the next month or so, as both Democrats and Republicans gather for their political conventions, voters will be beaten on the head with symbolism. The flag will be unfurled with regularity, the term "family values" invoked like a mantra. These symbols are intended to invoke the serenity of our distant past, the day when every family had 2.2 cars and kids, when Dad worked and Mom stayed home preparing aromatic meals. In 1992, both parents work in the majority of families that have both parents present, and fewer than one in five families conform to the ancient stereotype.

But labor market status, household headship, or even marital status does not define "family values." Neither do politicians. We do ourselves a disservice when we allow this rhetoric to substitute for proposals to improve our

economic condition. From where I sit, family values are clarified inside the house, economic conditions outside. If politicians paid enough attention to the outside, maybe family members could worry about that which happens inside.

King Features, July, 1992

I'M NOT DREAMING OF A WHITE CHRISTMAS

I am one of those people who still cringes when I hear the tune, "I'm Dreaming of a White Christmas." Yeah, I know, the white means snow, but there's something about the sentiment that doesn't sit well with me. That's why my holiday cards deliberately feature ethnic images, or plants. This year, I sent cards featuring either an enthusiastic black choir decked in Christmas robes, a chiseled black wise man, or a Kwanza graphic. When a friend told me I'd gone too far in my attempt to politicize the holiday, I was about to agree and declare myself a victim of political correctness overkill. And than I heard about the New Jersey Santa Claus that called a little black boy a monkey.

Monkey. That's an epithet that cuts almost as sharply as Marge Schott's six letter n–– word. It is seeped in a history that allows African American people to be dealt with and treated as less than human. We were treated as animals through much of our slave history, and are spoken of as animals even to this day. "Gorillas in the mist" is the expression the Los Angeles police officers used, as they left, to describe the scene of the Rodney King beating. They aren't the only folk who use animal terms loosely to describe blacks. But that it would come from a Santa Claus who is talking to a child is outrageous. It exhibits how vulnerable African Americans are to gratuitous insults, how powerless we are to protect our children from the venom that comes from fools.

Meanwhile, just a year ago, a black man sued a department store because he was not allowed to work as a Santa Claus. Public policy does not thrive on this stuff. World decisions are not made or broken by the petty racism that surrounds the Christmas season, nor indeed, all life in this country. Parents can shield their children from these silly Santas by creating their own celebrations. Or, they can decline to join in a "white" Christmas and celebrate Kwanza instead.

I know too many people who will dismiss the Jersey Santa as an isolated incident and decide that my diatribe is paranoid, petty and out of touch with the season. But these isolated incidents number in the thousands, and they are simply unacceptable. The persistence of this kind of racist minutiae explains the distance with which some perceive that which others call "America" — our flag, our holidays, our celebrations, our very existence. At a New Jersey mall, some children got wishes, but a black child got epithets. At a Detroit intersection, Malice Green got death, while white motorists get justice. There is a connection between a name-calling Santa and a baton wielding cop. And it's the connection that makes me cringe when I hear people sing "White Christmas."

King Features, December, 1992

KIDS AND TOYS

If I could resist my nephews' wide eyes, and were immune to their easy disappointment, I'd avoid toy stores altogether and make presents of books, bucks and trips. But these children are coached by peers and the media to ask for popular toys — Thundercats, Ghostbusters, Big Bird and everything else.

Smoking gun of war toys aside, shopping for a black male child makes it clear that toys are about something more than fun and games. They are designed to reflect society's stereotypes, to assimilate children, bring them closer to the "norm." In a world that makes it hard for black men to climb job ladders, is it any wonder that all of the superheroes are white? Even in play, the black child finds little positive reinforcement, few images that mirror his. In reaction to the paucity of images, Yla Eason created a black superhero, "Sunman." But like promotional ladders, distribution networks are hard to crack. "Sunman," like the black manager, is hard to find.

It isn't any easier to shop for black girls, or for any girls for that matter. Buying dolls reinforces the notion that girls and women should teach, nurture, and mother, change diapers and clothing, comb hair and tie bows. There is nothing wrong with nurturing, but there ought to be more gender-neutral toys, and more of us who take gender-neutral attitudes to toy stores. Shouldn't girls' toys reinforce skills like building, plumbing, and legislating?

While no toy I've seen qualifies as "worst offender," the toy industry seems out of step with present values, promoting violence for boys and domestic skills for girls. As a whole, the toy industry fails to reflect the cultural diversity present in our country, and gets an F- on the gender equity test. Between Thundercats and the Cabbage Patch, this aunt is ready to holler, throw up her hands, and turn into the Grinch. But then there are these wide-eyed boys.

I don't think that every girl who cradles a doll will choose nursing over doctoring, or that every black child who plays with a white superman is racially scarred. But I think toy buyers must be aware of signals they pass along to children when they give them toys that are reflective of society biases against blacks, women, and others. In the spirit of Christmas, I've been advised to "loosen up." I will when more toys are available that reflect my values as a progressive, peace loving, black woman, when the superhero under the tree looks more like the little boy who will tear open the wrapping. Till then, thank goodness for books and bucks.

USA Today, December, 1989

WE DON'T DO DUETS

In 1970, more than 71 percent of all adults were married; by 1991, the number had dropped to just 61 percent. It doesn't take an expert to figure out why the marriage rate is on the decline. Indeed, those with as little sense as Vice President J. Danforth Quayle, have tried their hand at an explanation. He says there is something askew with the family values promoted by the so-called cultural elite. Others suggest that the family values promoted by an administration that vetoes a Family and Medical Leave Act, not once but twice, are just a bit off course.

While the marriage level among the total population dropped between 1970 and 1991, the marriage level among African Americans fairly plummeted. The rate among whites dropped by 14 percent, while the rate among black folk dropped by nearly a third. As a result, by 1991, more than half of the black population was unmarried, and 37 percent had never been married.

As one of the world's greatest commitment-phobes, I am hardly an enthusiastic defender of an institution that reeks of patriarchy and tradition. But the data suggest that Terri McMillan is right — there are a whole lot of black men and women out there *waiting to exhale*.

Those flying solo with children under their wings are hardest hit by our weak economy. The average black woman worker earned about $330 per week in 1991, or a little over $17,000 per year if she worked the year through. But the average black family hardly did better — earning about $19,000 a year (compared to $32,000 for whites) last year. About a third of the black families considered middle class (with incomes between $25,000 and $50,000

231

a year) would be poor without two incomes. In many cases, marriage is both about finance and romance.

But half of all black adults are unmarried — and only one in that five is divorced. Why are black men and women evading the altar? We can't point the finger at jungle fever — only 231,000 of our nation's 53 million couples were black-white, with black men marrying whites about three times as often as black women marry white men. We can't point a conservative finger at the "destabilizing effects of welfare" as more than half of all states allow women with unemployed spouses to collect AFDC.

What we do know is that the marriage gap between African Americans and others was at about 10 percent in 1970. By 1991, that gap had almost doubled — 61.4 percent of all Americans were married, compared to 43.6 percent of all blacks. And we know that if it rains in white America, it's storming among blacks. If there are gender skirmishes in the white world, somehow they turn into all out wars among African Americans.

I'm not at all advocating marriage, but pointing out that our lower rate of marriage may have consequences for our children. That is, unless there are policymakers who are willing to talk about making a woman's wage a living wage for workers and their children. Pay equity, family and medical leave, child care, and fair wages have taken a back burner as politicians have argued about turning the economy around, as if this is done in a gender-neutral way.

As long as we don't do duets (but even if we do), the economic well-being of African American women workers is essential to the economic survival of black children. The Census data on marriage and living arrangements make that point all too clearly.

Emerge Magazine, November, 1992

HOLIDAY HUNGER

No matter where you live, you're no more than a stone's throw from the USA's growing hunger problem. More than 13 percent of our nation's families are poor. As many as ten million people, many of them children, go to bed hungry each night. Food banks in our nation's major cities are serving more people than ever; those who serve hot meals feed thousands each day. In economic good times and hard ones, during the past ten years these people have been busier than ever.

As we inch into the holiday season, we seem more willing to acknowledge the poor and the hungry than in other times of the year. Many of the hungry will receive gifts and baskets of food to make Christmas easier. But what is a hungry person to do on February 25 or May 17, months away from Christmas or Thanksgiving? More importantly, what will our nation's policymakers do to combat our hunger and malnutrition problems?

If federal expenditures are any indication, the answer is little or nothing. The dollars committed to provide free school lunches have actually fallen since 1985. Food stamp spending, up slightly, still serves fewer than the 22.4 million people who were served in 1981. Funds for women, infant and child (WIC) nutrition have grown more slowly than the inflation rate.

Even more than the symptoms of hunger, we have failed to address hunger's causes. Persistent poverty in the USA is the result of economic policies that have created unemployment, homelessness, and hunger. Our obscene military buildup of the 1980's was funded by social spending cuts. The poor and middle income are also likely to underwrite the greed that toppled the savings and loan industry.

Whatever the reason, how can we ignore the man who scavenges through garbage to find the makings of a meal? How can we turn our back on the youngsters who go to school with hunger headaches, or stay home because they can't handle their hunger? What about the women whose pregnancies compound their poverty and who eat so little that they give birth to infants at risk? In our $5 trillion economy, with federal spending totaling more than a trillion dollars, surely we can allocate enough money to fight hunger.

During this holiday season, private donations will rise, and the hungry will attract their annual share of attention. The dollars given to food banks help, as do the food baskets poor families receive. But what will they do on July 23? And how can our government fail to respond to the plaintive cry of a hungry child?

USA Today, December, 1989

"HOME ALONE" PARENTS AND DISPOSABLE KIDS

Although the children in my life, boys aged 6 to 9, are tickled and tantalized by Macaulay Culkin and the *Home Alone* movies, I find the flicks a responsible caretaker's nightmare. How could a child, no matter how bratty, be so overlooked that his family boards a plane without him? What tenacity must a preadolescent summon up to feed himself, clothe himself, and protect the home front? Granted, the Macaulay Culkin character is aided by benevolent writers whose goal is to make him the comedic hero. But despite his defenses, I shudder at the notion of leaving a young child alone for more than a few minutes at a time.

Truth is stranger than fiction, though, and a Chicago couple's Mexican getaway was obviously more important to them than their children, aged 4 and 9. David and Sharon Schoo left their young daughters, Nicole and Dianna, with copious notes as they jetted to Acapulco, Mexico for their vacation. The girls were expected to fend for themselves for ten days. When the couple was arrested at O'Hare airport in Chicago, angry onlookers taunted them with jeers and cries of "Scrooge." And the story of the couple's abandonment of their children has made national headlines.

But in many ways America has abandoned all our children. From the budget deficit that they will inherit, to the blackboard jungles that we call schools, our society has sent a signal that we devalue and disregard young people. The Children's Defense Fund's *State of America's Children, 1992*, is a document that makes the blood boil with anger, the heart sicken with shame. Every 13 seconds an American child is abused or neglected. Every minute, a teenager has a baby. Every 53 minutes, a child dies from poverty. Every 3 hours, a child is murdered. In many ways, America's children are worse off than the *Home Alone* boy or the Schoo girls. But the millions of children we treat as disposable and ignorable won't make the headlines that the Schoo girls made during this last week of the year.

According to the Children's Defense Fund, one in five American children live in poverty, with the number up by 4 million from a decade ago. Families with children make up one in three homeless families, with about 100,000 children going to sleep homeless each night. Anyone who disputes the notion that children are disposable need simply look at the number of apartment buildings that discriminate against families with children. Although such discrimination was banned by law in 1988, more than 12,000 families since then have filed discrimination complaints with the federal government. Their complaints may represent just a fraction of the actual discrimination against families with children in the housing market.

Internationally, our position on the status of children is worse than that of most of our trading partners and allies. More than 150 countries ratified the United Nations Convention on the Rights of the Child. The United States, along with South Africa, Iraq, Iran, Libya and Cambodia, did not. More than 127 nations, as a matter of public policy, mandate paid or unpaid parental leave for employees who have newly born or adopted children. Not the United States.

More than 70 nations provide medical care and financial assistance to pregnant women. Not the United States. Some 63 nations provide child allowances to workers and their children. Not the United States.

David and Sharon Schoo will pay a high price for abandoning their children over the Christmas holiday. They have been arrested and their children have become wards of the state. They will have to petition the court to see their children, and fight accusations of child abuse in the courts. Like the Schoos, this country will pay a high price for abandoning all our children in our policies and practices. But the neglect of children is so prevalent that there are few to taunt us and call us "Scrooge," few, besides advocacy organizations like the Children's Defense Fund, to chide us about the consequences of our shameful behavior.

King Features, December, 1992

THE EARTHQUAKE AND LIFE'S LOTTERY

On Tuesday night, a Santa Cruz reporter said his brother-in-law, on the top floor, survived the collapse of a three story building; two men perished on the ground floor of the crumbling structure. In the Marina, a dozen buildings burned and others were destroyed; thousands of buildings survived the earthquake. Thousands of people survived, hundreds died – life's lottery defines logic.

In the face of technology's breakdown, we retreat to traditional values, counting our blessings and thanking God. We trade fatalistic stories of what might have been – were it not for an impulsive change of route, I might have been on the freeway that crumbled. Except for a canceled appointment, a friend may have been stuck in an elevator all night. A taxi was crushed when a crane toppled – the driver, who left his car for a moment, was unhurt.

With one shrug of the Earth, the lights went out, telephone lines went dead, computers crashed. Thousands of commuters were stranded on the wrong side of the Bay.

Tuesday we insisted on instant communications. Fax it, please, no federal express for me. Today we've been forced to pause, not to smell the roses, but to survey the rubble, to put crammed schedules and split second arrangements into perspective. Tuesday, we made decisions by spreadsheet under the glare of track lights; today we make decisions by pen and paper in daylight, or decide that these decisions can wait.

With a humility that comes only from tragedy, we practice the patience and consideration of an era past. Traffic finds a rhythm despite the fact that lights don't work. We find camaraderie as we queue up for phones, for food, for ferries.

Too many in the Bay Area have built futures and dreams on landfill, but human inequity is no match for the might of Nature, for the ebb and flow of life that asserts itself despite the technological escapes we create. In the wake of this earthquake, there will be tales of triumphant human spirit — of businesses resurrected from the ashes, of homes rebuilt and families reunited. But for the moment we are left to ponder the mystery of life's lottery, to bow to nature, help our neighbors, and reconstruct our lives.

USA Today, October, 1989

HOW TO SEPARATE THE MEN
FROM THE BOYZ

A panelist at a session about education, I am clearly in the minority when I suggest that there is something wrong with the notion that we need all-male academies to "protect" young black men. Some of the aspects of these academies — lower class size, more teacher attention, an enhanced curriculum — interest me, but I maintain that girl children can gain from these educational improvements as much as boyz can. The conversation is heated, informed, enjoyable, but I lose my composure when one of the panelists moves from educational policy to personal relationships.

"Let me see a show of hands," she says. "How many of you here don't have men? How many of your daughters don't have men? So, you see, we have a problem and we have to do something about it." Bulls—t, I say, first to myself and then aloud. No matter where the conversational road starts, some of us can always find a path to talk about "having a man." But it occurs to me, as I watch my sisters check each other out, then raise their hands, that too few of us have taken the time to define what it means to be "a man." It's more than anatomy, it's actions and attitude. "Being a man" is about being respectful and respectable, responsive and responsible, relentless and irrepressibly focused. Unlike the men, the boyz are soft and coddled. They demand respect instead of commanding it, and are reactive instead of responsive. They're as cute, cuddling and clingy as most toddlers, but cute and cuddly grownups are candidates for therapy, not relationships.

How do you separate the men from the boyz? Let's start with the basics. *The boyz will give you a beeper number and a post office box, while the men will give you an address and telephone number.* I'm not exaggerating! Most folk reading this have run into the very firmly attached man who is still on the prowl. He wants to have both his cookies and his cake, but his challenge is to keep the cake crumbs away from the cookie jar. So, you can only call him between 5:30 and 5:45 on his office phone (not only is he fooling with his secretary, but his wife is coming by to pick him up at 6), or at 5:47 on the dot (synchronize your watch) at a pay phone. You can have him paged at a hotel (easier to ignore, my dear), or dial his beeper at some specific time. If you are willing to go through all that, either you have a mystery fetish or you know full well something shady's going on. You're dealing with a boy who gets cheap thrills from your calls, because he thinks he's getting away with something.

The next best way to separate the men from the boyz

is in approach. *The boyz need an audience to approach, hollering "hey momma" while surrounded by their friends*. Or they come on like they are on center stage, pelvis tilted, hair puffed and patted, with a rap so tired it's yawning. Sisters, this isn't about you, it's about their prowess. So when they ask you to "give up the digits," they need at least one witness to go back and testify how they "got over." Real men need neither an audience or an "Amen corner" to cheer them on as they approach you. They are confident that they have what it takes – themselves.

Boyz can't take a turndown and will tell you so, often in loud and unflattering terms. "You wasn't that cute anyway," sneer the boyz, and their surrounding chorus giggles and grunts. Men take a turndown in stride, maybe expressing disappointment, perhaps keeping the possibility of further contact open. Boyz respond to the polite but firm rebuff with a bunch of itch words, while men move on, maybe offering a card in case you change your mind.

Boyz have loose lips, but discretion is the better part of a man. In other words, *the boyz will brag about what all they can do for you and how good they'll make you feel. A man won't sell wolf tickets; he'll cash them.*

Boyz wear their pasts on their sleeves and will tell you who did what wrong and when. They want a pat on the head, a hug, something to make them feel better about the women who once hurt them. Real men separate the past from the present and don't bring old garbage into your new relationship. If old feelings surface, as they sometimes do, the boyz fret and pout, while real men talk about what they are feeling.

Boyz are always seeking someone better, even when they are hanging with you. They could get whiplash from checking other women out, or eyestrain from trying to peek into their binoculars on the sly. Not that a date is a cage, or that looking is touching, but while a man's eyes may stray (nothing wrong with that), real men make it a point of being attentive to the one he's with.

Boyz use the itch word a lot (and all those other less than pleasant words to describe women), and you have to know that if other women itch him, so will you one day. Men respect the women who used to occupy their lives, and decline the opportunity to run them down in general or specific terms. Listening to a brother talk about what a slut his last lady was, or what a greedy, grasping woman his ex-wife turned out to be makes me wonder what he'll say about me when he gets the chance.

Real men wear watches or at least know how to tell time, while boyz are masters of the approximate, as in "eightish" or "latish" or "sometime this evening." So, allowing for traffic and extraneous circumstances, the men will turn up within half an hour of the appointed time (or call), while the boyz may turn up anytime (or not at all).

Boyz whine, wolf, and waffle, and have a verbal style best suited to rap records. Real men know how to communicate without taking their voice up or down an octave or stuttering to obfuscate the matter at hand.

Boyz are great at games like "hide and seek" (in other words, one of the other women he is seeing has just entered the room), "show and tell" (as in look at all the goodies I have), "hit or miss" (as in their record in appearing as agreed), "search and destroy" (as in their hot/cold, approach/withdrawal, on again/off again action that many boyz have perfected), "now you see me now you don't" (as in their manner of exit). When men play games, the outcome is pleasure, not pain; the men, not the boyz, let you know about ground rules and give a clue of how you can expect to be treated.

Boyz wouldn't know truth if it was Sojourner, while real men combine truth with wisdom and discretion. In other words, men will act like boyz if too often pressed with the "where were you" question. Don't ask unless the object of your affection was supposed to be with you. Even then you ought not ever ask something you don't want to know (how will you feel if he replies, "Down in the Carib-

240

bean doing the wild thing with the girl of my dreams?"). But if you ask one of the boyz, you don't have to worry about hurt feelings. Boyz lie, often in elaborate, creative and amusing ways (the dog ate his car keys, the police locked him up, and baby, ain't no mountain high enough to keep me from getting to you but I didn't have any money for gas).

How can you tell the men from the boyz? It's in the actions and attitude, not the anatomy. There are boyz out there from 18 to 80. They look like men, walk like men, and if the body snatchers grabbed their brains they might even act like men. But when you hear the high-pitched whine, or the low-toned wolf, when you sort out the elaborate lie or play another game of hit or miss, you'd better know that this is a fish you'll either have to fillet (too much work) or throw back. And unless you are either a masochist or into early childhood education, my advice is to throw the boyish back into the sea to swim, drown, or turn into real men.

Being Single Magazine, October, 1991

HOW TO SEPARATE THE WOMEN FROM THE GIRLZ

I am one of these women who, in the words of a very good friend, "talks much stuff but takes none." I've spent a lifetime observing, but choosing not to play, little girl games, the eyeballing cajoling that some of my sisters call flirting or "managing a man." It is corny to say that I flunked recess in grade school because I don't play, but that's about the size of it, and recess is the only thing I flunked. My standard operating procedures are stark and no-nonsense, and they manage to keep me on the straight and narrow: (1) Beware of what you ask for cause you might get it, but if you want it bad enough, ask anyway. You can probably handle it; (2) If you don't get what you ask for, move on; a bird in the hand is worth two in the bush; (3) Don't confuse lust for anything but a chance at a risky good time; (4) Try for honesty without brutality, but get brutal before telling harmful lies; (5) Take anything a brother says over the phone or after dark with at least one grain of salt. If he is under the influence of anything (even reggae music or moonlight) make that two grains.

Sound tough and hard to handle? I like to think so. My rules don't keep me out of trouble, but they keep me feeling good about myself. And every sister has her own set of rules that she's developed as she's lived her life and learned from her experiences. Everyone, that is, except the girlz. These are the women, 16 to 86, who are stuck in a junior high time warp when it comes to their behavior toward the opposite sex. They haven't developed any rules, because they don't have any. They haven't even developed the weight of experience because they don't learn. The girlz are self-centered, catty, competitive, living life like it is just another high school moment. I mean, girlz just want to have fun, and men are mere toys for them to play with. Nobody ever told the girlz that when you give a dance you have to pay the band. Which means that far more often than anyone cares to recall, girlz bite off more than they can chew.

A man I know says there is some girl in almost every woman. He tells me this when he spies me in a dark corner of a restaurant, rubbing knees with a man I'm not supposed to be with, responding to a line I'm not supposed to believe, with a staccato giggle to top it all off, about to cross the line between good time and big fool. My friend said later, "Yeah, I saw the girl in you." And I had to laugh because that was the girl in me out for the night.

Scratch a woman hard enough and you might find something of a girl there. But you don't have to scratch the girlz cause they put their giddy and their gaming all the way out there all the time. Women may make an occasional catty remark, break an occasional rule, but the girlz have claws and no rules. What separates the women from

242

the girlz? It isn't age. I've seen girls of 8, women of 13. It isn't part performance. I've seen women stray into girl-hood, and watched silly-to-the bone girls show rare flashes of woman. What separates the women from the girlz? Good sense, dignity, purpose, and principle, tossed with a little humor, served with self-confidence. A woman is firm, a girl wishy-washy. A woman takes the long view on life, while a girl lives in the short run. A woman takes stock, a girl takes off. A woman picks herself up and dusts herself off after setbacks, while a girl waits for someone to do it for her.

Girlz wolf while women work it. Shahrazad Ali, author of the *Blackman's Guide to the Black Woman* is not only a girl, but a girl cruising for a bruising with (in her own words) an openhanded fist. Unwilling to simply give advice, she had to try to drag a lot of women down to make her million. In contrast, Oprah Winfrey is a woman, exuding a self-confidence and comfort that are inspirational. True, Oprah has had her girl days, like when she lost all that weight and got to crowing about it. But even then, with her millions, her shows and the helping hand she has extended to others, Oprah works it, size 16 or not.

LaToya Jackson is a girl, while little sister Janet is a woman. After all LaToya's acting out comes across as one long pout — a loveless, sexless marriage to punish her parents, a Playboy disrobing because her mother told her not to pose. Really, what would girlfriend do if Momma told her not to jump off a bridge?! *Girlz are reactors, while women are actors, and girlz will hurt themselves in order to do harm to others, while most women's agendas excludes self-inflicted pain.*

Telling a girl a secret is like taking out an ad in the paper. Since this honey lives for the approval of her friends (remember junior high?), she has at least a dozen folk she tells *absolutely everything!* So how can you expect girlz to keep your secrets, when they can't keep their own? *Girlz want to tell all, but women don't want anyone but the involved parties to know.*

Need more tips to tell the difference between the women and the girlz? Well *the girlz have a bad case of the gimmes*, while women can put material things into perspective. You ought to be able to spot a girl coming, hand out, mouth open. The first question out of her mouth is "what kind of car do you drive?" Your vehicle is not of immediate interest to a woman, who probably has her own. Don't get me wrong. It's not the sign of a woman (just a girl with more money than sense) to turn over her car keys, bury a man in gifts, and make her fiscal status known. But a woman won't mind picking up an occasional check, while a girl's lip will poke out so far that a bus stop can be built on it if she is asked to so much as pay for a tip.

A girlz favorite word after "gimme" is "honeydo." She thinks men were put on the world to do her bidding. A woman doesn't mind a helping hand, but she also doesn't mind using the word "please." Also on the subject of vocabulary, a girlz third favorite word is "we." Somehow girlz can bond with men they've gone out with only once or twice, and get down the aisle and into wedded bliss on the basis of a simple hello. A woman knows that there are no straight lines in life, and that the path between engagement to marriage may even be a rocky road.

Some of the queen bee *girlz can't stand to see another attractive person of the female persuasion in eye range.* They are jealous when another woman's name is mentioned, be it mother, sister, or random female relative. Women are confident enough not to compete with every other female person, girl or woman, in sight.

One difference between the women and the girlz is that women can spot a quality man, while the girlz can't tell a man from a dog. Sometimes they are so shortsighted that they don't want to. And then there are the "dog catching" girlz who would love to have roles in Spike Lee movies just so they can feed the brothers all the Alpo they can eat. Women walk on by the dogs, or stop to pet or play with them, but don't take them home or into their hearts.

If a woman, by chance, happens to get bitten by a dog, she gets her rabies shot and keeps on keeping on. The girlz wear their dog bites as a mark of distinction, sitting around and talking about the dogs that did them wrong. Women would rather be out in the mix, having a good time, working out, or improving herself. The girlz are mistresses of thrice-told tales.

Girlz are into manipulation and deception. They think "truth" is a fragrance that didn't catch on, and that people can be convinced to do things they don't want to. Girlz are practiced at the arts of hanging up the telephone, dating two or three men in the same circle, flirting with a friend's man, and masters at the "no show." If backed far enough against the wall, they can even fake a faint or dizzy spell to garner a little sympathy and get out of a lie.

Girlz would be women if they took reality pills two or three times a day, but girlz watch the soaps while women watch the news. This means that girlz are living in a fantasy world, and still think some man on a white horse is coming to their rescue; women know that a man might arrive in a Hyundai, not on a horse, and that the car might fall apart before it's paid for! Girlz want to be wined and dined every night, while between their own work and the recession, women save some nights for themselves, others for simple entertainment, and special occasions for wining and dining.

How, really, do you tell the women from the girlz? Girlz think "good sense" is something their grandmothers have, while women make sense, serenity, principle and dignity part of their everyday routine. My advice to the girlz – grow up and get real. It is never too late! The empty-headed ways that are cute at 16 grate at 26 and get more irritating the older you get. Take a page from a woman's book – or better still take the whole thing!

Being Single Magazine, December, 1991

ANIMAL RIGHTS OR HUMAN WRONGS

"We Shall Overcome." The song gave civil rights activists strength to engage in nonviolent struggle, fortitude to resist physical attack, forbearance to risk going to jail. "We shall overcome." Rarely a throat fails to catch at the plaintiveness of the verse, "Deep in my heart, I do believe, that we shall overcome someday," the hope inherent in the belief that right will triumph over wrong, truth over lies, human values over capitalism. That is, perhaps, why I was enraged at the image of animal rights activists singing "We shall overcome" as they protested the sale of furs in Neiman Marcus.

Has the struggle for justice for people been won? Is everyone in these United States earning a living wage? Or even the minimum wage? Not likely. How many homeless and hungry people did the "Animal Liberation Front" have to climb over so they could sing in Neiman Marcus? How many of them are exploiters, wearing textiles woven by women making minimum wage or less, sporting polyesters stitched by women in Thailand who earn less than a dollar an hour? How many of their flyers were prepared on computers whose parts were assembled in the *maliquador* zone in Mexico, where women can work as long as they don't have children, and are over the hill at 23? How many left their demo to eat a chicken dinner, the chicken plucked by a woman in North Carolina who earned a penny or so more than the minimum wage? How many flash diamonds on a middle finger, diamonds procured from South African soil by the blood and sweat of black men, laboring under apartheid? How many discriminate, violating the very principle of the song they sing, the "We shall overcome."

I was not impressed by the presence of Amanda Blake of *Gunsmoke* at the Friday demonstration. Black women, after all, had not the luxury of a television series, not until the 1980's, and hardly even then. Amanda Blake can afford to shrug her furs away, just like she benefited from the way Hollywood redlined black actors and actresses to the kitchen or the corner. If "Miss Kitty" managed to make a powerful statement in support of increasing minimum wages, I'd have a lot more respect for her than I would for her statements on animal rights. But increasing the minimum wage might cost the lady some money. Divesting herself of her diamonds might force her to find different ways to express love. Struggling for "animal rights" is the easy way out.

There were startling contrasts in the gentle way police dealt with animal rights activists and the way they deal with other protesters. Delores Huerta, the United Farm Worker leader who was badly injured by San Francisco police, might have appreciated such consideration. But Huerta was protesting the abuse of human beings that has been symbolic of the Reagan-Bush administration. How many animal rights activists are munching the grapes that are harvested by workers who are exploited? How many of them voted for George Bush? How many of them can sympathize with animals, not people? How many of them would dare to take a stand against hunger or homelessness, against unemployment or welfare? How many of them even hummed the words to "We shall overcome" before they got interested in the right of animals?

Have these animal rights activists ever served meals to the hungry? Have they ever donated clothes to the needy? Have they ever divested themselves of stock in companies doing business in South Africa? Or are such connections harder to make than their connections to the rodents that are bred to make fur coats? Do these animal rights activists protest the death penalty? Or do they shudder only when animals die? Have they ever fought for affordable child care? Or do they prefer to focus on the care of animals, not children?

Animal rights activists take the easy way out, because the animals whose rights they fight for will never talk back. People might, though. They might tell you that civil rights are not enough, that they want economic rights too. They might tell you that they want the same kind of job you have, same job, same home, same neighborhood, same tax breaks. They might tell you that they have the right to run for President and be taken seriously. They might thank you for struggling for their human rights, or they might be ungrateful, arrogant, even challenging. No wonder people who hum "We Shall Overcome" for the rights of animals can't get up enough enthusiasm to solve our nation's hunger problem. They know that the animals won't bite the hand that saves them, but they aren't as sure about the humans.

Sun Reporter, November, 1989

UP FROM SHARECROPPING

The Clarence Thomas story has been called affecting and inspiring, a tribute to how much of a difference hard work can make in a life. And if the paper facts fail to move one, the catch in the Supreme Court Justice nominee's voice is a reminder of the distance he has come. President Bush and his minions have attempted to use Judge Thomas' background as a B1 bomber, hoping its powerful effect will blow away any doubts people may have about Judge Thomas' fitness to serve on the Supreme Court.

This strategy relies on a collective ignorance on the part of the US Senate and the American public about the lives that *most* black people lived just a generation ago. Judge Thomas' grandfather is not the only black man who, despite success, was called "boy." Indeed, just a few weeks ago, Los Angeles City Councilor Mark Ridley Thomas was called "curly" by one of his colleagues on the Council, a remark horribly reminiscent of the derogatory "boy."

Judge Thomas' grandmother was not the only black woman who "suffered the indignity of being denied the use of a bathroom." Black women were also denied the opportunity to try on clothes at our nation's department stores in the forties and fifties, even in the nation's capital. Indeed, President Franklin Delano Roosevelt was alarmed at the possibility of a 1941 March on Washington (to protest segregation in the Armed Forces and in defense jobs) because there were few public accommodations for the estimated 100,000 African Americans who would have participated in the March.

Judge Thomas' mother was not the only woman who earned $20 every two weeks as a maid — nearly half of all black women worked as maids in the 1950s. As affecting as Thomas' background is, the United States Senate needs to understand that it is the background of many African Americans. The Thomas "up from sharecropping" story has been exaggerated, distorted, and turned into a "Rocky" story of a man clearing hurdle after hurdle of adversity. In fact, more than half of all black professionals over 30 are first generation college graduates, people whose backgrounds have much in common with Thomas'.

We have heard an awful lot about Myers Anderson, the hardworking grandfather that sent Clarence Thomas and his brother to Catholic school. What we have not heard is how common extended family help and support has been in the African American community. Had uncles and cousins and grandfathers not stepped in to offer a hand, many African Americans would not have had the educational opportunities that allowed them to move out of poverty.

From the age of 7 on, Clarence lived better than most African American southerners. He attended private school, the exception, not the rule during the fifties and sixties. His grandparents had the means that many lacked to pay for the tuition and uniforms that are a necessary part of a Catholic education.

None of this takes from the hard work Clarence Thomas has put into his career, nor minimizes the example his grandfather provided for him. But the drama in his story is the drama that many African Americans have lived since the sixties. His statement at his confirmation hearings segues with a statement that the late Patricia Roberts Harris made during her confirmation hearings as Secretary of the Department of Housing and Urban Development. When asked if she, a clearly middle-class black woman, could identify with poor black people, she movingly responded that her father had been a Pullman porter and she was not far removed from poverty.

In 1960, more than half of all black families lived in poverty, not because they did not work hard, but because segregation excluded them from many economic opportunities. People like Patricia Roberts Harris' father and Clarence Thomas' grandfather managed to both enjoy some economic success and to set their offspring on a path to prominence.

There are elements of the Clarence Thomas story in the backgrounds of many African American professionals. For the Senate Judiciary Committee to treat this man with deference because of his exaggerated "up from sharecropping" story shows an ignorance of black life and history. Their interest should focus less on his background and more on his qualifications for the Supreme Court.

King Features, September, 1991

WHY ARE THE BLACK CONSERVATIVES ALL MEN?

Michael L. Williams, the Department of Education's Assistant Secretary of Civil Rights, grabbed headlines last year with his independent ruling that college scholarships awarded on the basis of race were illegal. Williams joined the parade of black men — economists Thomas Sowell, Walter Williams, and Glenn Loury, and English professor Shelby Steele — who have bashed affirmative action, minority scholarships, and social programs. Many of these men were beneficiaries of the very programs they now oppose. What do they hope to accomplish by dismantling programs that offer African Americans an opportunity to close gaps created by decades of discrimination? And why are these publicly visible conservatives all men?

More than 25 years after the passage of the Civil Rights Act, the race debate continues. Gaps persist. Black family income is less than 60 percent of white family income. The black poverty rate is triple the white rate. Black student undergraduate enrollment, 1.2 million in 1986, represented about 12 percent of total enrollment. Since the 1970s, there has been little economic progress for blacks relative to whites, and a recent study by economist Bennett Harrison showed that a third of all black males ages 25 to 34, and one fifth of all black graduates, earned less than $12,000 in 1987.

There has been selective progress. One of ten black families (compared to one in four white) have earnings above $50,000. African Americans have entered a number of fields previously closed to them. A highly visible group of black people, mostly concentrated in the arts, entertainment, and sports, are symbols of this progress; indeed, their presence is often used to suggest that other blacks who aren't making it simply aren't trying hard enough. But this ignores economics, and most recent racial tensions are a function of transformations in the US economic structured, where productivity and wages grew half as slowly in the 1975-90 period as in the previous 15 years. The shift from a manufacturing to a service economy has cut the number of "good jobs" drastically. The Reagan Revolution worked. Unions are weaker, employers offer fewer benefits, and part-time employment opportunities grew faster than full-time ones in 1985-89. A bad situation, at least for the working class and the middle class, has been getting worse.

Still, some blacks are succeeding, and it comes back to that in many people's minds. If whites are doing poorly, why aren't blacks doing worse? (They are. In December 1990, when overall unemployment was 6.1 percent, black unemployment was 12.2 percent.) What advantages do these blacks have? It must be affirmative action, or quotas, those dreaded words used to conjure up visions of unqualified blacks invading positions of power. But there has never been any law mandating quotas (defined as a proportional share of opportunities). Nor does affirmative action mean unqualified people placed in jobs. It means employers (and educational institutions) do out-reach and solicit applications from people they never approached before. It means communicating to potential applicants that an educational or employment institution is now open. It may mean offering such incentives as scholarships to signal openness.

What about the charge that black students are less "qualified?" Do we mean by the highest standardized test score, though organizations like the Center for Women Policy Studies have shown that such tests are biased, especially against women of color? Are we saying a student with a 3.8 grade point average (GPA) is less able to handle college work than the student sitting next to her who has a 4.0 GPA?

What we really have is an adjustment problem here. The rules on how the goodie pot got divided up were made by the good old boys to serve the good old boys. Word of mouth (with lips moving in those all-male clubs) was as responsible for employment information as open advertising. Enter the Civil Rights Act. The law didn't fix everything, but at least it defined the parameters for lawsuits. We learned you could have more clients and make more sales but still not earn partnership status if your partners didn't think you were "feminine enough" (*Price Waterhouse v. Hopkins*). We learned you could be humiliated on the job, and called all kinds of names but have no legal recourse (*Patterson v. McLean Credit Union*). We learned when the managers are white and the workers nonwhite, some employers call that "business necessity" *Ward's Cove v. Antonio*). Meanwhile, white men learned how to holler "reverse discrimination."

Like them, black men who bash affirmative action use sports metaphor – rules of the game, the level playing field. These black men tend to be high achievers who may feel diminished by the notion they got where they are because of affirmative action. Thus the hankering for a "fair fight" on a "level playing field."

How do we define "winners" in a capitalist patriarchy? You either make the most money or have the most status. But after Ronald Reagan made racism acceptable, and George Bush popularized it with his use of Willie Horton as a campaign symbol, no black man can possibly have the status of a white man. Some of the black men who are affirmative action bashing are really trying to affirm that their status is the result of a fair fight.

Given the image of African American men in the media, such an attempt is understandable. Black men have been portrayed as lazy, irresponsible, unemployable, and criminal. Shelby Steele uses the word "stigma" quite a bit in his book, *The Content of Our Character: A New Vision of Race in America,* and clearly the current media image of black men is incredibly negative. But that negativity comes from without, not from within, and Steele is writing about an inner stigma, inner negativity. He coins phrases like "race fatigue" (tired of talking about race) and "integration shock" (the way black people supposedly behave in integrated settings). Steele assumes that if he feels fatigue and shock stigma, then so must the rest of us. And he is ready to dismantle a policy that has opened doors because he can't stand the stigma.

Steele's book is devoid of socioeconomic content and analysis. Yet I can't recall any nonfiction book by a black writer getting such critical acclaim in the past decade, not Derrick Bell's *And We Are Not Saved,* not John Edgar Wideman's *Philadelphia Fire.* Perhaps Alice Walker's *The Color Purple*, or Toni Morrison's *Beloved* got such a response, but fiction markets are very different from nonfiction.

Why the acclaim? The applause for Steele's book, like the acceptance of Michael Williams's announcement, signals an unspoken agreement between white and black male conservatives. The white men are desperately trying to preserve their perquisites; while the black men are desperately trying to prove they can fight the good fight with white men and win. Women don't see the world in such combative terms. Life is not so clear cut for those well acquainted with the double shift, with dashed hopes and broken promises. Level playing field? Words that don't even enter women's vocabularies.

From a sociopolitical perspective, this is all the more true of African American women. We head 46 percent of all black families, and now shoulder multi-generational responsibilities as the caretakers of crack babies, as members of the "sandwich generation." We are often buffers between social and criminal institutions and the black male, the person who negotiates the school system for her children, the juvenile justice system for her adolescent, and the criminal justice system for her brother or spouse. This is not to say that every black woman has to deal with social deviance, or that every black man has problems with institutions. But it is important to note that black women, like most women, bear heavy family responsibility. Society's differential treatment of the black male places an additional burden on the black woman. And women seem far less concerned about a level playing field than about the location of the field, the context of the race, and the issue of whether hierarchical competition is the best way to do allocations. We are certain that life isn't fair, and few of us see life as a game.

There may be black women conservatives, but they are rendered invisible by media that are both racist and sexist. Indeed, as Steele skyrocketed to notoriety, the loudest black female voice in the press was that of Shahrazad Ali, a self-published writer whose poorly written *The Blackman's Guide to Understanding the Black Woman* suggested that the black man "get control of his woman," and advocated domestic violence. The contrast between Steele and Ali was reminiscent of a decade ago, when the most widely read black writers were Williams Julius Wilson (*The Declining Significance Race*) and Michele Wallace (*Black Macho and the Myth of the Superwoman*). Then, as now, black women's voices were heard only when we spoke of black-on-black relationships, especially black male-female relationships. Black men's voices are the ones that are heard in discussions of black-white issues.

Black male conservatives are exercising their masculinist game playing prerogatives by closing the door on affirmative action and other social programs. In essence, they are placing a higher priority on rules and appearances than on outcomes and equity. So while a handful of black male conservatives speak of fair competition and level playing fields, a larger number of African Americans realize that competitions can't be fair when the rules are rigged, that playing fields can't be leveled when one side is weighed down with generations of inequity, and that in economic crisis those who don't write the rules will end up holding the short end of the stick.

Ms. Magazine, March/April, 1990

THE DUKE IN BUSH AND WILSON

David Duke has reviled our nation with his racist and anti-Semitic past and his Klan background, his racially divisive rhetoric, and the way that this message has gotten such wide acceptance among Louisiana voters. Better late than never, even President Bush said he'd vote for Edwards over Duke, preferring to hold his nose and vote for a Democrat and scoundrel instead of the man his own rhetoric helped nurture. There's denial here, on the part of the President, but also on the part of the politicians and editorial writers who have promoted parts of the Duke message.

Take California Governor Pete Wilson, a Republican moderate. Reacting to a survey that says 20 percent fewer Californians describe our state as "the best place to live," he has announced that the growing number of welfare recipients is partly responsible for the decline in the standard of living in the state. He is also dismayed by the number of new immigrants that come to California. In blaming welfare recipients and immigrants for the state's financial problems, Governor Wilson is offering a milder version of the Duke message. Here is what he is really saying: if it were not for these people of color, then white people might be living a bit better. His words pack the same racial wallop as Duke's.

Polls say the glitter on the California dream is tarnished, but I say life in America won't ever be what it used to be. Politicians have two choices — they can exploit fears and hark back to the past, as Duke, Bush, and Wilson have done, or they can offer visionary options for our much-changed future, but few Democrats or Republicans have offered such options. In trying to recapture the America that used to be, nostalgics forget that the past wasn't too pretty for some of us, mostly people of color and women. But as long as an uncertain future is compared to distant, distorted memories of a pleasant past, the future is a clear loser.

These are the stark realities: the white proportion of the population is both shrinking and aging, while the black, Latino and Asian proportions of the population are growing. The labor market won't ever again generate the employment security that it used to, and more and more of us will balance an economic tightrope, regardless of our race. World markets are shrinking and "globalization," not "nationalization," is the name of the game. The pace of change has been so swift that we do not know what our nation will look like in a decade.

But we do know that our government could reduce economic uncertainty by taking on key economic and social policy reforms like family policy, unemployment insurance extension, health insurance, employment and training, and other issues. Instead of tackling economic issues, some of our politicians have chosen to indulge in racially divisive rhetoric, blaming economic uncertainty on people of color, not on their own inaction.

It is easy to condemn David Duke as a racial extremist who does not belong in public office. Why is condemnation slower coming when so-called "responsible" politicians like President Bush and Governor Wilson mirror Duke's sentiments to defend the status quo?

King Features, November, 1991

IS BUCHANAN A BIGOT?

In the beginning, I really didn't care whether conservative pundit Pat Buchanan was a bigot or not. He seemed more an extremist than anything else, but his CNN barking "from the right" and his columns seemed more effective at staking ideological ground than shaping public policy. His comments about "taking America back" (from whom, one might ask) seemed anachronistic and narrow, his opposition to affirmative action no more severe than the President's. Is Buchanan a racist? Three months ago, I'd have shrugged and said "who cares?" But then, three months ago, he had not placed so well in the New Hampshire primary. Three months ago, few took the Presidential noises he was making very seriously.

Now Buchanan has been boosted by the 41 percent of the Republican votes he got in New Hampshire and says he will aggressively challenge President Bush in every primary. And his rhetoric taps into an anger that many Americans are feeling, an anger that has caused the Governor of California to blame immigrants and welfare recipients for our budget woes (that's "America first"), an anger that gave David Duke a sizable vote in the Louisiana gubernatorial race last November.

Using terms like "take America back" implies that it has been taken over — by African Americans, Latinos, other people of color. But historical accuracy would suggest the opposite, that white immigrants took America away from the native peoples who lived here. Unemployed whites don't want a history lesson, though. They want jobs, they want opportunity, and they want their superiority as white people to be affirmed. That's why they so bitterly oppose "quota bills" that simply provide people of color and women with a fair shot at jobs they've been excluded from. It may be Pat Buchanan's fault that his constituency seethes with anger at people of color, but if he deliberately ignites the anger to get votes, he's fanning flames of racial hostility.

It doesn't help that Buchanan is a graduate of "Ole Miss," the citadel of white supremacy. There were whites who said black people would attend the University of Mississippi over their dead bodies, the University's mascot is an old "Reb" colonel. Those things that Pat Buchanan holds sacred are the same things that some of us hold in contempt. In taking America back, would Buchanan have the Rebel flag fly from every flag post?

I remember being chilled to the bone by a column Buchanan wrote suggesting that LA motorist Rodney King should be grateful that he was simply beaten by the LAPD. His column seemed a barbaric endorsement of the heavy-handed and racist tactics of the police force. More genially, Buchanan is apt to hark back to the fifties as America's "golden age." But his golden age was a nightmare for most African Americans. It was a period of harsh segregation, of Bill Connor's dogs, of limited (if any) voting rights, of the back of the bus. In Buchanan's golden age, more than half of all black women worked as maids — it was the only work we could find, often even with college educations. Is this the past Buchanan wants, a past when black people were both grateful and quiet, and when white people ruled supreme?

Buchanan has also made anti-Semitic remarks, but Jewish leaders have treated Buchanan with kid gloves. Buchanan has said many of the same things about Hitler that Muslim minister Louis Farrakhan has said — that the man was "great" and a political genius. But Buchanan is an insider, and Farrakhan supported Rev. Jesse Jackson, an outsider. Buchanan's bigotry is the acceptable bigotry of all white golf clubs and all male dining clubs. The pundits who are still eviscerating Jackson have exempted their buddy, Buchanan, from the same harsh analysis. "I don't like to use the label 'racist,'" said Buchanan's *Crossfire* host Michael Kingsley, letting his colleague off the hook. So much for the left.

I'm a member of the "duck" school, myself. If it walks like a duck and quacks like a duck, then it's a duck. Buchanan's "take America back" talk sounds like bigotry, his statements about welfare and African Americans sound like bigotry, and some of his columns resound with bigotry. You don't have to wear a hood or post a "whites only" sign to be a bigot. In today's political landscape, all you have to do is use the carefully crafted rhetoric of "taking America back."

King Features, February, 1992

LEADERS AND LEGENDS

How would Malcolm X respond to gansta rap? Would there be common ground between Rev. Martin Luther King and the nihilistic drug generation? How would Thurgood Marshall rule on campus speech codes? While I don't know the answers I can't help but think of these leaders in a turbulent time when the issue is not customs that put us on the back of the bus but questions of who owns the bus.

BLACK FIRE: MALCOLM'S MESSAGE

"Malcolm was our manhood, our living black manhood! This was his meaning to his people. And in our honoring him, we honor the best in ourselves."

— Ossie Davis
February 27, 1965

"If, to protect my relations with the many good white folks who make it possible for me to earn a fairly good living in the entertainment industry, I was too chicken, too cautious, to admit that fact when he was alive, I thought that at least now, when all the white folks are safe from him at least, I could be honest with myself enough to lift my hat for one final salute to that brave, black ironic

gallantry, which was his style and hallmark, that shocking zing of fire-and-be-damned-to-you, so absolutely absent in every other Negro man that I know, which brought him, too soon, to his death."
  — *Ossie Davis,*
      The Autobiography of Malcolm X

The history of black survival in white America is a history of adaptation, assimilation, accommodation, with rare bursts of rhetoric, of defiant courage, of rebellion, Denmark Vessey, Nat Turner, Malcolm X, Huey Newton, Michael McGee — those voices of rebellion are voices of a defiant courage. They are men who have ignored all their mama's admonitions, who have rejected the black male model of go along to get along. The men who lift their voices in a defiant courage that speaks black/white, right/wrong, retaliation pay a price for the words they speak, a price that is usually disgrace or death. Or deportation — Marcus Garvey.

"That was then and this is now," I can hear the skeptics say. No need, now, for Malcolm's defiant courage? No need now to confront injustice? No need now to articulate the issues without fear? Black men who climb the corporate ladder find a trick bag on each rung, the challenge of assuring friends, foes and competitors that they are not "threatening," but affable. Smiling. Non-incendiary. That there is no anger, or that anger can be masked. But what can be done to make the legacy of inequality, the statistics that report that 40 percent of all black men (compared to about 25 percent of all white men) over age 25 are not in the labor force. Dropped out. Gone away. Ground down by assimilation, adaptation, an inability to mask.

"We wear the mask that grins
and lies, that hides our teeth
and shades our eyes."
  — *Paul Lawrence Dunbar*

Every black person has an automobile story. I was

262

driving a convertible out of the Los Angeles Airport when a member of the LAPD decided to stop me to check on my license and registration. My companion, a thirtysomething black man, immediately assumed the position, hands up behind the head, head bowed down. After a few minutes, the matter was successfully resolved, and I was back on the right track to my destination. Back on the right track, almost. The sour taste left in my mouth because a black man was smart enough, astute enough to assume the position polluted my afternoon and evening. My brain knew enough to know that my friend's silence was wise. I'd seen enough of the videotapes of the beating of Rodney King to know just what the LAPD is capable of. But another part of me, my heart, broke into tiny little pieces at the sight of a black man bowing his head in the face of capricious law enforcement.

Malcolm didn't bow his head. He didn't bite his tongue. He didn't kow-tow or curry favor with white America. And that is the enduring nature of his legacy, his hold on black America. No voice has been as defiant, as eloquent, as painfully honest, as racially confronting in the 27 years since his assassination. Every African American man (the exclusion of women is another story) called leader has had something to lose, some need to compromise, to "go along to get along" in the face of scrutiny. Every one of these leaders has seemed able to calculate, on the spot, the costs of defiance and the benefits of accommodation, to tailor their public comments accordingly. This set Malcolm X apart from them, in his life and legacy. Ossie Davis celebrated Malcolm, because Malcolm did what he could not do; put his own mouth to a microphone and voice the anger of a people.

A black stockbroker who makes six figures a year says Malcolm's legacy keeps him sane. He has all the trappings of white success, the condo in New York, the car he pays more to garage than some folks pay for rent, the designer suits with shoes to match, the cachet to get a table at most restaurants even when the maitre d' says there is no room. He also has a set of Malcolm X's recorded speeches, and keeps a well-thumbed copy of Haley's Autobiography of Malcolm X at the side of his bed. He can recite line, chapter and verse of Malcolm, with jocularity, intensity, or bitterness, depending on the moment. "What do white racists call a black man with a Ph.D.?" he sometimes chuckles darkly, quoting one of Malcolm's Harvard speeches. "A nigger."

You wouldn't see the Malcolm in this man to look at him. He is shades of Ron Brown, not Malcolm X. When he shakes off his Malcolm speeches and walks into the world, he meets everyone with a smile and a kinetic handshake. An affable fellow, the white folks say. But what do you call a black man who can double your profits? In his face you call him a rainmaker, behind his back you call him a nigger. Kevin has been frisked by the security guards at the Wall Street Building where he works. They didn't expect a big black man to bring his pristine sandwich (fried chicken would have been too stereotypical) back inside the building after it was closed, except to steal. He has been stopped driving his BMW for no good reason, and gotten no tickets, just that vague law enforcement back and forth that questions why a black man is driving this car. He doesn't hail a cab in New York, but calls a car service so he can make sure he gets a ride. When the white partners in his firm ask how it's going, he smiles that Dunbar smile and says, "Okay," thinking of Malcolm X.

> *"He was a kind of alter ego for people who were too vulnerable and too insecure to say what they really felt regarding our situation in America."*
> *— C. Eric Lincoln*

When the Spike Lee version of Malcolm X's life hits the screen, the man who was once a black American icon becomes more strongly identified as part of American popular culture. Many will focus on the fact that when Malcolm came back from Mecca, he ceased to call whites "blue-eyed devils." It is important to remember that even as he distanced himself from condemning individual whites, Malcolm X continued to condemn racist institutions, to demystify white people for those black people who were clearly intimidated by them. Some will see his description of "devils" as evidence of Malcolm's derision for fools who have all too often attempted to impose institutional power over African American people. Malcolm's philosophy may have evolved, but he had no illusions about the tendency of even well-meaning whites to attempt to dominate blacks.

> *"Every time that whites join a black organization — before you know it a black will be up front with a title, but the whites, because of their money are the real contributors."*
> *— Malcolm X*
> *The Autobiography of Malcolm X*

> *"The white man is not inherently evil, but America's racist society influences him to act evilly. The society has produced and nourishes a psychology which brings out the lowest, most base part of human beings."*
> *— Malcolm X*
> *The Autobiography of Malcolm X*

As a member of the Nation of Islam, and even after his expulsion, Malcolm X did not bow down to white America, but set himself up in stark opposition to those who expected bowed head, bended knee, turned cheeks from black men. More than that, he challenged those blacks who wanted white reality to be their own, whose anger was muted by their need to get along. Wannabes, Malcolm called black leadership. An observer to the March on Washington, he later talked about black need for white acceptance and the role that compromise had on the Washington March.

> *"They ceased to be angry, they ceased to be uncompromising. It ceased to be a march.*

It became a picnic."
— Malcolm X,
"Message to the Grassroots,"
November 10, 1963

Go along to get along. This is the American reality. Bite your tongue. Compromise. Get into the mix. The dynamic of tokenism, that phenomenon that gives one or two of us voice if we are well-behaved, has produced visible black success. But at what price? A third of the black population lives in poverty. One of every two black children born today is born into poverty. Many of those who call themselves leaders were involved, not in critical issues of income distribution, but in elections for the past year. Malcolm called our misplaced priorities "tricknology."

"In this deceitful American game of power politics, the Negroes (i.e., the race problem, the integration and civil rights issues) are nothing but tools used by one group of whites, called Liberals, against another group of whites, call Conservatives, either to get into power or to remain in power."
— Malcolm X,
"God's Judgment of White America," December 4, 1963

For most African Americans, the March on Washington was not a picnic, but the single action that spurred the passage of the Civil Rights Act. And for some black folks there is an ambivalence about Malcolm X. He was our shining Prince, said Ossie Davis, but where was his kingdom? He was a scathing critic of black leadership, but he offered no competing reality, no solutions. Weeks before his death, he described his philosophy as "flexible," "evolving." Much of Malcolm's legacy is the promise of what might have been, the organizations he might have developed, the many ways he might have worked with others to improve the status of black Americans.

Twenty-nine years after the March that Malcolm criticized, Rev. Jesse Jackson is still talking about bathrooms. In the speeches he gave much of this fall, as he registered voters for the Democratic ticket, he reminded African American people that while we thronged on Washington, we could not use public accommodations, because of the enduring nature of Jim Crow. Jesse is still talking about bathrooms because he wants to remind us that the hundredth anniversary of *Plessy v. Furgeson (1896)*, that Supreme Court ruling on separate but equal accommodations, is upon us, while separate, unequal realities for many black Americans persist. I've seen black people squirm when Rev. Jackson speaks of bathrooms, well-dressed, comfortable black people who have escaped the reality that Malcolm X spoke of so well. Their discomfort is the painful legacy of the oscillation of progress and poverty, of the mixed path that black Americans have trod since the passage of the Civil Rights Act of 1964.

Some thought the struggle ended when the Civil Rights Act passed. That legislation, after all, outlawed discrimination and set forth an enforcement mechanism. Since 1964, the refrain from whites has been "What do black people want?" as if the passage of a law is balm for the Gilead of a century of post-Emancipation unequal treatment. The irony is that black folk have always wanted to believe that America would do them right. This belief is, perhaps, responsible for the muted nature of our struggles. John Blassingame and Mary Berry speak of the "paradox of loyalty," the number of African Americans who have fought for the right to fight for their country. Black folk have both chafed at racism and exclusion, and stood eagerly, like damsels deserted at a ball, hoping white America would come to its senses and ask for that one, affirming, dance. Many on the outside envied those on the inside. Except Malcolm.

Malcolm said we should not wait for white America to do right. He said that left to its own devices, white America would not/could not do right. He challenged whites and blacks to work for justice, offering "the ballot or the bullet" as paths to the right thing. Some shuddered at mention of the bullet, and said that Malcolm X was a violent man, but in equalizing the ballot and the bullet Malcolm made it clear that civic action was a real alternative to violence. A more violent man would have preferred the bullet to the ballot, but Malcolm X placed them on equal footing at a time when use of the ballot was denigrated. When Malcolm said black people should seek justice "by any means necessary," many thought that meant he was stirring up violence. But he was merely a mirror that reflected black American's frustration and anxiety.

> *"It takes no one to stir up the sociological dynamite that stems from the unemployment, bad housing, and inferior education already in the ghettoes. This explosively criminal condition has existed for so long it needs no fuse; it fuses itself spontaneously, combusts from within itself."*
> *— Malcolm X,*
> *The Autobiography of Malcolm X*

Malcolm X was an enigma. No movie, no book, no recorded speech can measure the trajectory of his growth. And while there are black men who look to his words for strength to fight or to assimilate, there is no way to measure those touched and inspired by his defiant courage. Most of those who will see Spike Lee's film were not born when Malcolm was assassinated. They can only imagine the water faucets that said "white" or "colored," the bathrooms that were closed to us. They don't have to use their imaginations to visualize a United States Senate that has but one African American representative, a managerial class with an even worse ratio. For these youngsters defiant courage is a real alternative to the discouragement so many in our society offer them, an inspiration, as empowerment, and in Ossie Davis' words, "our manhood."

> *"I don't think any black person can speak of Malcolm and Martin without wishing that they*

*were here. It is not possible for me to speak of
them without a sense of loss and grief and rage;
and with the sense, furthermore, of having been
forced to undergo an unforgivable indignity, both
personal and vast. Our children need them, which
is indeed the reason that they are not here. And
now we, the blacks, must make certain the our
children never forget them. For the American
republic has always done everything in its power
to destroy our children's heroes, with the clear
(and sometimes clearly stated) intention of de-
stroying our children's hope. This endeavor has
doomed the American nation: Mark my words."*
— *James Baldwin, 1972*

Many will view this Malcolm-mania as driven by a Spike
Lee-directed, Warner Brothers-distributed film. That does
disservice to both the man and the myth. For many, the
reality of Malcolm's defiant courage was soothe, salve,
strength and sanity even before it hit the big screen. Some
of these men wear "X" caps; others carry briefcases. Some
of them have dropped out of the labor market. Some in-
corporate Malcolm's message, poised to fight racism "by
any means necessary."

This is the Malcolm X legacy of defiant courage — that
voices will be raised even in the face of positive political
moderation and a changing of the guard. Mark my words.

San Francisco Weekly, November, 1992

ARTHUR ASHE:
GRACE AND CHALLENGE

I am one of these people who is joyfully "addicted to
the printed word." If I'm not writing or talking, then I'd
rather be reading than doing almost anything else. For the
last week, I've been on one of my "reading jag" periods,
where nothing would satisfy me but the turning of a page.

So I ran through about a dozen books in a week, trying to satisfy the craving for print. I read a couple of mysteries, a couple of unpublished manuscripts, some fiction (including a wonderful collection of short stories by Edward Jones, called *Lost in the City* and based on Washington, DC), and some autobiography. Among these books was Arthur Ashe's last effort, co-written with Arnold Rampersand, *Days of Grace*. This gentle and reflective work, literally written on Arthur Ashe's deathbed, offers insight on a man many of us have admired, appreciated, but often disagreed with.

Arthur Ashe describes himself as a "race man," but he does not mince words when he exhorts the African American community to get up off our collective butts (he would say rear ends) and do better. The book begins with his April, 1992, "outing," the public announcement that he had been diagnosed HIV-positive and suffered from AIDS, and ends with a poignant letter to his much loved daughter Camera. Between the outrage at his outing and the caring missive to his daughter, Ashe pulls no punches and emerges as a firm and conservative man who, despite race consciousness, bent over backwards to make sure that his consciousness did not translate into racial bias.

Indeed, while Ashe railed against the immature tennis court behavior of folk like John McEnroe and Jimmy Connors, carped about the money habits of some of his triflin' friends (his words, not mine), and announced that he voted for George Bush because he wasn't a "yellow dog" Democrat, some of his harshest criticism is leveled at African Americans. In a chapter title, "The Burden of Race," Ashe speaks of racial dignity and morality, about issues of standards in life and athletics. He was critical of conspiracy theories, of the controversy whirling around the drug Kemron, purported to cure AIDS, and takes on the race consciousness of a range of people, from Al Sharpton to Len Jeffries, to Jesse Jackson. During his lifetime, Ashe had principled collisions with a number of folk, the most visible that over NCAA Proposition 48, which requires ath-

letes to have a C average and 700 on the SAT test. Prominent coaches like Georgetown's John Thompson clashed
with Ashe on this issue, but what emerges from Ashe's
book is the dignified notion that he could agree to disagree and maintain his dignity.

Despite his inherent dignity and conservatism, Ashe
does not let our country off the hook. "The need for us to
be at the bottom seems integral to the identity of the nation. At every turn, our character and competence are questioned," he writes in *Days of Grace*. The difference between his times and these, though, is that African Americans who came of age in the early sixties were determined
to answer questions of character and competence with
excellence. Today, even those who are committed to excellence are not committed to answering the questions of
those who dare raise questions simply on the basis of skin
color.

Some people are nostalgic for those simpler times,
when the African American credo was turn the other cheek,
was "We Shall Overcome." For some folk these are solutions of the past, solutions that made sense before the
economy's downturn also turned the clock back and
brought the sheets out of the closet. Since 1980, the tone
of race discussion and the terms of the race debate have
changed. Few can consistently manage Ashe's quiet civility. Sometimes the "in your face" response to racial nonsense is required.

Arthur Ashe learned to get in folk's faces during the
Free South Africa Movement when he and boyhood friend
Randall Robinson (along with Mary Frances Berry and others) were locked up for their protests outside the South
African Embassy. Indeed, his last hospital stay was preceded
by a picket outside the White House to protest immigration policy against Haitians. Ashe's political consciousness
was clearly heightened in the years since he beat Jimmy
Connors at Wimbledon, since he deliberately distanced
himself from politics.

In reading *Days of Grace*, I found several places where Ashe articulated positions that I vehemently disagree with. His opposition to affirmative action, despite his acknowledgment that African Americans are "perhaps" due reparations and still face bias, for example, struck me as strange logic or an inadvisable pragmatism. But while I found points of disagreement, I found no breach of caring, and reading the book made me wonder what Ashe would think — of Lani Guinier, of *Reno v. Shaw* (the decision that rejected the drawing of a "black" Congressional district in North Carolina), of the current Supreme Court. Ashe's voice is one we will miss, but his book is a reminder that we lost a giant and a gentleman when we lost Arthur Ashe earlier this year, a man whose challenge to African Americans is part of his enduring legacy.

Sun Reporter, July, 1993

MAXINE WATERS:
THE WILL TO TRANSFORM

Maxine Waters had hardly been sworn into Congress when she was asked to join House Majority Leader Bill Gray in a fact-finding mission to the Persian Gulf. She says as soon as she got there, she was certain we were going to war. "As far as the eye could see, there were tanks," she said. "We were ready for war."

I heard Congresswoman Waters address a group of women foundation executives on Monday in Chicago. It was the first time I've seen her in action since she went to the Congress. Max is always a moving speaker — fiery, dynamic an incisive critic of the unequal way the nation works. Before she went to Congress, she made her mark on the California legislature, crusading on behalf of the "have nots." I wondered if the stifling atmosphere of Congress, the old boy nature of the place, would dampen her fire. The answer is no.

But in her own words, she has had to grapple with herself, to "hold on to herself," as she watches politicians who she says are often "cowards" fold in the face of intimidation. What's lacking is leadership, said Congresswoman Waters. People take polls and more polls and then they poll the pollsters. They don't raise their voices when they know policies are wrong. They go along to get along.

When the first vote was taken about whether to bomb Iraq, 173 legislators were opposed to the bombing. Says Maxine, "Then the intimidation started." People started twisting arms, calling in chits, building the pressure. And the votes started dwindling. Hours later, when a motion was made to commend President Bush for his "excellent leadership in the Gulf crisis," only six votes opposed that motion. Maxine Waters was one of the opposing votes, and she told us that she was prepared to be the only vote. That's political courage! But then, again, this is the woman who introduced divestment legislation at the state level six times before it passed.

Where were the other 23 members of the Congressional Black Caucus (actually, she was joined by Congressman Dellums in her "no" vote)? Where were the Democrats? Where were all the legislators who say they were for peace? Indeed, where are they now that Saddam Hussein is exterminating thousands of Kurds each day. Is a Kurdish life worth less than a Kuwaiti one because Kuwaitis have cash and Kurds don't? Why did it take so long for President Bush to provide humanitarian aid?

Many of these questions have retreated from the front lines of inquiry, in the same way that Colin Powell (remember him?) has retreated from the headlines. Too many people are already engaged in the act of rewriting history, turning this into a three-day rout, turning ambivalence into unqualified support. The Republican Party is attempting to cash political chits from this war, while the Democrats, doing business as usual, are mealy mouthing their way around the issue. Between the two parties, there is not an ounce of political courage or human compassion, except for the all too scarce presence of people like Maxine Waters.

When Congresswoman Waters says she has had to hold onto herself, she speaks of the difficulty of maintaining sanity, managing frustration in a country where power corrupts and where the impulse is to go along to get along. Go along to get along brought us the S&L crisis, as the complaints of whistleblowers were so frequently dismissed that bank examiners stopped complaining. Go along to get along brought us 70 percent cuts in employment, and training programs, where our nation rolled over and played dead in the face of Reagan-Bush rhetoric about the poor. Go along to get along brought a 65 percent decrease in the money we spent on federal housing, or, in other words, brought us much of the homeless problem that we currently grapple with.

In this go along to get along atmosphere, it is sometimes difficult, sometimes impractical to maintin a righteous anger at inequity. But in "holding on to herself," Maxine Waters has held on to her pre-Congressional dream of a better world, held onto her will to transform a bad situation into a better one. Where is our collective will to transform our society? Or are we content to get along?

Sun Reporter, April, 1991

THE THURGOOD MARSHALL CHALLENGE: EQUALITY

It seems like the end of a civil rights era. Retired Supreme Court Justice Thurgood Marshall died Sunday afternoon, taking his gravelly voice, his compelling conscience, his blunt repartee, his irascible ways, leaving America with the challenge to make equality of opportunity a reality not just a "dream."

In many ways, it seems that Marshall thought he could

rest easy and that's why he left. Once, he said they'd have to carry him out of the court, that despite the wishes of President Ronald Reagan, he would not step down. He walked out of the court with the pointed observation that a black snake and a white one both bite. But one wonders if he didn't leave resting easy with George Bush out of the White House. Like Reagan, Bush was not one of his favorite people. Indeed, he once referred to Bush as one of "the dead."

When I heard Thurgood Marshall tell stories or bite back at fools, I was reminded of somebody's grandfather, old and crusty and not too inclined to tolerate nonsense. But there was nothing crusty about his legal opinions. Marshall was sharp, incisive, and unapologetic about being a social engineer. He once said the Constitutuion was flawed, but he figured he'd helped fix it with his legal work.

Social engineering is a word conservatives sneer at. Let the market work, they say. But deriding social engineering is like jeering at the driver who stops to change a flat tire on her car. Social engineers simply try to ameliorate the excesses of predatory capitalism, a capitalism that was compatible with slavery, then de jure discrimination, and now de facto difference.

Marshall's dissent in the Croson case was an example of his scathing indictment of our social and economic system. Justice Sandra Day O'Connor, who reportedly wept when Justice Marshall announced his retirement from the Court, wrote that the city of Richmond needed to prove past discrimination before implementing a set-aside program. She essentially asked that we show the world our chains, and Marshall took her up on it. In his dissent, he reminded her and the world that it had not been so long since African American people were forbidden to own the tools of trade. He brought history and morality to bear as he dissented, demanding that the court consider the matter of economic justice.

While Thurgood Marshall made an impact on the Supreme Court, his greater contribution may have been in those pre-Supreme Court days, when he traveled thousands of miles through the South in his role as attorney for the NAACP Legal Defense and Education Fund. He argued the *Brown v. Board of Education* case, and though his success came "with all deliberate speed" (judicial speak for take your sweet time), it impacted every facet of American life. First the classroom doors opened, then the university doors, then the boardroom doors. That we have even a toenail (and in some cases only a toenail) in some of these doors is due in part to the mammoth contribution of Thurgood Marshall.

I feel privileged to have heard Marshall speak on several occasions, most recently when he came to the Bay Area last August to accept an honor from the American Bar Association's section on Individual Rights. At this event, I was reminded of Marshall's unremitting opposition to the death penalty, a penalty that has been reinstated in several states. But who is most likely to get the death penalty? African Americans, that's who. Marshall's ceaseless and relentless quest for justice in cases where mistakes are clearly fatal speaks to his commitment to the correct, not the expedient. Many have retreated from opposing the death penalty, including those among the clergy who say they are horrified by the atrocity of some crimes. Should our society be in the business of killing? Absolutely not, said Thurgood Marshall.

Our society has been shaped by Marshall's action and agitation, both as an attorney and as a Supreme Court justice who had all of "us" in mind. Black or white snake, they both bite, he said. We will miss that commentary. But we are also challenged by the Marshall legacy. Marshall's death raised an important question. What have you done to close the gap between blacks and whites, to move us toward the path of equal opportunity lately? I'd direct that question at the current Supreme Court, a court that seems determined, despite personal affection for Thurgood

Marshall, to deny opportunity to many in our country.

Our nation's greatest tribute to Justice Thurgood Marshall would be renewed commitment to closing gaps, to providing equality of opportunity. After the words of remembrance, the songs, the eulogies, will there be such a commitment?

Sun Reporter, August, 1992

THEY DON'T MAKE 'EM LIKE THEY USED TO

My sister called me late the other night and we talked nearly an hour, the conversation touching on everything from food to fools, leadership to lingerie, travel to temptation. Of course we got to every woman's topic, the "brothers," but we didn't sing the blues for long. Instead of speaking of "no good," we talked of good instead, of men like Dr. Martin Luther King, Jr., Frederick Douglas, W.E.B. DuBois, and others as symbols of an era past.

I'm not fascinated by these men because of their reputations. Instead, I'm passionate about them, and others, because of their very brilliant writing, their service, their closeness to the black community. King, Douglas and DuBois have written timeless words, phrases as relevant twenty or fifty years ago as they are today. DuBois predicted that the major problem of the twentieth century would be the color line, and the accuracy of his prediction is reflected in the fact that twenty years after cities burned, blacks are still isolated from power centers in white America. Douglas put the concept of social change in perspective with his stirring words "Power concedes nothing without a struggle." And Dr. King took the movement to the people, with a March on Washington that remains unsurpassed twenty five years after it happened.

All of these men were versatile. Douglas was a publisher and an orator, a soldier and a government administrator. DuBois defined the term "scholar-activist." King was a preacher, a civil rights leader, a scholar. All the men left legacies.

With very, very few exceptions, it is almost sad to note that they don't make black men like they used to. Though not every man of the century past was a Douglas, DuBois, or King, these men had peers who were almost as stellar as they, as accomplished, as committed, as dedicated. Now, too many brothers are jockeying for a corporate position, a government contract, a BMW, or a white woman. Too many of the redundant buppies (if black people weren't upwardly mobile we'd still be picking cotton) are running away from our community, chasing a dream that is also a nightmare. Too many college freshmen are convinced that race is not a problem. Too many high school students think drugs are the answer.

But two black men stand out in my mind as wonderful, contemporary men who should walk in the company of Douglas, DuBois, and King. Dr. Carleton Goodlett, the publisher of *San Francisco Sun Reporter*, shares the diversity and vision of the three giants in his varied and accomplished career. "Doc," as we call him, expanded the window of opportunity for black journalists in California with his publishing efforts and his vigorous encouragement of young journalists. Dr. Goodlett is also a physician, a peace activist, and a pillar of the national civil rights community. He will be honored on October 22, and the kudos are well deserved.

Another of our living giants is M. Carl Holman, the President of the National Urban Coalition and a driving force behind the Black Forum, a national roundtable of heads of black organizations. But I first met Holman through his work, when I was assigned "American Negro Poetry" in a literature class in high school. Once upon a time I could quote every line of his poem "And On The Shore," a poem that manages to be a soldier's poem, a love poem, and civil rights poem. In his poem "And to the Leaders," Holman exhorts the group he later became part of: "Fire on your tongue, fire in your heart/Hold the helm in the dirty weather/When war and prejudice have done their part/ Lead us all out together."

Holman won prizes for his writing and was a professor at Hampton Institute and Clark College. He founded a newspaper, *The Atlanta Inquirer*. Then he served in the Kennedy and Johnson Administrations before coming to the National Urban Coalition. Like DuBois, Douglas, and King, Holman has a vision for black America. Right now part of that vision is our mandate to "Say Yes to A Youngster's Future" which is one of his programs..

There is an amazing symmetry in these men's work and careers. When I contemplate them, one after the other, I marvel at their brilliance, their accomplishments, and their commitment to black people.

They just don't make 'em like they use to, brothers like this with visions and dreams. And our communities suffer because there are so few Holmans and Goodletts, so few descendents of DuBois, Douglas, and King.

Sun Reporter, October, 1988

DR. MARTIN LUTHER KING - MORE THAN JUST A DREAMER

Dust off your vocal chords; practice your swaying. For the next six weeks – from the time between the Martin Luther King birthday celebration and the end of Black History Month, you are going to be singing "We Shall Overcome," holding hands with folk you probably cannot stand as you sway to the music and say "we shall overcome someday." Someday? Like when? In many ways these six weeks of swaying and singing are as much about postponing struggle as anything else.

Every time we sing "We Shall Overcome Someday," we are putting equity, equality, and economic justice on an indefinite time line. "Be patient," say the policymakers. "We're getting there," say the pundits. "What do black people want," say those who think that enough is enough. Though "We Shall Overcome" has a strong, sentimental message, the fact is that I'd rather sing "today" or "by 2000" than someday, especially when someday, in some minds, is in the distant future.

Issues of racial justice take on a soft haze during the time around Dr. King's birthday, during Black History Month. All too often, we gloss over the harsh bite of injustice past, and idealize a struggle that has cost thousands of lives. This softening is best seen in the way we quote Dr. King out of context. Everybody remembers that he said things about "having a dream," about "the content of our character." Yes, Dr. Martin Luther King, Jr. was a dreamer, but he didn't die dreaming, he died fighting for fair wages for garbage workers. King might have talked about a color blind society, but he also talked about remedies for those who experienced past discrimination. King might have talked about love, but he also talked about the evils of economic exploitation. Somehow, we are able to remember that King had a dream, but to forget that economic justice was very much a part of his dream.

Thus, Ronald Reagan was the President who signed the official King holiday into being. Would he have done so had not King's image been so sanitized? Are Americans really willing to celebrate King's dream, with all its implications? Are we willing, like King, to "have the audacity to believe that people everywhere can have three meals a day for their bodies, education and culture for their minds, and dignity, equality and freedom for their spirits." Are we aware that our social and economic policies deny millions of Americans dignity and equality, and that people like Governor Pete Wilson would deny even more with his efforts to blame the poor for California's economic troubles. Pete Wilson will probably show up someplace singing "We Shall Overcome," and then go back to his office in Sacramento to find some more poor people to bash.

We need to reclaim the real King, the man who was a social and economic redistributionist, the man who said "If the world is two-thirds water, why should we pay water bills?" We need to reclaim the King who argued that economic exploitation and racism are connected. This is the King who would have taken the Imperial Foods fire in North Carolina to the nation, reminded us all that we smack on five pieces of Pioneer or Kentucky Fried Chicken for $3.99 because women work for $4.25 an hour to process those chicken parts. This is the King who would have looked at the carnage of 10 million officially unemployed people and connected it to an obscenely rising stock market. This is the King who would have mounted a campaign for national health insurance. And that King, the one who stands for economic justice, is the one who is often missing from the singing, swaying, celebrating that goes on in his name.

Dr. Martin Luther King, Jr. was much more than a dreamer. He was an activist, a teacher. He was a motivator. There was more than rhetoric in his words; there was dignity and an acting plan.

We sell ourselves and the struggle cheap when we remember King only for the dream he had. We mustn't lose the dream, but we must absolutely cling to Dr. King's penchant for action. Martin Luther King was not shot because he had a dream, but because he was prepared to do something to make his dream come true.

Because of his dream, he threatened the status quo, but few who say they follow in his footsteps have posed such a threat. No, the status quo of unequal pay for equal work, of poverty for some and riches for others, remains intact even as we celebrate. All the singing and the swaying hasn't changed the bottom line, or made the dream of economic justice any more attainable.

Sun Reporter, January, 1992

DOUBLE BUBBA AND THE NEW POLITICS:
WHAT'S RACE GOT TO DO WITH IT?

Have race matters changed much because we have a President who cries on cue to gospel music? Truth is, the price of his victory was as coded a racial conversation as George Bush's Willie Horton. Bush had Horton, but Clinton has Sister Souljah and Jesse Jackson, and the notion that equal opportunity is somehow divorced from equal outcomes. While President Clinton is an improvement over President Bush from a social policy standpoint, he has done absolutely nothing to advance the debate on race.

DOUBLE BUBBA AND THE OPTIONS

When Arkansas Governor Bill Clinton chose Tennessee Senator Al Gore as his running mate, I started humming to the tune of *Three Blind Mice*: *Two white boys, two white boys, see how they run, see how they run, they both ran into old NYC, the ticket has no place for folk like me, I guess this is the way it is going to be, two white boys.* People are saying that Gore strengthens Clinton, but both Cuomo or Bradley might have done the same. They are saying this is a sign of change, this "new generation" ticket. But the line I like best comes from a *New York Times* writer who described the ticket as "Double Bubba."

The problem is that there is a lot of Bubba going on during this Presidential season. When you bear in mind that both Bush and Perot call Texas home, and that Arkansas borders Texas, what we are left with in the general election is three very similar men battling each other. Maybe it is a generation thing. Ross Perot went to the NAACP talking that "you people" stuff that never fails to set black skin crawling. "You people" speaks to separate, different, bottom. Usually sneered, even when delivered with saccharine, it never fails to distance. After the fact, Ben Hooks and the new Perot campaign co-chair, progressive Abyssinian Baptist Church (in New York) minister Calvin Butts, tried to put a positive spin on it. "He didn't mean it maliciously," Butts told Katie Couric on the "Today Show." Mean it or not, Eleanor Holmes Norton and Texas Governor Ann Richards had it right when they noted that people who spend time around black people don't use "you people" language.

Calvin Butts speaks for all of us, though, when he talks about the many ways the Democratic Party has taken the black vote for granted. And what are we going to do? Cut off our noses to spite our faces? I mean, if for no other reason than the Supreme Court nominees he is likely to appoint, there are reasons to support the Democratic ticket. On the other hand, Bill Clinton's clear mistreatment of Rev. Jesse Jackson, combined with his views on "responsibility" (to make a whole third of the platform document a call to responsibility seeks to reinforce notions that people who use social programs are somehow irresponsible), makes me look askance at the man.

What about Perot? Only a party loyalist would dismiss him outright, especially given the excitement and energy he brings to the table. Does he bring anything else? His relations with the African American community in Dallas, his home base, have been strained by his notions of control and law enforcement. Teacher's unions don't support him because of changes he supposedly pushed through the school system. But few will bad-mouth him on the records, mostly because he is powerful, perhaps vindictive. Also Texans seem reluctant to badmouth each other.

On the other hand, Ross Perot has been so unspecific about his plans for the economy (which most perceive as his strong point) that it is hard to compare his record to that of Clinton or Bush. He has tripped over his tongue more than once during his non-campaign, then retreated to the safe corner of his non-candidacy. In one conversation with a Perot staffer, the man defended Perot on the grounds that the non-candidate is simply a "volunteer" who is "giving" his time to the American people, unbound to be specific until his candidacy is declared. That's crafty, but it isn't honest, and from where I sit does little to advance Perot's candidacy.

Nor do all these stories about how good his daddy was to "his" black people. All the cotton has been chopped, and all the wood has been hewn, and so these stories of blacks who needed white patronage (Clarence Thomas aside) are weak, tired, and trifling. And they serve no one well, not even candidate Perot, who seems to take such pleasure in recounting them so often. If he wants to tell some black people stories, he needs to tell us how many African Americans sat on the Board of Directors at EDS, the multi-million dollar corporation that he founded. Or, he might want to tell us how many black businesses have contracts with his Perot Electronic Systems.

It is interesting, though, that many entrepreneurs support Perot, and that in Washington, DC, a good number of these entrepreneurs are African American. Indeed, the DC headquarters is run by an African American woman who runs her business and does a television show about small business success. When asked why she supported Perot, she didn't even pause before saying "economics." The perception is that Perot will get business, especially small business, jumping.

Since all the candidates remind one of Bubba (or Bozo, in the case of Bush and Quayle), the question for most voters is which Bubba do you want? Bubba doing business, Bubba dissing Jesse Jackson, Bubba tackling environmental issues, with every Bubba doing all he can to avoid the issue of race. It is alarming that, just two months after Los Angeles sizzled, Bubba triumphs. In the name of winning an election, the Democratic Party seems determined to place some issues at the periphery, so that even the very visible leadership of Ron Brown and Alexis Herman (convention CEO) is diminished, a bit, by the way race has been minimized.

The more I think about the Bubbas, the more I wonder whether the Rev. Calvin Butts has a point. Maybe there's more than one way to call African Americans "you people."

Sun Reporter, June, 1992

HEARD ON THE FLOOR

Do you remember the miniseries *Roots*? It was hidden somewhere in the recesses of my mind until I heard a black man on the floor of the Democratic convention refer to the Rev. Jesse Jackson as "Toby." If you remember it like I do, there was Kunta, captured in Africa, came here in chains, named randomly, "Toby," and insistent that his name was Kunta. It took white folk to chain him to a tree and beat him for awhile, beat him to bitter, weary submission, before he was willing to respond to the question, "What is your name," with the dreaded syllables, "Toby."

I stopped and asked the brother what he was saying about Jesse, but he looked at me as if he was about to call me Toby, too. "Who you writing for, black girl," he sort of sneered. "Are you going to leave out of here and interpret black people for the white media?" So I guess I had to jump back. I asked the brother which white man he was

286

representing. Cause you know, I told him, that there isn't a black candidate in this picture. How you gonna ask me, I told him, what I'm doing, when it is perfectly clear what you are doing.

Once we played the rhetorical game, we took a minute to talk. It seems that the description, "Toby," was being used by more than one delegate to describe Jackson. Now before you bolt, Toby is better than Tom. Tom submitted because he wanted to, but Toby submits because he was beaten into submission. And then there is the estimable soul, Tobias, who submits because she/he (no, this is not a gender thing) can make some money on the deal.

The black delegates calling Jesse "Toby" would whether Bill Clinton even met the Rev. three-quarters of the way. In his acceptance speech, Clinton made it his business to mention most party leaders, but Jackson was unmentioned. Jackson went out of his way to meet Clinton. He gave up an endorsement, though tepid, before the convention opened. He referred to Clinton in his rousing speech, and gave him compliments. But he got nothing (and in fairness, it isn't clear that he has asked for anything). To his supporters he seems like one so addicted to the approval of the Democratic Party that he is willing to take any kind of treatment, no matter how shabby.

The press had a field day. David Broder proclaimed DNC Chair Ron Brown the "new black" as if we are allowed only one at a time. The *New York Times* struck a death knell for Jackson's rhetorical supremacy by declaring his speech tepid before he was even finished. But even as the headlines were published, the tears that streamed down delegate faces as the Rev. Jackson spoke, the outright borrowing of Jackson's rhetorical style by Bradley, Cuomo, Gore and Clinton, spoke to the influence Jackson has had on the Democratic Party. Further, the young brothers and sisters who were staff aides for Ron Brown and Alexis Herman all paid some dues in the Jackson organization. That, too, was part of the Jackson legacy.

But the Democratic National Convention has never seen a Jackson film. We've heard Jackson's words that evoked powerful images of those excluded, but we haven't seen Jesse Jackson's mother talk about her hard times, nor heard Jackson's contemporaries talk about his life as a youth. We haven't had his wife face the camera and feign a southern accent (she wouldn't have to) and talk about how they met and married. We haven't seen the home videos of the five Jackson children.

The reason I raise the issue of a film is because much of the 1992 convention was public policy by personal biography. It was beyond the feminist adage of "the personal is political." It was, "hear my biography, feel my pain, this is what propels me." Except there are few forms of acceptable pain. Who wants to hear about the pain of being dog-bit on a picket line? Will that drive Democrats to tears? We heard of a child wounded by a speeding car, but what about a child wounded and battered by simple hunger, rat bite, snake bite? We heard this once, when Rev. Jackson spoke of Sugar Ditch, Mississippi, a town where there was no sewage plant in 1984. We heard that Bill Clinton's mom was a single mother; Jesse reminded us of the Biblical single mother, too. We have to take policy beyond personal biography if policy is to respond to the needs of the broadest spectrum of Americans.

I think the Democratic ticket of Clinton and Gore can win the election in November because they are better on issues than Bush and Quayle. But if they try to win this election on the basis of their biographies, there may well be a problem. I don't know that Clinton or Gore understands the meaning of the word "Toby." And unless they understand what I heard on the floor, they cannot understand how alienating the simple sight of two white men standing over a black man, bowed, is to some of us.

Sun Reporter, July, 1992

SISTER SOULJAH TOLD THE TRUTH

Homicide is the top cause of death of young black men. And "the white man" isn't killing them, these young men are killing each other. They go by names like Moochie and Pookie, either sell drugs or buy them, and stay out of school. Some have been spurned by the mainstream economy, and can't find legitimate jobs. Many see drugs as the only economic opportunity available to them. These young dealers who "pack" guns as regularly as their school-ground brothers carry knapsacks, aren't the majority of black youth, but there are enough of them to color the quality of life in inner cities. They've divided urban areas up into turf, and peace be on the soul that somehow crosses a line, or who stands near someone crossing a line.

Some of these young men will shoot faster than they will blink, and they'll shoot over the smallest of offenses, a "dis" or a grudge. Maybe you looked at one of them the wrong way. Maybe your shoulder bumped one of theirs in a crowded mall. Maybe you said hello to one of "their" women. The rule is shoot first, ask questions later. Even if the victim is another black youth, a child, a woman who might have been in the way. Street rules, some of these young men will tell you, not missing a beat. Kill or be killed.

These are the young men Sister Souljah was speaking of in her now-celebrated *Washington Post* quote, young men who have learned easy, early, that black life is cheap. They know they can get away with shooting another black man, woman, or child. They know that few police resources will go to finding the person who pulled the trigger in another drive by shooting. These young men would shoot a cousin, a brother without missing a beat. So what makes anyone think they'd hesitate before shooting someone white?

That's what Souljah said, in context or out. If you are prepared to shoot a black person, you are also prepared to shoot a white person. The only thing that might stop these young men from shooting white is the ugly realization that the chances of getting caught are greater, and so are the penalties.

Candidate Clinton set up a straw woman in his attack on Sister Souljah. In some ways, he is no better that Dan Quayle attacking Murphy Brown. It is interesting that both men used women to make a strategic point that had less to do with these particular women than with drive-by rhetoric. In many ways both men are no better than the young men who shoot first, ask questions later, because both shot off their mouths before understanding the issues.

If Bill Clinton wanted to go before the Rainbow Coalition to talk about urban conditions, he might have talked about the inequity that make urban violence so easily acceptable. He might have talked of gun control or ways to bring marginalized black youth into the economic mainstream. Instead, he called a young rapper a racist because she told the truth.

Clinton took exception to Souljah's assertion that she didn't know any good white people. Plenty of urban youth share her experience. The white folks they meet, the teacher who doesn't have the time of day for them, the social worker who can't be so bothered, the police officer who would as soon bust head as write a traffic ticket, are hardly perceived as good white people. Clinton says he's a good white man, but how many urban youth has he touched? And how many has he alienated with his attack on Sister Souljah?

If Pookie would shoot his brother on a "hummer" or kill a cousin over a misspoken word, white Americans can't expect any special consideration from the Pookie they created. Some of us were reminded of that in the anger that erupted after the LAPD brutality verdict. Governor Clinton avoided the anger and the ashes in Los Angeles, and now he seems to be avoiding Souljah's truth.

King Features, May, 1992

CREATING NEW RASCALS

"Throw the rascals out" has been the rallying crying of voters from California to Colorado, from Massachusetts to Mississippi. Some voters have taken harshly to the rascals, turning out a governor in Mississippi, and a hand-picked Bush candidate for Senator in Pennsylvania. Others have chosen to treat the rascals generically, opting for term limits in some cities and states.

Term limits offer voters the opportunity to make a clean sweep through City Halls and State Capitols. But they are also stupidity insurance. They protect us from ourselves, from those old time politicians we love and are loath to turn out. Term limits assume that voters are a group of indiscriminate sheep that need to be reminded of the evils of incumbency. But term limits ignore the notion that there are some evils worse than incumbency.

Let's talk money. If the playing field is level and City Hall is swept, who will we replace the rascals with? Those with name recognition usually created it through some combination of public service, private money, and a publicity machine. Who has private money? Who are they loyal to? Certainly not the masses of people who are clamoring for reform. There are fifteen minutes of fame in store for almost every American, but dollars can turn fifteen minutes into fifteen years. And few reformers have the dollars to nudge their way into the political establishment.

Term limits? Perhaps. But what about limiting campaign spending? What about making television time available for every candidate whose signature base suggests some threshold of support? What about limiting the role that political action committees play in channeling funds to candidates? Term limits ensure that we get rid of our old rascals, but these limits can't determine the kind of rascals voters will replace them with, and the ways concentrations of power and privilege influence our choices of new rascals.

291

Try this scenario on for size. Jesse Helms has to leave the US Senate because North Carolina votes term limits in. So he finds his clone, some man named Helms, Jr., who talks his talk, walks his walk, and spouts his position. Helms campaigns for his man, brings his considerable power and influence to bear on his behalf. Helms, Jr. is elected, despite spirited opposition, because some people consolidate power and others don't. What have term limits accomplished in this case? The same kind of power with a different face!

But North Carolina is a lot less likely to support term limits than a state like Colorado is. Which means that North Carolina gains influence, nationally, while Colorado loses it. North Carolina Congressional representatives and Senators move up the seniority ladder, while Colorado legislators rotate through the bottom. How can anybody talk about term limits without taking on the seniority system in Congress? To offer one without the other is to suggest that reformist states deserve to be penalized in the national legislative process.

The popular support for term limits taps into a profound dissatisfaction at politics us usual. But the President's enthusiastic support of this measure raises questions. What does George Bush have to gain from term limits, especially when we limit terms of office but not the way elections are held?

It is impossible to defend career politicians of either party, whether they are named Bush, Kennedy, Thurman, or Helms. But it is inappropriate to focus on term limits without focusing on the other way these men can use their money to clone themselves and consolidate their power. If Neil Bush runs for Governor of Texas today, despite his checkered past with the savings and loan industry, what role would his family name and money play in ensuring his election? What chance would an outsider have? When we throw the rascals out, what will we get in their place?

King Features, November, 1991

CAN BLACK PEOPLE BE RACISTS?

Arkansas Governor Bill Clinton attended a Rainbow Coalition meeting, but instead of dealing with the urban issues that he was expected to deal with, he took the time to attack Sister Souljah, who had been quoted in the *Washington Post* as saying that blacks who kill blacks ought to kill whites instead. Clinton called the young sister's remarks "hateful" and "racist," "filled with the kind of hatred you do not honor." Ironically, or perhaps intentionally, Sister Souljah had appeared before a Rainbow Coalition group the day before Clinton did.

Will Sister Souljah play the same role for Clinton as Murphy Brown plays for Vice Present Quayle, a vehicle through which to vent feelings and frustrations. Quayle has made Murphy Brown a symbol of "decaying family values," even though the woman chose to have her child instead of an abortion, even though the fictional Brown can well afford to raise her child alone, and even though the father of Murphy Brown's child withdrew his marriage proposal and "punked out" on her. What is Bill Clinton trying to say by harping on Sister Souljah? She's an articulate, well educated 25-year-old who has studied both in Spain and at Cornell University. In the aftermath of the Los Angeles rebellion, I was impressed by her assurance, and by the fact that she seemed to have an understanding of the social, economic, and political forces that shape the status of African American people. Is Bill Clinton trying to make Souljah a symbol of so-called black racism so that he can draw some of the votes of the Reagan Democrats?

Why did Clinton, like Quayle, choose a woman to make his point through? Why are we women always the example of that which is wrong with society? Both men are affirming women's status as powerless by using them as vehicles through which to make their points. Why don't they, instead, use men as such vehicles. Quayle, for example, could have talked about the man who walked out on Murphy Brown as a symbol of the male irresponsibility

that forces women to head households in increasing numbers. Clinton might have talked about some of the economic forces that lead to black-on-black violence, or about
some of the (mostly male) black leaders who have avoided
dealing with this problem. But then Clinton might have
had to take on an equal who would fire back in a way he
can't afford to be fired on as he scrambles for votes. So he
chose to make his point by putting down a woman.

Clinton's behavior is at odds with the portrait he likes
to paint of himself, of a man who appreciates strong
women. Not only strong and forceful, Souljah is also a role
model for young African American women. Clinton is apparently willing to alienate that segment of the population
to pander to southern whites who are fond of talking about
"reverse discrimination" and "black racism."

Can black people be racists? If you simply define racism as prejudice, perhaps. But I think racism is prejudice
combined with power, and from that standpoint African
American people simply cannot be racists because we do
not have the power to prevent anyone from attaining their
economic or political goals in this country. I've been dis-
puted on my views. An Asian man told me that the black
people who "targeted" Korean business owners were racists that destroyed the economic hopes and dreams of hundreds of families. But let's play that one out. Then what?
And how will who be treated? The LAPD has been vigorous about finding, and attempting to prosecute, any arsonists. And given the Simi Valley verdict, the arsonists are not
likely to get "justice." Indeed, any black man or woman is
likely to be accused of arson, whether involved or not.
That's not power.

What about the men who were arrested for beating
Reginald Denney, the white truck driver who went to the
corner of Florence and Normandie and hollered racial slurs
before he was beaten? They have yet to see the light of
day, though one has a mother who is willing to put her
house on the line so he can make bail. They might have

had the power to administer the beating, but the "just us" system has the greater power.

When Sister Souljah says that the black people who are killing each other ought to kill white people instead, she is saying that drive-by shootings would stop if people took them seriously. People don't take shootings seriously when black people are killed, but they pull out all the stops when the victims are white. If you don't believe me, compare Rodney King and Reginald Denney, the Central Park jogger and Tawana Brawley, and so on and so on and so on.

Can black people be racist? I think not. But Bill Clinton's most recent remarks suggest that white people can sure be fools.

Sun Reporter, May, 1992

WHAT IF CASPER WEINBERGER WERE BLACK?

The day after Christmas, I was dissing George Bush and his cronies, including Casper Weinberger and Elliot Abrams, on KGO. How dare the President pardon his slimy cronies, I raged. Didn't he know it made him seem guiltier than guilty, that it put his fingerprints squarely on the Iran contragate mess? Does he really want to go down in history as a crook, a felon, a dishonest fool? I was on a roll of anger, outraged at this President's arrogance. And most folks seemed to agree with me. But I had to pause and laugh at the logic of one caller.

"You've defended the LA rioters," the caller said. "Now how would you feel if Casper Weinberger were black." For a minute I was speechless if only because the notion of a black man being that crooked stunned me. And then I was tickled because I thought it was funny. But the man raised a question, and at some point it makes sense to look at it. What if, indeed, Casper Weinberger were black?

Well let's put a few others in the notorious set in black face. Don't forget that the man who discovered the Watergate break-in was African American. He lost his job as a security guard. He found another low paying job. Meanwhile, those who were convicted of Watergate trouble have found success. G. Gordon Libby has a syndicated talk show and advises people on security matters. Either Halderman or Erlichman was "born again." Richard Nixon has been rehabilitated and may collect millions of dollars from the government on his Watergate tapes. Who says crime doesn't pay?

The black man who blew the whistle got no glory, no bright lights. The white men who committed crimes ride off into the sunset with their goodies.

The Los Angeles rebellion is another place where we can talk about race, although this is not a black and white situation. Some twenty white cops beat Rodney King near to death and not a one of them has served a day of time. Four black men are accused of beating Reginald Denney near to death, but another four black folk rescued the man. Those who are accused of beating Denney have had bail set so high it would make your head swim. What if Rodney King was white? What if Reginald Denney were black? What has race got to do with it? Ask the cops — Theodore Wind, Ted Bresinio, Lawrence Powell, Stacey Koon — who walked away from beating Rodney King unscathed. Ask the men who have served hard time for allegedly beating Reginald Denney.

What if Casper Weinberger were black? Would he have ever, given his race, been able to scale the heights he had, to land a senior position in the state department, to launder money and deal for hostages. Not. So I can't fathom a Casper Weinberger with melanin in his skin. A black man with those negotiating and criminal skills would be more likely to be a drug dealer than a state department official. If Casper Weinberger were black, there probably wouldn't have been an Iran contra scam.

What amazed me about my conversation with a man who wished Casper Weinberger black was his anger, and his blind spots, at my unapologetic African American identity. Because I have defended African American people, he apparently thought I could make some major leap and defend a fictional black Weinberger. It is as if an African American identity has no structural context, as if you need simply spray a stick figure with melanin to get me in his corner. The fact is that one could look at a Weinberger and laugh at the very notion that he might be African American.

But it seems that we will play this game of "what if" as long as white folk are defensive and African Americans are unapologetic. It's an old conversation, a turgid one, but one that never fails to fascinate.

Sun Reporter, December, 1992

IF YOU GIVE A DANCE YOU'VE GOT TO PAY THE BAND

California political legend Jess Unruh was neither the first nor the last man to describe money as the mother's milk of politics. With the Presidency priced at $60 plus million post-primary dollars, a Senate seat like Illinois going for about $8 million, and even a measly City Council race causing a six-figure investment, Unruh's words have that timeless quality to them. To put it another way, if you give a dance you've got to pay the band.

What kind of music is the African American community willing to pay for? Is it that canned jazz, all form and no substance? I've been involved in enough fundraising endeavors to think so. I'm exasperated at the person with the six-figure salary who wants to see and be seen, but doesn't want to pay, or the person who doesn't mind spending money on the clothes and the trappings, but balks at writing a hundred dollar check. These folk don't mind gobbling the munchies that cost ten or fifteen bucks a head, but they think twice about writing a check that covers the cost of their nosh and leaves a candidate with a few dollars for a campaign. They've got the concept of "networking" mastered, but not the mechanics of politics.

I mean, if I had a nickel for every sequin a sister wore to a fundraiser, I could probably finance the campaign of the next President of the United States. With one in seven black families earning $50,000 or more, enough of us look like we could be givers. Is the look consistent with the checkbook? Some of those seeking funds say "no." And yet if our candidates want to compete, they need the same direct mail operation, the same media penetration, the same staff as others. While volunteer hours and "grassroots efforts" can sometimes substitute for dollars, money is still the oil that makes campaign wheels churn.

Of course, there's a flip side. "We don't have the same resources that the larger community does," says Yolanda Carraway, who raised money and headed the Voter Education Project for the Jackson campaigns in 1984 and 1988. "Fundraisers keep going to the same people, and they get tapped out. It is probably a bit harder to raise money from African Americans than from others." Carraway says there are exceptions. "Jesse Jackson goes to a church and passes the hat and everyone gives. Candidates like (Illinois senatorial candidate) Carol Mosley Braun and (1990 North Carolina senatorial candidate) Harvey Gannt can raise money all over the country because their elections are perceived as causes. And they draw from a group greater than the black constituency, they get money from women, from liberals, from others. But in general, black candidates have a hard time raising funds."

Some say the heavy spending on campaigns makes a good case for campaign finance reform. Illinois Senatorial candidate Carol Mosley Braun, stunned by the hefty sum she has to raise to "play" in her November election, says she'll make this reform a priority if elected. And during the primary campaign, some Democratic candidates eschewed PAC money because they said some industries had too much power and influence over the political process. At the same time, women's groups like EMILY's list (EMILY is an acronym for *Early Money Is Like Yeast*) are "bundling" contributions to women candidates to make the point that women are prepared to support their own. At one reception during the Democratic convention, more than $750,000 was raised to support women candidates.

African Americans could do the same thing – pool our money to support those black candidates who move our agenda. We could be as narrow and focused about it as women are, spending our dollars on those candidates who move our agenda. In 1990, more than 83,000 African Americans earned more than $75,000 per year. If each of them spent a paltry $100 on a BANG (Black American Politicians Need Gold), there'd be $8.3 million to spread among our candidates, and some accountability to be demanded as well. If African Americans aren't writing the checks, can we expect to be political players? Enough of us are running to suggest we can give a dance. Are enough of us giving to pay the band?

Emerge Magazine, November, 1992

SIGNALS AND SUBSTANCE

Is President-elect Clinton really a good ol' boy? Lord knows I want to think he is. Not for any other reason than I want to feel something akin to optimism about the direction of this country. Not for any other reason than it is time for the tide to turn.

I wasn't persuaded by his appointment of Vernon Jordan as one of the heads of the transition team. With all due respect to Brother Jordan, we all know what this one is about. Jordan has so completely paid his corporate dues that in an astonishing example of double standards, the

New York Times got on his case for serving on corporate boards. Venting at the *Times* for double standards against Jordan is a diversion, but it is useful to note that they've never got to fussing at any white man for his corporate board membership. That said, the appointment of Jordan to head the transition team suggests that a black sensitivity comes to the table. The Jordan appointment doesn't speak to much more than sensitivity, though. Even in his civil rights heyday, Vernon Jordan came out of the Urban League movement, a movement that stands more for corporate assimilation that for structural change.

I looked with interest when Clinton walked down Georgia Avenue. It takes more than a walk through the hood to make the man a homeboy, and the inside scuttle-butt on the walk says it was a payoff on a bet to DC Coun-cilwoman Charlene Drew Jarvis. At the same time, when is the last time a President-elect, or a President for that matter, walked through the African American community stopping to talk with entrepreneurs? Hmmm, I had to say to myself. Not leaping, not even leaning, simply hmming.

My ears perked up with Clinton's selection of cluster group heads, especially as I noted Dr. Johnetta Cole's pres-ence as head of a cluster. Indeed, several women and people of color are represented in the clusters. I had to move from hmmm to hum on this one. Good sign, Bill Clinton, I said. Thumbs up, I signaled. But still just a hum.

I have to admit that I almost boogied out of my chair when I learned that Bill Clinton asked our own Maya Angelou to read a poem at his swearing-in. I keep thinking of Maya's poem, "America," (*"the gold of her promise has yet to be mined . . . the fruit of her labor, the crops and the grain, have not eased the hunger nor the great pain"*) and shivering with absolute glee at what this wordsmith can say about the direction of this country. Hmm, no longer hum, looks like a winner to me. It looks like time to pause for the cause, to take a moment and celebrate the progress, to say "right on" for the recognition and the symbolism that President-elect Clinton is bringing to his transition process and inauguration.

Except. And there always has to be an except. Except we need not celebrate so hard. A transition team head at the top doesn't mean jobs for the 2 million black unemployed on the bottom. A poem isn't going to feed anybody or turn any cities around. Am I the Grinch who stole the party? Possibly.

Actually, I'm concerned at the way discussion has turned since the economic indicators have perked up. With last quarter growth at 3.9 percent, the best it ever was in the Bush presidency, there are grousers who are now saying it isn't necessary to jump start the economy. But we all know where business as usual leaves the African American community. A day late, a dollar short, and jobless.

Then the December 14-15 economic summit is now not a summit but a retreat. Before it is over with, it may be downgraded yet again to a speakout. Bad sign.

And finally, this whole macroeconomic approach to the economy promises much to the country in general, but little to those stuck in pockets of poverty. We need targeted urban policy. We need policy targeted at the structurally unemployed. And, based on research that shows that the rising tide floods the black boat instead of lifting it, we need specific attention focused on black unemployment.

Bill Clinton hasn't gotten that yet. He's got the symbolism. He's got the poetry. Has he got the policy? I'm beyond humming to celebrate the signals. But I'm waiting for the substance.

King Features, December, 1992

THE SILENCE OF THE LEFT

This is a memo to President Clinton. The election is over. It doesn't make sense for you to run from pillar to post drumming up support. Get down to business!

This is a memo to the left, to the people who call themselves "liberals" and "progressive." The election is over. The bad guy lost. The not so bad guy won. Please don't tell me you are so relieved to see George Bush gone that you have lost your powers of creative dissent. Where are the voices lifted to protest Clinton's broken promises about the Haitians, his gratuitous attacks on those who receive public assistance, his moderate economic stimulus package? Are you so willing to give Clinton a chance that you won't risk criticizing him?

Some 260 Haitian refugees are trapped in a legal limbo on Guantanamo Bay, unable to return to Haiti where they will face political prosecution, and unable to enter the United States because they are HIV positive. Many have pleaded with the President to become personally involved in their plight. Instead, he has reaffirmed the policy of turning boats of Haitians away, or of taking those fleeing to Guantanamo Bay.

I've seen full page ads to support the immigration of Russian Jews, embassies surrounded over the rights of black South Africans. Rev. Jesse Jackson and the NAACP have raised their voices in support of the Haitians. But where is the left?

The left is also missing in the discussion over welfare reform. President Clinton says he wants to start a comprehensive program that will make welfare a helping hand not a way of life. The "up and out" program he proposes will offer recipients two years of education and training, but that's it. What kinds of jobs can people get after two years of training? Are those jobs being created? Can they support a family?

To be sure, about half of those women on welfare have graduated from high school and can land a job after two years of training and assistance. But what about those who dropped out after sixth or seventh grade? Will two years turn these folks into literate workers? I keep hearing people say we should give the President time to flush out the details of his proposal, but the silence of the left on this issue is disturbing.

But the lefties who went along with the notion that "it's the economy, stupid" ought to be drawn and quartered for their silence on the tepid economic stimulus package that has been proposed. The President hasn't said a word about raising the minimum wage, and the job creation he proposes is a drop in the bucket when 10 million Americans are officially unemployed. Where are the "progressive" and "radical" economists who can deconstruct Reagan-Bush economics faster than they can say "infrastructure investment?" Without agitation on the left, those who would reduce the size of the stimulus package will find it easy to do so. The left has been silent, and I'm not sure why.

The only national exception to the silence of the left has been a recent meeting of the National Rainbow Coalition. There, Rev. Jesse Jackson pledged to monitor President Clinton's promises. Jackson has made good, too, traveling to Guantanmo Bay in support of the Haitians, and joining a handful of protesters outside the Supreme Court in support of Haitian rights.

But the National Rainbow Coalition is a small slice of the left. Where is the rest? The silence of the left may be a well-intentioned attempt to give the President a chance, but it can also be interpreted as total acquiescence to policies that fall far short of putting people first.

King Features, March, 1993

HAS THE CONGRESSIONAL BLACK CAUCUS COME OF AGE?

Last year, the 26 members of the Congressional Black Caucus sat with bated breath as they wondered how much their numbers would increase. Less than a year after the election of President William Jefferson Clinton there are 40 members of the CBC, and an additional group of Cabinet members and senior staffers in the White House who bring influence to the table. What a difference a change makes! A year ago, the President could give less than a full damn about what black folk thought, and demonstrated his indifference by his invisibility. Now, President Clinton has made overtures to African Americans, especially with his short speech to those gathered at the Congressional Black Caucus dinner Saturday night.

Before we give Mr. Clinton "Massa" laurels for coming to the CBC dinner, let's note that this is the same President who thinks black women are nothing more than basketballs, friends and colleagues to be slam dunked. The first victim was Dr. Johnetta Cole. Then there was Lani Guinier. Dr. Jocelyn Elders said her confirmation hearing turned her from steak to chopped meat. Antoinette Cook, a woman who was slated to head the Federal Communications Commission, hasn't been asked for a quote. Massa came to the plantation Saturday night, perhaps because he needs support on controversial matters like NAFTA and health care. But has Massa had an attitudinal adjustment?

In many ways it doesn't matter. Massa isn't the issue, the strength of the Congressional Black Caucus is. The Caucus represents nearly ten percent of the Congress, more than twenty percent of the Democratic vote. Should President Clinton pay attention to African Americans? He had better if he can count votes!

If he can count votes, President Clinton had better understand that the Congressional Black Caucus has come of age. When a president passes a budget package with 2 votes, the notion of a 30 something vote bloc ought to be notable and worth consideration. In other words — President William Jefferson Clinton, meet Congressional representatives Kweisi Mfume and Harold Ford. Meet the members of congress who can rock your world with the votes they represent.

The members of the Congressional Black Caucus have taken their new clout to the max by sponsoring the open debates on race that Lani Guinier called for when she was abandoned by the President. CSPAN broadcast a conversation between Guinier, Princeton University scholar Cornel West, Civil Rights Commissioner Mary Frances Berry, and Judge Leon Higginbotham; and then a talk between Minister Louis Farrakhan, NAACP Executive Director Ben Chavis, Rev. Jesse Jackson, Congresswoman Maxine Waters, and CBC Chair Mfume. Besides old rhetoric, there was also the possibility that African American people could come together along ideological lines. And the fact that these sessions spilled over with participants spoke to the need for an African American dialogue. At the same time, the need for unity seemed to stifle some of the analysis that might have taken place, especially in the second discussion. Too many people thought Minister Farrakhan took the high road by handing out an olive branch. Too few saw his leader-busting "Final Call" that smacked the hand that might have taken the olive branch. I find it fascinating that Jackson and Chavis were so subdued in the face of Farrakhan's fire. Was this the best way, the most expedient way, or the mollifying way to face Farrakhan.

The day after this debate the *Washington Post* told the world that the Congressional Black Caucus and the Nation of Islam had agreed to work together. The announcement had a mixed reception. African Americans rejoiced that some of "our leaders" ended up on the same page, especially after the debacle of Farrakhan's exclusion from the 30th Anniversary of the March on Washington. Others (including myself) wondered if good sense had gone out the window with the notion of a partnership with an organization that does not speak to the equal rights of African American women.

From where I sit, the Congressional Black Caucus has gained clout but has not yet come of age. We come of age when we are able to engage in a dialogue of constructive criticism, not a dialogue that rushes us to a unanimity that is based on more rights for some African Americans (men) than others (woman). We come of age when we reject demagoguery and rhetoric for analysis. From where I sit we took a step backward from the issues raised by Guinier, West, Higginbotham and Berry when the race debate continued by Final Call headlines that asked "let my people go." Malveaux to the Minister: when will you "let my sister go" and "let the rhetoric go?"

King Features, September, 1993

EQUAL OBJECTS

My grandmother was such a product of the segregated South that her every conversation was peppered with the question: "white or colored." To her, more whites than Blacks behaved scandalously, partly because whites have more opportunity to do so. When Blacks were the object of scandal – like boxer Jack Johnson or Congressman Adam Clayton Powell – it was as much because they were Black as because of any misbehavior. Far too often the law had been written, bent or unevenly applied to topple a black man who had climbed too high.

When I think of 2 Live Crew, I think about race and censorship, but I also think about my grandmother's question. If she'd heard the Live Crew on the radio and asked "white or colored," she'd have expected an opposite answer. Redd Foxx, Pigmeat Markham, and the bawdy tradition of black comedy notwithstanding, she'd have been scandalized by four young black men prancing around a stage barking "me so horny," further scandalized by the way their lyrics, videos and album covers objectify black women.

But equal right often means the equal right to be a fool, a scoundrel, or, indeed, a sex object. The four black girls posing on the 2 Live Crew album cover, butts out, may well be "as nasty as they want to be." The album cover ought to spark discussion about gender roles and black women, but because of the way 2 Live Crew has been treated by the legal system, it more often sparks discussion about the First Amendment and race.

The 2 Live Crew aren't the only black men embroiled in scandals that objectify Black women. As the FBI tape on DC Mayor Marian Barry's sting illustrates, one black mayor has claimed his equal rights to adultery and indiscretion, and the pawns in his game were black women — his mistresses and his wife. But by using an ex-lover and the promise of sex to trap the DC Mayor, the FBI didn't draw the line at using black women as objects.

Criticisms of Mayor Barry's behavior and to 2 Live Crew lyrics have been mumbled, not shouted, in the black community because the "white or colored" question of a generation past is far too relevant in the way the legal system has treated these men. The FBI and the Broward County sheriff have transformed these scandals into causes, and the gender issues raised by the treatment of women who decorate arms and album covers have been swallowed by the cause. "White or colored," in entertainment and politics, women are too often treated as objects, our issues too often pushed to the back burner.

USA Today, June, 1990

QUOTAS - MYTHS AND REALITIES

There is only one operating quota in the United States and it is this: there shall be at least one dumb white man in the White House at all times. Popular wisdom would suggest that the 1989-93 dummy is Dan Quayle, but if we look at the way politicians have handled the Civil Rights Act of 1991, the real dummy is President George Bush.

Bush is true to racist form when he talks about a "quota" bill. Nothing in any legislation sets aside job slots for people, but he and his cronies persist in pushing this matter to the hilt. In the 1990 political season, Jesse Helms used a "white hands" commercial, the text of which went something like this: "You really needed that job, but they had to give it to a minority." The photo is of white hands tearing up a job application. Yet there is no law that forces an employer to give a job to a minority, just a law that prevents an employer from discriminating.

No matter. In politics there are lies and big lies. The white hands commercial got Jesse Helms elected over Harvey Gannt, and now Governor Pete Wilson's vote not to override the President's veto of the Civil Rights Act of 1990 meant that the five court cases which weakened the Civil Rights Act of 1964 make it more difficult for people to sue against discriminators.

Since the 1990 Act was vetoed, there have been interesting new cases that further weaken rights. The Supreme Court ruled in February that the Civil Rights Act of 1964 does not apply in other countries, so that American firms can discriminate if they are headquartered elsewhere. The Court has also ruled that employers can force workers to sign an agreement that they will not sue even if they are discriminated against. That opens the door for employers to force people to sign such agreements as a condition of hiring, further disadvantaging those who already face discrimination.

Meanwhile, a recent Urban Institute study shows that white workers were favored over black workers in the hiring process at least 20 percent of the time, while black workers were favored over white ones 7 percent of the time. The Urban Institute concluded that unequal treatment in hiring African Americans is "widespread and entrenched" and could discourage young black men from entering the job market.

Most firms know that enforcing civil rights and participating in affirmative action programs is good business. But thanks to President Bush, negotiations between the

Civil Rights Roundtable and a business forum were abruptly halted. Bush called in political chits to keep people from talking about how to make a civil rights bill work.

The worst part of the whole thing is that President Bush keeps engaging in divisive rhetoric. Whenever he says "quota bill," he stirs the embers of racial economic competition that is largely a function of our changing economy, not any advantage that blacks have over whites. Both black and white workers lost in the 1980s, but you'll never hear President Bush talking about that. You'll never hear him say the 31.5 percent of all workers earn less than a poverty wage, up from 25 percent in 1980. You'll never hear a commercial with a voiceover talking about the rich getting richer, or about tax breaks to corporations. Instead, this man seems stuck on the notion of "quota bill."

Like I said, the only operating quota in this country is one dumb white man in the White House at all times. With the Bush-Quayle combination, however, we seem to have exceeded the quota and come up with two racist and myopic dummies.

Sun Reporter, November, 1990

DOUBLE BLIND IN A DOUBLE BIND

What did you pay for your last car? A Northeastern University law professor found that white men get the best deals. In a "double blind" study, which is especially accurate because the testers don't know they are looking for evidence of discrimination, Professor Ian Ayres found that when the dealer's price of a car was $11,000 (which means the sticker price $13,465), white men were able to negotiate prices of $11,362, white women $11,405, black men $11,783, and black women $12,237. The man who did the study said that bigotry was part of the cause of the price discrepancies, but that another reason prices were so different was that dealers try to make money however they can.

This information came in the same week when a black Justice Department attorney launched an attack against scholarships for minority students. Michael Williams, himself probably the recipient of some minority student scholarships while he was at Harvard, has joined Glenn Loury and Shelby Steele in attacking the black students trying to follow in his footsteps. These folks say that affirmative action, minority set-asides and scholarships give us an unfair advantage. Apparently they haven't bought a car in awhile, or they'd know what unfair advantage *is*.

White men still get the best deals our society has to offer. Why? Because in positions of power, they offer the deals to each other. Whether it is a price break on a new car, a stock tip, or a job opening, white men get first bids unless the law does something to open doors to others.

Not only do white men get first dibs, but they also have been socialized to think that keeping the benefits to themselves is benign behavior. What harm can come, surely, from sharing a few tips on new opportunities over a cup of coffee at the Olympic Club? What's wrong with telling your best friend about the internship opening up? His son, no doubt, would be a prime candidate for it. What's wrong with cutting a buddy a deal on a car, when he will shoot a little business your way in return.

White women, black men, and black women have less business to shoot back. They've got hardly a foot in the door of the boardroom, not enough of a foothold to cut deals. And even when they have that foothold, the image is that they do not. Does it make economic sense to bargain hard with people you perceive as powerless?

Affirmative action doesn't offer any special advantage. It just forces white men who call their friends when opportunities open up to make a few more phone calls. Minority scholarships don't violate the Civil Rights Act of 1964. When minorities are underrepresented in colleges and universities, they offer them assistance so that they can compete.

Between the car study and the Department of Education decision, African Americans are stuck between a rock and a hard place. On one hand, there is clear evidence of racial bias in the economic marketplace. Then there are the handful of black conservatives, making like Chicken Little, crying "there is no racism, there is no racism, so take away the scholarships and affirmative action." Like alcoholics in denial, they are so addicted to the approval of the whites around them that they are MORE willing to assume the playing field is level than fight to level it.

In his book, *The Content of Our Character*, Shelby Steele speaks of "race fatigue," his utter exhaustion with the way race can work its way into almost every situation. It isn't so, Steele says, in his collection of essays. All people need to do is to work hard.

Steele's fatigue won't alter the facts. Race raises its ugly head at the strangest times, in the strangest places, in the most unexpected of ways. In the car dealership. In the Christmas spirit (Chabot College student Michael Whiteside was told he was too dark to be a Santa at Southland mall). And so on and so on. Being tired won't change things, fighting the system will.

Black conservatives have rushed to the altar of hard work as if they are the first to worship there. They forget that those they've tarred and feathered as "underclass" and "lazy" are hard workers, too. But while some are working hard to survive, others are working hard to limit their chances for survival by knocking down the ladder they once climbed, asserting that ladders are no longer necessary.

Sun Reporter, December, 1990

OPPORTUNITY AND OUTCOME

For William Jefferson Clinton, the withdrawal of attorney Lani Guinier's nomination as Assistant Attorney

General is simply one of a series of snafus that has characterized his perilous Presidency. For African Americans, the withdrawal was a painful reminder that the rules of the game change whenever we play. Wiping away tears, the President claimed he had not read Ms. Guinier's legal writing. He went on to say that he cared about equal opportunity not equal outcomes. A wise person might ask what the difference is between opportunity and outcome. The President, and indeed much of white America, seems to be avoiding that question.

If we have equal opportunity, how do we end up with such dissimilar economic and political outcomes between African Americans and whites? How do African Americans end up with unemployment rates twice those of whites, wealth levels a tenth as high? Does the system work, and are African Americans a flawed group of people who fail a "fair test?" Or is the system flawed by institutional barriers so that the difference in economic indicators is the result of a system skewed against African Americans? Obviously, I think it is the latter, not the former, that the process is flawed, not the people. Apparently, the man at 1600 Pennsylvania Avenue disagrees.

To care about opportunity without caring about outcomes is to let individuals and institutions off the hook, to say that good intentions are good enough. How many times have you seen the tag line in the job ads, "We are an equal opportunity employer?" How well does that jive with the sprinkling of non-white faces that are hired? Do we ever ask how to reconcile the statement "equal opportunity" with the outcome of an overwhelmingly white professorial? Or is mouthing the words enough?

Equal opportunity means paying attention to methods of recruitment and advertising, interviewing and evaluating, hiring and promotion. And the only way to figure out if an equal opportunity statement is working is to measure results. If black employment was 5 percent ten years ago and it remains 5 percent, it simply isn't enough to talk

312

about equal opportunity. Something isn't working, and it is clearly the process! And whining "quota queen" when someone raises the question about outcomes might be an effective way to rivet attention away from the problem, but it is an intellectually dishonest way to deal with the very real issue of economic, political, and social disparities among whites and African Americans.

If an electoral district is 50 percent African Americans, but the electoral outcome is always white, it makes sense to raise questions about the outcome. If African Americans don't register and don't vote, perhaps that accounts for the outcome. But what if there are barriers to registration and voting? Does someone become a "quota queen" because she/he raises those questions? Just a year ago, the Democratic Party spent time and energy looking at the electoral process because they were concerned with electing a candidate. Rev. Jesse Jackson led students to a registrar of voters in a rural county where student registrations had previously been shunned. There was no teary repudiation of that activity on the part of people like President Clinton because that served the purpose of his election. Sounds like there was at least one case when concern about outcome transcended concern about opportunity!

These issues of opportunity and outcome are critical when the Supreme Court has decided, again, that the burden of proof in discrimination cases is on workers, not employers. When a Missouri guard was denied a promotion on a fabricated basis, the Court found that lying is not illegal, and more importantly, it is not discrimination. Indeed, in his majority opinion, Justice Antonin Scalia referred to the way the black prison guard was treated as "less" than discrimination, though not completely fair. Just what does it take to "prove" discrimination, a videotape of KKK meetings on the job site? What about the outcome – a man was denied opportunity.

In another Supreme Court decision, Justice Sandra Day O'Connor wrote the majority opinion that ruled against creating the majority black North Carolina Congressional seat, because race based boundaries are unconstitutional. *New York Times* columnist Neil Lewis characterizes O'Connor's opinion as one that asks, "Can't we ever get beyond race?" Indeed, a careful view of Lani Guinier's writing suggests she, too, might have had questions about the way the district was created, but she never had a chance to make that point because intellectual charlatans on the far right had discredited her with the epithet "quota queen," and because the President failed to stand by her.

But the uncomfortable answer to Justice O'Connor's question is that we can't get past race until and unless we get to the heart of questions about opportunity and outcome, until we do some hard bean counting and harsh analysis of the overrepresentation of African Americans among the poor and the unemployed. We can't get past race until we decide that it is the system that is flawed, not the people. We can't get past race until we figure out how to make our economic and political system generate more palatable results.

Black Issues in Higher Education, July, 1993

WILL EVERY WOMAN HAVE HER YEAR?

"Ain't I a woman?" asked Sojourner Truth. What does it mean to be a woman in the year after the highly-touted year of the woman, a year that advanced the interests of some women, but utterly ignored the interests of others. Or, as a Mills College student Constance Wiggins wrote in her poem, "Year of the Woman":

> *Seems like...*
> *A practical joke and*
> *I'm not laughing*
> *Crumbs from the table and*
> *I'm still hungry*
> *A Band-aid solution and*
> *I'm still bleeding.*
> *I've had enough!*
> *Let the men have next year.*

WILL EVERY WOMAN HAVE HER YEAR?

You can count the panhandlers on your fingers outside Madison Square Garden. New York City has done a good job in putting on a pretty face for the 100,000 or so people who have converged here for the Democratic National Convention. The Democratic Party has done cosmetic surgery as well, tucking away its fissures and disagreements to put on a happy face. But just like the panhandlers will never totally desert the Garden area, the dissent in the Democratic Party, though muted, remains beneath the surface.

The first day that I went to pick up my credentials, I spotted a small black woman folded into a storefront near the Garden. She says something, and I say hello. When I walk by, again, she smiles and I notice her missing front tooth. On Tuesday we exchange a few words about the convention. "Lots of people are walking by here, looking like money, but they don't leave any," she says. When I drop a few coins in the paper cup she carries like an extra limb, she smiles and says, "See you tomorrow."

Ellen Malcolm of the women's campaign funding group EMILY's (Early Money is Like Yeast) List says this is the year of the woman. More than half a million dollars are raised for the seven women Democrats who are running for the United States Senate, and Malcolm specifically mentions the fact that two black women – Carol Mosley Braun and Anita Hill – have helped make this the year of the woman. Hill for her candor in the House Judiciary committee hearings, and Braun because of her tremendous primary election victory over Senator Alan Dixon.

Indeed, women have been showcased during this convention, upbeat women with windswept hair and jewel colored suits, women who have been identified as the "rising stars" of the party. They are mostly white, but the Democrats have bent over backward to be inclusive. Congresswomen Maxine Waters seconded the Clinton nomination, and Texas Railway Commissioner Lina Guerreto spoke at the platform presentation Tuesday. Perhaps it is the year of the woman inside Madison Square Garden. But outside, where a woman is cadging for coins, it is nothing but business as usual.

The woman at the Garden is not the only woman one ignored in this "year of the woman." Until Rev. Jesse Jackson spoke, there was no mention of women at the periphery, women like my panhandling friend or like the women who clean toilets at Madison Square Garden. Rev. Jackson spoke with passion, and with personal knowledge of the women who worked in a chicken processing plant in Hamlet, North Carolina, women who watched their co-workers burn to death because the policy of Imperial Foods was to lock the fire door to prevent theft. Jackson spoke with more passion than any of the windswept women might, of the lives of women who have not been airbrushed or sanitized for prime-time television consumption. And he spoke bluntly of these women, who were called "lazy" and "b—ch" because plucking 90 chicken wings a minute isn't good enough.

No speaker reminds us more powerfully than Jackson of the economic justice behind "Democratic ideals." In weaving together the lives of Haitian refugees, coal miners, Jews fleeing Germany, interred Japanese, and displaced textile workers, Jackson reminded those attending the convention that the world is not a made of balloons and ticker tape, and that the Democratic Party must be broader than the delegate base represented there, a base that had an average income of $50,000 and nearly 200 fewer African Americans than in 1988.

I was hoping that one of our "rising star" women could have done what Jackson did, used her 15 minutes of fame to breathe life into the predicament of working women who earn an average of $20,600 for a year of full time work. Oh, the women candidates said the right things about child care, about men not "getting it," but too often their words rang of rote and not compassion. In the "year of the woman," too many women candidates remind me of Clinton and Gore with dresses on.

I looked at the storefront doorway Wednesday, hoping for a glimpse of a woman who hasn't had her year yet. But her gap-toothed smile and her coffee cup were gone after two days. Will her concerns and those of other women

at the periphery be swallowed up by the hoopla of "the year of the woman"?

King Features, July, 1992

GENDER AND POLITICS, BIOLOGY AND IDEOLOGY

Former San Francisco Mayor Dianne Feinstein announced her candidacy for the United States Senate on Ash Wednesday (what was she giving up for Lent?) by noting that there needed to be more women's representation among our nation's most select body of legislators. While I'm enthusiastic about former Mayor Feinstein's possible presence in the Senate, I wonder whether she, and those others who are touting women's representation, have thought its impact all the way through.

It was a woman judge in Florida, Mary Lupo, who refused to allow testimony from women who said William Kennedy Smith attacked them in the past. Had a jury heard from those who had to fend off Smith, they might have found him guilty of rape. Instead, Lupo positioned herself as an adversary to prosecutor Moira Lasch. This woman is one I'd not mind missing from the bench.

Another is Los Angeles Judge Joyce Karlin. This woman sentenced a Korean American shopkeeper, Son Ja Du, to probation in her brutal slaying of a young black girl. Latasha Harlins was shot in the back, but it was classism and race, not gender, that motivated Judge Karlin to decide that this is one black life that had little value. A videotape shows the altercation, the deliberate shooting of a young girl in the back. The record shows a woman judge excusing the death of a girl-child who was not allowed womanhood.

In the wake of Professor Anita Hill's riveting charges against Judge Clarence Thomas, in the aftermath of a jury's stunning affirmation of Desiree Washington's charges against Mike Tyson, people have been talking about

318

women's empowerment. But if both of these cases say nothing else, they remind us that women aren't always on the same side. There are women who support abortion rights and those who oppose them; women who believed Tyson and Thomas, and women who looked askance at charges against those men.

And that's politics — what happens when women collide in the workplace? There are women secretaries who say they won't work for "women bosses," women flight attendants who seem troubled when women passengers ask for assistance. For some of us, gender is a bond, but for others it is the plexiglass wall that divides. The plexiglass wall is strengthened by films like *The Hand That Rocks The Cradle* and *Fatal Attraction*, films suggesting that women's only bond is envy.

But these concerns are swallowed or unspoken as candidates like Dianne Feinstein talk about the need for more women in public office. Just what will these new women do? Will they raise women's wages, provide more child care, more access to choice, stronger laws against discrimination? Will they protect white women, privileged women, all women?

I agree with women like California candidates Dianne Feinstein and Barbara Boxer, like Congresswoman Patricia Schroeder. There need to be more women in the House, the Senate, the Judiciary. But then there are women like Mary Lupo and Joyce Karlin who give me pause because their gender is less important to them than their politics. Do the women who say they want more women in high places see past biology to ideology?

King Features, March, 1992

WILL THE YEAR OF THE WOMAN TRICKLE DOWN?

Now that the confetti has been swept from hotel suites and the champagne glasses have been tossed into waste-baskets, perhaps it is time to reflect on the gains that have come from this "year of the woman." Yes, women's representation in the United States Senate has tripled. But how quickly will this phenomenal gain trickle down to other working women?

The representation of women in construction jobs is 2 percent, just about what women's representation in the Senate was before the election. While the men of the United States Senate may chafe at the presence of their new female colleagues, it is unlikely that Senators Feinstein, Boxer, Murray and Braun will experience the same hazing as women in construction sites. Chicago Women in Trades, a support and advocacy organization for women working in the skilled trades, has done research on the working conditions of women in construction and report most face unpleasant working conditions.

Fifty-seven percent of those surveyed were inappropriately touched or asked for sex. 86 percent heard unwelcome sexual remarks. 60 percent were given the dirtiest assignments. Half had to deal with remarks about race or ethnicity. While the sanitary facilities at the United States Senate are being altered to accommodate the new women Senators (before this, Barbara Mikulski and Nancy Kasselbaum had to use facilities three flights removed from the Senate chamber), 80 percent of the women surveyed by Chicago Women in Trades either had no toilets or dirty toilets.

Chicago Women in Trades has designed a model future worksite that contains no sexual graffiti or pictures, clear policies on sexual harassment, more women than the usual 2 percent, and separate bathrooms and changing rooms for women. But they're the exception. In general, as women enter untraditional worksites, they encounter resistance.

Consider the report of the Presidential Commission on the Assignment of Women in the Armed Forces. The Bush-appointed commission voted to continue excluding women for ground and air combat, citing camaraderie, among other things, as a reason to keep women out of combat. Men might get so distracted by working with women, the line goes, that they'd become less effective. Rather than train men to treat women equally, the Presidential Commission thinks it more expedient to simply exclude women.

Reasons of comfort have always been used to bar women at the gates. All male clubs can't make room for women because male members are used to their locker room banter and old boy bonding. They can't let women use single sex athletic facilities because then they might be forced to wear trunks — an incredible inconvenience. Senate Majority Leader George Mitchell seemed to yield his perquisites with more grace than many, noting that "appropriate steps (would) be taken to meet the needs of all the senators." Unfortunately such steps haven't been taken for women in the rest of the workplace.

Indeed, the challenge for the women in the Senate is to make sure their gains trickle down to the rest of us. It is one thing for the Senate Majority leader to order construction of a new bathroom for women. It is quite another for construction workers to cut the crude comments, snatch down the smutty pictures, and let their women colleagues in the trades do their work. This year of the woman will be a flash in the pan if there is no connection between the former and the latter, if the distance between women in the Senate and their working sisters is the same as the distance between powerful and powerless men.

King Features, January, 1993

NO MEANS NO

Thursday evening. I am at Nordstrom's to meet a colleague. We have tea in the Pub, then I head for the express elevator to go downstairs. Two young brothers join me in the elevator and we nod, how you doing. And then one of them says, let's cut the chit chat, you've got to buy a paper, sister. No thank you, I say, but he doesn't get it. He launches into a staccato patter that is overwhelming, offensive. I tell him that I said no because I do not *want* the paper. Get with the program, he says. Again I say no thank you.

But it is not as polite as that. It is really oppressive, offensive. These young men, members of the Nation of Islam, selling the *Final Call*, feel like they can harass me in this elevator, that they can wear me down with words. When I say no, I mean it. And I have the right to say no.

Some will say I'm quibbling. The Nation, and Minister Farrkhan, do some good things and send out some good messages. But I'm about to think they do more harm than good. Because in my encounters with young black men selling whatever, there seems to be the supposition that they can push as hard as they want, say whatever they have to say, to get a dollar from me for a paper. They don't hear me when I say "no." They don't respect my right to "no." They think if they talk faster, run it quicker, that they will convince me. Or they don't care what I think, they are just out to hear themselves talk.

My elevator encounter wasn't the first time I've run afoul of the brothers in the Nation. I was walking down Market Street a few months ago, just trying to get to the chiropractor to get my back straight. A young man who told me his name was Anthony 3X demanded, not asked, that I buy a paper. No thank you, I said, walking fast. He began walking behind me, hassling. "Why not," he said, "you'll buy anything else, the white man's paper, why not mine." "Is that really going to make a sale?" I turned on him and said. I was furious, sizzling, ready to throw down.

322

"You ought to be ashamed of yourself," I told the brother. "You aren't going to follow a white person down the street, hassling them. You aren't going to run this stuff by too many black men, cause some of them will take you on and tell you where to go. You must think black women are the only folk vulnerable to your nonsense (I used another word), but I'm not. You cannot harass me, I have the right to walk down Market Street."

To me this is the root of it. These young men have contempt for black women. We are at the low end of the food chain for them. They are pulling at our guilt strings, and if that doesn't work, trying to intimidate us. But what they are really doing is selling Minister Louis Farrakhan's vision short. Because each encounter I have with them chips away at the regard I have for the Nation of Islam. I wonder if they teach young men that their contempt for women is acceptable.

The worse of it is the response I get from women friends when I talk about this. "At least they are not selling drugs," one friend says. "At least they are trying something positive," says another. Give me a break. If their positive experience jeopardizes my right to get in an elevator and have peace, my right to walk down the street, then there is something wrong with their positivity. Can someone explain the simple meaning of a two letter word to these brothers? No means no, means get away, go away, I am not interested, forget it, not this time, back off. It does not mean follow me down the street. It does not mean continue the conversation. It is a declination.

I do not mind, understand, the request, but I mind the deafness to my reply. And I mind it more when I read about Mike Tyson and his rape of a young sister in Indianapolis. Yes, I believe her before the jury comes back with a verdict. Tyson and trouble go hand in hand; this is a man who has never heard no. The frightening thing is that respectable men, hiding behind shaved haircuts and Muslim bow-ties, behind degrees and business suits, are all too often no different or better than Mike Tyson. They don't hear, don't see, don't think that a woman's voice is worth paying attention to. No is not a word that enters into their vocabulary.

In all fairness, let me say that I am not talking about all black men. There are the good guys, bunches of them, whose good names are tarnished by a few bad apples. But good guys aside, the fact is that a woman cannot walk down a street without getting hassled, and that some of this hassling takes place both on the street and behind closed doors. No, there's nothing wrong with a look or a comment, but there is such a thing as back off. Anybody listening?

I am jarred by the fact that an organization that says they want the best for black folks seems to condone the street harassment of black women by black men. I am amazed that so many men, black and white, cannot hear the word no. And I am disheartened by the fact that some find this a trivial matter. Not.

People are standing outside an Indianapolis courtroom asking if Mike Tyson can get a fair trial. All I want to know is if anyone has checked his hearing and comprehension, and that of the thousands of other men who don't understand that no means no.

Sun Reporter, June, 1992

OLDER WOMEN'S DEPENDENCY: A TIMELESS IMAGE

The woman is almost sixty, and it shows. She wears the starched white uniform of a nurse or home health aide, and carries herself with the stiff dignity of someone used to working hard for her living. Her cracked knuckles and rough skin suggest that she is not afraid of using elbow grease or getting down on her knees and scrubbing floors in order to survive. Her cushioned white shoes suggest that many of her sixty years have been spent standing on her feet. She accompanies a wheelchair-bound woman down a city street, a woman not fifteen years older than herself. The two women are tenuously connected by their age (both, over 60, are considered "elderly" by many), bound by their gender, separated by their economic status and probably their race, connected by their predicament of being old and alone, and separated by the way they survive this predicament.

It takes little to establish that the woman navigating the wheelchair has always worked in low-wage jobs as a home health worker, cleaning service worker, private household worker, or nurse's aide, earning an hourly wage that puts her at the bottom of the pay distribution. At the same time, it is obvious that her charge is protected by her economic past. Perhaps her spouse died recently, leaving her a pension. Perhaps she was a single career woman who put 40 years into the labor market and left having built up a pension history for herself. Although she is being cared for, her position is far from secure. If the insurance company that invested her pension funds chose junk bonds, her ability to afford the help she gets may be jeopardized. If her certificates of deposit exceed $100,000 and they are held by a bank that has been affected by the S&L debacle, her income is also at risk. When the interest rate dropped, a move that was heralded as "good" for the economy, so did her income. For that matter, if her disability persists or worsens so that she requires full-time care, even a generous pension income will not be adequate. She will then be forced to "spend down" her savings in order to qualify for public assistance with which to pay nursing home fees.

In what year are we observing these women? It could be 1950, when more than half of all black women worked as private household workers, and when the typical black woman could be found in some caretaking role. It could be 1990, when despite changed occupational status, black and brown women were far more likely to be home health aides and other service workers than white women. Could it be 2030?

The women on the city sidewalk, one sitting in her wheelchair, the other maneuvering it past urban roadblocks, are a common sight, but one from which we often avert our eyes. After all, aging poverty is everyone's horror, a horror increased by the sight of bag women sitting on park benches and homeless women clamoring for space in shelters. These riveting images play on our fears — could it happen to me?

Unfortunately, the answer is "yes." In a political year, when all the talk is of family values and jumpstarting the economy, few have spoken of the elderly, especially the elderly poor who live alone (most of whom are women). And for too many older people, poverty is an accident waiting to happen. Sure, economic downturns affect us all, but when the economy goes sour and people are clamoring for jobs, few employers will hire an elderly woman, even if she is able to work.

It is easy to look away from an image of elderly women's dependency, but with the "baby boom" aging and not saving, it makes a lot more sense to stare that image down.

King Features, July, 1992

NO PEACE IN A SISTERLY SPACE

The dress has an exciting, vivid print. Big green leaves and muted gold swirls, tan, brown, and a little yellow. Belted at the waist, it emphasizes the woman's taut figure. But the print looks out of place with her lime green shoes that are a throwback to a fashion nightmare. And when the woman turns from the counter in the candle shop toward me she looks fifty, not thirty, and the dress looks like she borrowed it from one of her children.

I had been concentrating on the wild print of the small brown woman's dress because I didn't want to listen to her words. I'd finally roused myself from the hypnotic rage

I felt at the Senate Judiciary Committee's treatment of Anita Hill to move out of my house, to move around streets with folks, and I made my usual Saturday stops — to the health food store, to a progressive book store, to the small, pungent, smelly candle shop that a friend runs.

But everywhere I go there is the buzz buzz buzz about Supreme Court nominee Clarence Thomas, about Professor Anita Hill. In the bookstore and the health food store, support is strong for Hill. I have deliberately avoided one of the "bars in the hood," cause I know what to expect there from the conversations I've had with black men who combine fiction with justification to support Thomas. I have even declined to talk to my own male sibling, the fault lines of our relationship about sexism so strong that we both sense this is a conversation we cannot have without doing what may be irreparable harm.

I expected solidarity, sisterhood among my women friends, but it was not there. One of my closest friends told me that she is the mother of a teenager, that any man can stand accused. I tell her she did not raise her son to pull stunts like those Thomas was accused of, but her love for her son and her image of Hill as "treacherous" clouds her vision. And in the candle shop where the smells and sounds so often soothe, I am jarred, nearly slapped by the force of one black woman's feelings against another.

"I hate that b___h," said the woman in the lime green shoes, with such vehemence that I jump. She launches into a tirade about one black person tearing another down. All around me there are black women, a couple of whom look like they could take this woman on if they wanted to. But they sit silently, crowded into a bench, arms folded against their chests. When I can't take it no longer, I offer a tentative comment. After all, I didn't come to the candle shop to fight or debate, just to buy a white candle to burn for peace in my home, for quiet thoughts, to relieve myself of the anger that grips me when I consider the way Professor Hill has been treated.

Hill's allegations had barely been made public, when Arizona Senator Dennis DeConcini gave the first clue that she would be treated badly. "This lady," he described her, "Mrs. Hill, Miss Hill or whatever." Whatever? DeConcini went on to say that the allegations were "unfortunate for Judge Thomas." He never could quite bring himself to correctly refer to Professor Anita Hill, reducing her to a "some lady" both in her words and in his actions. If the allegations were unfortunate for Judge Thomas, what did DeConcini think the experience was for Professor Hill?

His October 7th comments were mild in comparison to the comments later made by Senators Specter, Hatch, and Simpson. These three stooges led the lynch mob that attacked Hill and defended Thomas, whose sudden identification with black history and culture was amazing. After days of self-effacing comments and references to his dead grandfather, I half expected Thomas to approach the Committee with a harmonica and burst into song, further establishing himself as the nonthreatening handkerchief head they sought. His anger and empty threats ("I would rather be dead than go through this") suggested that there was truth to Hill's allegations.

But there was no hearing that in the candle shop, in a tiny space full of women either too weary to argue or too outraged to shut up. I am stunned by the anger and harshness some of these fiftysomething women express toward Hill. She should have known better, says one woman. If he talked dirty to her, why did she follow him from one place to another, said another woman. The woman who owns this shop is as smooth as icing on cake, she doesn't say anything, just smiles and moves her customers out of the store. But in this space there is no kind word, no empathy for Anita Hill. These women have led hard lives and know what it is to swallow pain and indignity. As far as they were concerned, the hurt had happened too long ago to matter. What Clarence Thomas had to lose was greater than her pain. She didn't have to say anthing, she brought this pain on herself. These women who might have combed Anita's hair, held her between their knees when she was a girl, were now, with hard eyes and harsh hearts, condemning her.

Support for Professor Hill comes from the strangest places. Two white women friends offer $10 each to help pay for the *New York Times* ad placed by African American Women in Defense of Ourselves. Just a block down the street, at a deli where I resolve not to talk politics, an Italian man says his heart breaks for "the little professor." But too many black women say this is an indignity we are supposed to bear, that Hill should have been silent, even those who had stories to tell themselves. The most heart-breaking story I hear is from a sixtyish woman who was raped by the man of a house she worked in as a maid when she was fifteen. "I didn't tell anyone," she said. "Who could I tell? The missus would have fired me. My brothers would have fought the man and gotten into trouble. I prayed I was not pregnant; I left the job at the end of the summer. On my last day of work the man crushed up some bills, stuffed them down the front of my shirt, and patted me on the ass. I took that money—almost a hundred dollars—and put it toward my college costs. I guess you can say he bought my silence."

It seems to me that some black women's resentment against Professor Hill was resentment that she found a voice when they could not. Indeed, because the black women's burden is lightened by class, educational status, and generation, many black women could distance themselves from Hill, depicting her as "other" even in the community of black women. When one of the three stooge Senators mentioned her "proclivities," a weak attempt to insert the issue of sexual preference into the discussion, the gap widened even further.

The women in the candle shop spoke of the accomodating that they must do to live, the juggling of pressures and personalities, the weighing of whether a nasty remark is more effective than a simple cold shoulder. "You single women don't have to follow the rules, you don't have all these burdens," one woman said gently. So in addition to everything else, some sisters held Professor Hill's independent status against her.

Black women are the targets of everyone's ire, even of an ire we turn against ourselves. Politicians scream "welfare" and our images are conjured up. They say "entitlement" and there we are again. "Illegitimate child" and can't you see some black woman, belly distended, sitting at a hospital? Black men do some of the screaming, too. In the days after the Senate Judiciary Committee hearings, brothers in suits showered black women with more contempt than most rappers. "She must have wanted it," "She was jealous," were the kindest of the statements. Dog Dogget, the egomaniac who fantasized that everyone wanted him got his 15 minutes of fame as an "international business consultant" (aka unemployed huckster with frequent flyer miles). Few were as harsh or as crazed as he in their assessment of Hill, but his performance set a tone for some of the other things black men said about black women.

A San Francisco State University political science professor told his class that career black women were one cause of the black family's deterioration. His remarks were timed to follow the Senate Judiciary Committee interrogation of Hill and his scapegoating of black women made local headlines. But Professor Robert Smith, like Clarence Thomas, seemed to forget where he came from and what is important. Here are the facts. Black women work because they have to, not because they are "choosing" careers over men and family. Without black women's work, about 40 percent of all two-earner families would be in poverty, not at a middle income level. True, a few black women are on the fast track. Of 12 million adult black women, 89,000 earned more than $50,000 in 1989 (or fewer than 1 percent of all black women). About 229,000 black men, 2 percent of all black men, earned more than

$50,000, along with 1.5 million white women and 8.6 million white men. On the other hand, 7.4 million black women had incomes below $10,000, and that's 62 percent of all black women!

In many ways this is all about distance — between the sister at the bottom and the sister at the top, between the sisters at the top, and the brothers at both bottom and top who resent their success, between black folk and white folk and the ways we see history. The complexity of those differences hit me where it hurt — in a place where I had only known peace, there was no peace, just tension high. On the telephone with friends, there is not always the understanding ear. Even in my family, with a brother whose sexism is in stark contrast to the feminism of his four sisters, I had to hear, just once because that was when I dropped the phone back into the vicinity of the receiver, "If she didn't like it, why did she keep working for him." The *New York Times* printed a piece by a black male scholar who said this was how black people talked to each other, and two nights later, in my role as radio talk show host, I was asked if it wasn't true that black women preferred to be called "b___h" than "baby?"

But here is the bottom line. Supreme Court Justice Clarence Thomas was confirmed because he invoked the image of a black man hanging. They don't make ropes for black women's lynchings or destroy us with high drama. Instead, it is the grind of daily life that wears us slowly down, the struggle for a dignified survival. Black women work the same endless days white women do, but when we juggle work and family, we also bear the burden of the racism that shapes the composition of our households. We are not lynched, just chipped at by the indignity swallowed, the harassment ignored, the gossamer thread of job security frayed by last hired, first fired. We have been taught silence, and Anita Hill's lifted voice is evidence that she finally found the Sojourner within her.

I finally got the candle I wanted, something white and

aromatic, soothing. I brought it home and lit it, and watched the rest of the hearings against the flicker of the flame. I didn't find peace where I sought it, but I found it in myself, and was reminded that such is the definition of a true Sojourner.

The Black Scholar, Spring, 1992

RACIAL HARASSMENT ALSO A WORKPLACE PROBLEM

When the drama of workplace sexual harassment is played out in blackface, as it was when Professor Anita Hill came forward with her charges of sexual harassment against Judge Clarence Thoimas, what effect does it have on other workplace issues? Gender concerns override matters of race for some women, and people are sensitized about sexual harassment. Indeed, as a friend told me angrily last week, "Scratch any woman and you'll find a sexual harassment story." The Thomas hearings have certainly motivated discussion about appropriate behavior on the job between men and women. But in all the discussions I've heard about behavior, I've heard little about the racial hazing and harassment that so many workers experience.

Brenda Patterson is one of many black workers who was on the receiving end of race discrimination in the workplace. Her case, perhaps, illustrates why many do not use the judicial system as a remedy. Patterson sued the credit union where she worked for a full decade in a case that went to the Supreme Court, *Patterson v. McLean Credit Union*. She was subject to racist comments from the start — when she was hired as an accounting clerk her white supervisor told her that her coworkers would dislike her because she was black. The only African American employee at her bank, Patterson was the brunt of an endless stream of racial remarks and workplace hazing. Her supervisors and coworkers told her that black people were, by nature, slower than whites, then they piled extra work on her to see if she could do it. She was ordered to dust and sweep the office, something no other accounting clerk had to do.

Patterson was laid off in 1982, even though people who were on the job less than she were retained. She brought a lawsuit against her employers for denying her a promotion, for an unjustified layoff, and for racial discrimination on the job. She and her attorneys fought through district court, to the court of appeals, to the Supreme Court which found, in 1989, that discrimination is not allowed at the point of hire, but that it is acceptable after hiring. This woman's case of a decade of harassment and hazing has still not been resolved at this moment. Indeed, between all the courts, claims of racial harassment and discrimination have been dismissed, and the only pending action she has against McLean's Credit Union is based on whether she was unjustifiably denied a promotion.

People like Brenda Patterson could get justice if Congress could pass the Civil Rights Act of 1991, a law that makes it clear that racial harassment on the job should be illegal, and that employers who harass should be subject to strong legal penalties. Although the House of Representatives passed the legislation in April, President Bush has said he will veto the legislation in its present form. Indeed, he vetoed a version of this Civil Rights Act in October 1990, and the Senate failed to override his veto. Brenda Patterson has been jerked around by the judicial system, and concerns of people like her have been ignored by the same legislators who wonder why Professor Anita Hill did not officially complain about the harassment she experienced!

All the vocal women's groups have raised their voices about sexual harassment like the kind Professor Hill experienced. Their voices are more muted when it comes to protesting the racial harassment experienced by women like Brenda Patterson. To be sure, groups like NOW are on record as supporting the Civil Rights Act of 1991. But they have focused their support on issues of gender discrimination, and have said little about racial discrimination. Their silence is, perhaps, the reason that so many black women looked askance at women's protests outside the Thomas hearings. Perhaps they wondered, as I did, why women in Congress would storm the Senate on behalf of a Professor Hill, but not a Brenda Patterson. As sexual harassment issues take center stage, who will speak up about race discrimination?

King Features, October, 1991

RECONSIDERING THE ANITA HILL EFFECT

I was having a conversation with a white woman politician, chiding her about her record on issues affecting women of color. "When I talked to Anita Hill...," she replied, using the black women law professor's name like a mantra, like a cross held up to ward off offending vampires.

"Let's pull an Anita Hill on him," I heard another woman say, speaking of blowing the whistle on a man that she found offensive.

"We need to Anita Hill this issue," wrote a columnist, speaking of riveting attention toward subjects badly neglected.

Noun. Verb. Pronoun. Adverb. Icon. Mantra. Political Effect. More than a year after the Oklahoma law professor made accusations against Associate Supreme Court Justice Clarence Thomas, it seems to me time to reconsider this "Anita Hill effect" and the extent to which it has trickled down to African American women.

I make this point not to criticize Hill, because my support for her actions in the October, 1991 Thomas confirmation hearings remains unwavering. But I resist the attempt to deify her, to turn her name into a household word, some noun, some verb. And I make the point because there are so many women who are invoking their past support for her as a symbol for other working women, but their actions don't suggest such support.

"The Anita Hill effect" has been cited as a factor in the Senatorial candidacies of some eleven women, and the victories of four new women (Carol Mosley Braun, Barbara Boxer, Dianne Feinstein and Patty Murray) in the 1992 elections. Hill's testimony has also been credited with giving voice to women who had long been silent about matters of harassment, including women in legislative staffs, corporate offices, and university campuses.

While it is clearly likely that dissatfaction with sexual harassment was present before Hill spoke up, her testimony empowered some women to pursue their claims of sexual harassment.

After the dust from Hill's testimony settled, it appeared that those women who gained strength from her voice were not evenly distributed by race, class, and occupational status. Indeed, it was mostly professional women who stepped to the forefront with their complaints about sexual harassment. Perhaps it is logical that these women should have been the first to benefit from the "Anita Hill effect." They, like Hill, are well educated and articulate, able to present their cases and explain themselves in a credible manner. But without questioning the merit of these cases, it is important to note that the earliest recorded examples of sexual harassment in American workplaces took place at the bottom of the occupational hierarchy, not at the top.

Private household workers, clerical workers, hospital service workers, and restaurant staff all earn pay at the bottom of the occupational spectrum. They are as likely, if not more so, to be sexually harassed as their professional sisters. And they are more likely to be women of color than are professional women. They don't make good copy, they are not necessarily articulate, and one can't build as good a movement or an effect around them. They are the voiceless women who may have been empowered, but also maybe not, by "the Anita Hill effect." When I think of Anita Hill, I also think of Brenda Patterson, the named plaintiff in *Patterson v. McLean's Credit Union*, one of the five cases that was part of the Civil Rights Act of 1991. We've never heard of the Brenda Patterson effect because the racial harassment Patterson experienced didn't rally women's groups around her. And yet the regular racial hazing she endured was as harsh as the harassment Hill experienced.

Was the Anita Hill effect responsible for President Clinton's lifting of the ban on importing RU486? Most working women aren't lining up to take a Concorde to get morning after pills for their personal use. The company that manufactures RU486 doesn't want to distribute it here. Lifting the ban is a symbolic step that helps women at the top. Where is the relief for women at the bottom?

The Anita Hill effect brought us Senators, sensitivity, and symbolism. But the effect, like icing on a cake, seems stuck at the top of the occupational spectrum. It will take more than humming the mantra "Anita Hill" or invoking her testmony to imply a movement to transform the "effect" into gains for women at the bottom.

King Features, March 1993

CAN BLACK AND WHITE WOMEN BE ALLIES?

They just don't get it, screamed a group of Congressional women, storming the United States Senate during the Supreme Court confirmation hearings of Justice Clarence Thomas. I applauded the seven women who raised their voices against the ultimate white boy's club, but I shuddered when I saw the lone black woman in the group, Rep. Eleanor Holmes Norton, bringing up the rear. It reminded me of black women's history, of the way we had to nudge and elbow our way into the suffrage march down Pennslyvania Avenue in 1919 because there were those white women who had discouraged our willingness to walk for women's right to vote.

Not much has changed between 1919 and 1991. Then, as now, black women had to fight for a place among feminists, and we often had to settle for bringing up the rear. And then, like now, we had to face the wrath of black men when we spoke up about our gender interests. Black and white women are bound by those interests, by the need for affordable child care, for family and medical leave, for pension plans that consider widows. But as close as these issues bind us, there are others that push us apart. When white women talk about getting relief from the burden of housework, they often look to a woman of color to relieve that burden. Fewer black women clean white women's houses in 1991 than 1919, but the arrogant assumption of white women that someone is ready and waiting to shoulder their burden is often irksome.

More than that, there are the economic realities. While more than 40 percent of black women head households, just 15 percent of white women do. More white women than black, then, have access to male earning power. In other words, they have the means to put out the message that "they don't get it." Their husbands, fathers, and brothers are the advertising executives that advise them in how to package their message. Black women who head households give support instead of receiving it from the men in their lives.

Generations removed from the 1919 suffrage march, white women expect black women to join hands with them and confront men who "don't get it." But because black men have so much less economic power than white men, black women are torn between supporting their men and defending their gender interests.

Black and white women can't be true and honest allies until and unless white women understand that the economic status of black men is part of the black feminist agenda. Platitudes like equal pay have to be expanded to include black men before they can appeal to most black

women, despite the feminist rhetoric.

USA Today, November, 1991

GIRLS AT WORK, BOYS AT SCHOOL

The Ms. Foundation's effort to promote National Take Our Daughters to Work Day seemed to be a modest effort to promote the career aspirations of girls. Too modest, I thought, when I first heard of the notion. Daughters should go to work not just one day a year, but, perhaps, more often than that. Girls should be exposed to working professionals and role models and reminded that there are a range of opportunities for them in life. In the realm of public-private partnerships, there should be internships for girls to expose them to the possibilities available to them.

Women's work is no secret from girls or boys. In 1988, 30 million children had employed mothers. As the "jobless recovery" proceeds, women's work becomes more crucial to family economic survival, with women's work representing the difference between poverty and middle-class incomes in many cases. But despite women's work effort, women still earn less than men, even in similar jobs, with similar education, doing similar, if not the same work. The average (mean) full-time male worker earned $34,900 per year in 1990, compared to $22,700 for the average full time female worker. Among college graduates, full-time men earn $49,000, compared to $36,300 for women. Among those earning over $100,000 per year in our society, 1.7 million are white men, 206,000 are white women, 31,000 are African American men, and 15,000 are African American women.

Occupational differences account for at least part of the difference. Women are still woefully underrepresented in the "prestige professions" like law, medicine, and management, and overrepresented in lower paid clerical and retail sales jobs. The purpose of the Ms. Foundation's National Take our Daughters to Work Day seems to be to close some of the gaps in representation and pay that women still experience in the workplace.

But while the girls went to work, the boys stayed at school, and some of them didn't like it. Press coverage of girls at work included, all too often, chiding from the boys who said that they wanted to be treated equally, that they didn't think girls needed the special exposure to the workplace that they got on April 28. At least one of the male anchors I watched deliver the news looked into the camera and gave it a full smirk, as if to say "how's that for equality, ladies."

The young men that I saw complaining about women at work have learned, all too early, how to cloak themselves in white male petulance. As teens, they are complaining about daughters at work. As college freshmen, they'll be complaining about affirmative action programs and Women's Studies, and forming groups like the National Association for the Advancement of White Males. As labor market entrants, they'll fuss that the "best qualified" person ought to get the job, and they won't wonder if "male" and "qualified" means the same thing to them. Either they don't see the gaps between men and women in the workplace, or they are choosing to ignore them.

Men, especially white men, have experiencd tremendous advantages in the labor market, while both discrimination and the pressure to juggle work and family has relegated many women to unequal wages, and the persistence of the gender wage gap is something we just don't hear enough about these days. The Ms. Foundation for women talked about girls' self-esteem as their reason for organizing a day to take daughters to work. In addition to self-esteem, they should have focused on issues of unequal pay to make it clear the workplace exposure is about something more than a feel-good "girls day." It is also about women's economic survival.

King Features, April, 1993

DISCRIMINATION OR STUPIDITY

"Women earn less and pay more. That's the double jeopardy," said consumer advocate Ralph Nader. A study released by his Center for Responsive Law indicates that women pay more for haircuts, automobiles, drycleaning and alterations, and sometimes even medical care. Frances Cerra Whittelsey, author of the report, says there are two reasons women are charged more at the cash register. Car salesmen believe women are suckers who won't bargain for better prices. Dry cleaners overcharge women because of something called "traditional pricing," or because they rationalize that they spend more time and energy on providing services to women than to men.

Nader says that women's groups have looked at inequities in the labor market but not in the consumer marketplace. I agree with him, but in consumer markets women have more power than we acknowledge. There is nothing to prevent a woman who shops for a car from picking up a consumer magazine to learn how much a dealer typically marks up a car. There is nothing to prevent a woman from calling one of the many consumer services to get a better car price. There is absolutely nothing to prevent a woman from bargaining for an auto. When I read that men and women pay different amounts for cars, I conclude that the difference is part discrimination, part stupidity or laziness.

I don't know that men look harder for bargains, and there's documented evidence that white men tend to offer white men better prices on the first quote. A Northwestern University study showed that white women paid about $150 more for identical cars than white men, and African American women paid $800 more than white men. And a *Prime Time Live* special documented an auto dealer offering a white consumer a much better deal in terms of down payment, financing, and price than a black consumer. That's discrimination, pure and simple, and such discrimination is against the law, and should be punished. But there's no law against shopping around.

Some women have taken cleaning establishments and department stores to court to contest the issue of price discrimination. Some have walked away with winning settlements. But price descrimation will continue as long as women allow it to continue. When someone walks into a barbershop and sees one set of prices for women and another for men, and sits down in the chair, accepting the price difference, she is signaling her agreement with the discrimination. A more effective tactic might be to walk out.

Of course, one might argue that women have less time for shopping around than men, and that women are less inclined to walk out of an establishment when confronted with unfair pricing. And it is true that women who both work in the labor market and have families shoulder a "double day," which means that convenience often takes precedence over smart shopping. I say that the only way price differences are narrowed is for women to say something about them.

Once upon a time, Ralph Nader's work was at the cutting edge of the consumer movement. But this study on price discrimination is disappointing, because it states the obvious. People should be informed shoppers and be prepared to walk away if they don't get fair treatment. People should complain to consumer protection offices when they encounter incompetence or fraud. Women should stop spending on items that are impractical and overpriced.

That's good advice for women and for men. In many ways, smart shopping is simply not a gender thing. To attempt to make it so diminishes real claims of discrimination in the labor market and the economy.

King Features, May, 1993

PRAYING TO A GENDERED GOD

Although I consider myself a Christian, I don't go to church very often. I think it has something to do with my upbringing in the Catholic church, where the men were always in charge, the women "handmaidens." Never mind that these maidens were the backbone of the church, the women who brought the flowers, sold the raffle tickets, taught the children, visited the sick, fed the pastor, washed his garments, polished the chalices, filled them with the wine, the body and blood of Christ as we were taught. They may have filled the chalices, but they could not feed others from them. In the Catholic Church women were, still are, second class citizens. I grew up in that, chafed under it, and yet when I hear somebody sing "Praise God From Whom All Blessings Flow," I begin to hum, hum, to feel comforted. I kind of get into the soft, melodious voices of the people around me, the notion that my burden, light or heavy, can be laid down in the church. Praise God, the words seem like cold water on parched lips, and I understand why the black church has been such an enduring institution. At the end of a week of unequal wages, praise God. At the end of a week of insult and indignity, praise God. Turned away from opportunities, praise God. Praise God, that is, or go mad. Because there has to be some order to this, some order, divine order.

But is that order necessarily male? The singers make it so. Praise God from whom all blessings flow, praise **him** all creatures here below. Him. Why is power, authority, even divinity, always vested in a man, or in the masculine gender? Why must I praise "him" not "her"? We all have to praise somebody, but why is it that in a congregation, the church is 70 percent women, ministering to a handful of men? When the gender message pounds my ears, I find my knees buckling unwilling to bend. I can't pray to a gendered God, especially when those of the opposite gender seem to revel in oppression. I can't pray to a gendered

342

God, because doing so buys into the notion that there is a masculine trump card that cancels out all the feminine.

And if I ever could, no I can't anymore. Not after the Reverend T.J. Jemison of the National Baptist Convention not only led a prayer rally for Mike Tyson, but apparently tried to convince the woman who accused him of rape to drop her charges. Now the Baptists are running some scam called "Mercy for Mike." Is there any mercy for the women who prop them up on their awful pedestals, women like Desiree Washington who teach in their Sunday schools, work with their needy? Mike Tyson may have given the Baptists a few million dollars (five, it is reported), but has anyone told the brother that he can't buy his way out of hell?

There seems to be a conspiracy to silence women's voices, to make women's images invisible, but the conspiracy goes beyond the black community, beyond the farce of "mercy for Mike." The conspiracy is as deep as the notion of an all-powerful "him". Even the "hymn", then, of the ritual is suspect. This is how we have always done it, my church friends say. But until a hundred years ago, the way black people always did it was last. Don't tell me how it used to be unless you really know. To hark back to a glorious and old tradition as to suggest we get back to brown nosing and begging. And that just isn't going to happen.

Except in our churches, where only a few will allow women in the pulpit as ministers. Where pastors and leaders mimic other men in power in their abuse of women. Lying, cheating, and stealing, in the name of the Lord is more the exception than the rule, but it is getting to be a common exception. Why does Rev. Jemison have such sympathy with Mike Tyson? If he thinks rape is acceptable behavior, then all of us need to think about boycotting church.

As much as I read my Bible, I cannot read into nonsense. And it is not the Bible, but a mortal man who decided to throw the weight of one of Black American's largest congregational groups to Mike Tyson. Rev. Jemison not only turned my stomach, but he also reminded me of how hard it is to kneel to a gendered God.

NO. No, I'm not on the warpath. This is in response to a reader who asked why I'm swinging at the Muslims, the Links, and everyone else. The fact of the matter is that we black people have to do better. There are a range of things we can't blame on the white man. A white man didn't tell Mike Tyson to rape a child. A white man didn't tell some fool members of the Nation of Islam to hassle me in an elevator. A white man didn't tell San Francisco Links to talk good talk and walk a different walk. Let's get real, folk. The black community has been blistered and bashed, but when black people claim Mike Tyson as a role model, what are whites to do but follow suit? And while we can all run down the psychological and sociological theory of deprivation, we also know how to draw lines and set limits. Or do we?

All of this Black History Month, I have wondered what the world would be like if we could banish white people from the hemisphere. Would black people have a more egalitarian, more human, more just world? In the absence of white people, would we be kinder, more giving, more caring? Or have we been socialized otherwise?

The Afrocentrists might remind themselves that it was black people that sold other black people into slavery. Yes, I know, there were different kinds of slavery, some more brutal than others. I also know that cash changed hands. Not a condemnation, not a recommendation. A reality.

It seems to me that black women who are propping up "the brother" might want to ask what would happen if "the brother" was in charge. Would there be less gender discrimination? Less rape? Less sexual harassment? No, these aren't the only problems in the world, but they are among

344

the problems that many black women deal with each day. And you don't have to be on the warpath to try to stare reality down.

Sun Reporter, February, 1992

LANI GUINIER AND THE ANITA HILL EFFECT

Less than two years ago, the white men of the Senate Judiciary Committee peered before the long table that separated them from University of Oklahoma Professor Anita Hill. No matter what their intentions, the Senate came off as a bunch of bullies, as a bunch of white boys all too eager to pick at, pick off an African American woman. Now they've done it again, but not facing a sister from across the table. This time around, they've scurried, like rats in the dark, into White House corridors to pressure the President to pull the nomination of University of Pennsylvania Professor Lani Guinier for Assistant Attorney General for Civil Rights.

Not that President Clinton needed much pressuring. This man has the backbone of a jellyfish and the disingenuous character of a prevaricator. After 20 years of knowing someone, he says he has read none of her work and if he had he would never have nominated her. Too many people are too knowledgeable about White House briefings on Guinier's work for Clinton to get away with that one. As an *LA Times* writer said, it is the adult version of "the dog ate my homework." Clinton not only denied Guinier the opportunity to speak for herself, but his actions have tarred her, marred her character, and perhaps disqualified her for future public service.

Let's look at what they called her — a "quota queen." Sounds like an upscale "welfare queen." But the real "q" word is not "quota," but quisling. Our President, simply, is a wuss.

Besides Guinier, the only attractive character in this whole fiasco is Attorney General Janet Reno, who stood behind Guinier despite all the flap. Guinier also enjoyed the support of the civil rights community and scores of organizations like the NAACP and the National Political Congress of Black Women. The women's community stood behind her, too, including the NOW Legal Defense and Education Fund, the Women's Legal Defense Fund, Equal Rights Advocates, and the National Women's Political Caucus. But the President bailed out because he could, because he doesn't have to respect those who stood behind Guinier, or because he thought he could buy them off with a few crumbs.

Indeed, while the Congressional Black Caucus has spoken sternly to Clinton, some of the moderates have advised leniency saying "we have to work with him." The President invited a group of black leaders to the White House Saturday and plied them with platitudes. Is that all it takes to modify us for the public lynching of one of our best and brightest? Because make no mistake, Lani Guinier was lynched. Hung with a rope made out of *Wall Street Journal* lies, with President Clinton like one of those Southern whites who peered from behind the shutters of his locked home because he had no stomach for the fight.

The most disgusting group who participated in the Guinier lynching were the women of the Senate who chose not to fight for her. Some of the women who were elected because of the "Anita Hill effect" won't support a woman much like Anita Hill. Senator Dianne Feinstein is reported to be among them, but I couldn't find out because her San Francisco office seems to be staffed by lobotomized automatons who neither answer phones courteously, take messages, or give out fax numbers. And where was Senator Carol Moseley Braun? The biggest villain here, certainly, seems to be Senator Joseph Biden, who chairs the Judiciary Committee, didn't want to face off with another African American woman.

What has Lani Guinier done that has caused so many to distance themselves from her? The law professor has taught, written and litigated, all with civil rights in mind. She worked for the NAACP Legal Defense and Education Fund, and for the Justice Department between 1977 and 1981. She has written that civil rights are not black rights, but American rights. She says the white minority in South Africa should have guaranteed seats in that country's governing body. But you wouldn't know it to read her opposition.

An Administration that has found room for conservative David Gergen ought to have space for a moderate like Lani Guinier. If it does not, if Senators Biden, Boxer, Braun, Feinstein, Mikulski, and Murray turn away from her, they have also turned away from the millions of African American women who both support Guinier and wonder if the "Anita Hill effect" offers anything for us.

My editors asked me to contemplate Father's Day, and I started to do so when the Guinier case broke. But when I watched Lani Guinier's, press conference Friday, I could not help but think of her father, Ewert Guinier, who headed the African American Studies Department at Harvard for a time. He organized a panel on Blacks and the Labor Movement for the Association for the Study of African American Life and Culture in the seventies that I participated in, and remembered how, after the formalities were done, he mentioned that I ought to meet his daughter. Ewert Guinier passed away just a few years ago, but in watching Lani Guinier speak for herself, I was reminded of Dr. Guinier's fierce intelligence, his brilliance, his integrity. Lani Guinier indicated that her father was the victim of a "quota of one" at Harvard, denied a scholarship because one had already been given to an African American. Attorney Guinier was victim of a quota, herself. Only white males are allowed controversial views in the Clinton Administration.

King Features, June, 1993

WHEN A QUEEN'S CROWN TURNS TO ASHES

In the days that led up to the Japanese royal wedding, pundits were agog with comments about the not-so-young prince and his careerist wife. There were comparisons galore — would the Japanese couple bicker like Charles and Diana or settle into amiable partnership like Bill and Hillary. And there were those cultural arrogances, Western women writing how much they pitied the princess-to-be for her acquiescence to traditional ways without considering, it seemed, the factors that surely must have influenced her decision to accept a royal proposal.

In the middle of all this, CNN's Mary Tillitson led into a talk segment by noting that "all little girls dream of being princesses." Not black girls, I thought, then said aloud. Because when words like princess and queen are applied to white women they are words that imply power, influence, and other things. Somehow the word "queen" has been so twisted that when it is applied to African American women, it is used as a term of derision.

First there was Ronald Reagan's proverbial "welfare queen." When did the receipt of public assistance elevate one to royalty? The woman in question, I understand, perhaps received $16,000 in benefits in a year. Where is the language to derisively describe the rip-off of savings and loans, the subsidies of weapons manufacturers? There seems to be no comparable disgust for that type of rip-off artist. Indeed, their denouement is all too often followed by headline-making redemption. Ivan Boesky's duplicity is punished with a short jail term and a $20 million dollar settlement from his former wife. Neil Bush's savings and loan involvement garnered him a defense committee run out of the Bush White House. Far from "queens," these men are perceived as captains of industry. No, I don't want to be queen.

University of Pennsylvanian law professor Lani Guinier was described by the right as a "quota queen." Since Guinier never argued in favor of quotas, the queen appellation was obviously bestowed upon her because the Clint Bollick-Paul Gigot crowd wanted to make this woman an object of their derision. "Quota queen" – hardly. Guinier was just a thoughtful African American woman who took seriously the notion that we should try to solve some of our nation's racial problems. Her law review articles, her support of cumulative voting, hardly make her a "quota queen."

Now some of the reprobates on the right have decided to describe Dr. Jocelyn Elders as a "condom queen." There's that "q" word again, and again it is used in unflattering terms. Elders, like millions of Americans, is concerned with the teen pregnancy that is a scourge in our nation. Unlike the unrealistic rights, who preach abstinence as the only solution, Elders has insisted that sex education is important, and that school-based family planning clinics are part of the solution. Derailed in Arkansas by zealots who beat her at the budget process, Elders still managed to get clinics in about 20 of 319 school districts. As Surgeon General, she wants to preach the message about curtailing teen pregnancy, much as Antonia Novella preached the nonsmoking message and Everett Koop preached the AIDS prevention (among other) messages. For this she has earned the contemptuous title – "condom queen."

It seems to me that much of this name-calling is part of the discomfort our society has with African American women of conviction, women like Jocelyn Elders and Lani Guinier. These women, in the vernacular, don't "know their place." So the right has invented an ironic rhetoric to cut them down to size. "Queen" in some cultures suggests honor. For African American women, it suggests the opposite.

White women don't get it. They hear the rhetoric and, even if they dislike it, don't understand why it cuts so closely to the quick. But they don't understand why "water buffalo" was a racial slur either, why a young white man's hurled epithet, when viewed in historical context, is yet another attempt to defeminize African American women, make us animal, beast, broad shoulders for burden.

The defeminization theme seems consistent when we look at those others who get the "queen" label – drag "queen," closet "queens," the sexually ambiguous. In some ways the "queen" tossed at strong women both connects them to the despised "welfare queen" and attempts to raise questions about black women's sexuality. If we can come to the table with all this strength, this courage of conviction, does that make us any less women? Not at all, when in the words of Sojourner Truth, "I plowed and planted and not a man could head me, and ain't I a woman?"

The white right has turned a mythical queen's crown into ashes when perching it on the head of those strong black women who frighten them. Black girls don't dream of growing up to be princesses, and many of us reject the label "queen" as well. But thanks to the example of women like Sojourner Truth, Lani Guinier, and Dr. Jocelyn Elders, we don't reject the responsibility to speak, loud and strong, about those things that ail our nations.

Sun Reporter, June, 1993

CLINTON SHUFFLE OR BACKBONE TIME

I don't usually watch Rush Limbaugh. The jokes that so many find entertaining fall flat on my ears, his bombast more an irritant than a tickler. But I was in New Orleans last week, too full of spicy food to fall asleep, too teased by the jazz band I'd just heard to meditate. Instead, I engaged in that all American sport, television grazing. And somehow I came upon a pair of black lips, distorted beyond recognition. Then the angle of the camera widened and the lips were connected to a face, and it was Dr. Jocelyn Elders talking. And then there was Rush Limbaugh, imitating her. I kept wondering whether those garlic shrimp I'd eaten were fodder for a nightmare, but the big white man on the screen wasn't surrounded by wiggly lines, and he wouldn't disappear. Rush Limbaugh was imitating Jocelyn Elders, distorting her views and mocking her voice, and this is the garbage that passes for entertainment/policy analysis serious discussion.

We've been down this road before. Remember the *US News and World Report* line on Lani Guinier – "strange name, strange hair, strange views." Now, what did her hair and name have to do with anything, and by the way, is the name George Herbert Walker Bush, or for that matter, Mort Zuckerman (publisher of *US News*) any stranger than Lani Guinier? Those who bashed Guinier, those who are now bashing Elders, use the personal as the foundation for their nonsense and move on from there.

The issue is not the Elders-bashers, though. It is the man who made the nomination, President William Jefferson Clinton. Will President Clinton stand by Jocelyn Elders when her confirmation hearing takes place this Friday? Or will he succumb to the same pressures he succumbed to with the Guinier nomination? Will the band play the music for another Clinton shuffle, or is it backbone time?

As I listened to Rush Limbaugh distort Dr. Elders' record, I marveled at his use of symbols to incite opposition. To let Limbaugh tell it, Elders supports the distribution of contraceptives in the schools. He said elementary schools, then made some poor joke about giving condoms out in kindergarten, and I could just see some poor blue-haired soul calling her Senator or Congressman in enraged opposition. The fact is that Elders has opened school based clinics to reduce the high rate of teen pregnancy in Arkansas, and she has persuaded legislators to set aside money for Norplant. But the Arkansas birth rate for teens stands at 78 per 1000 girls aged 15 to 19, and the availability of contraceptives is likely to reduce that rate. Nowhere has Elders advocated distribution of condoms to elementary school aged children. It's just another Limbaugh myth.

Of course, Limbaugh is not the only one. Jocelyn

Elders' nomination is opposed by the Concerned Women for America, the American Family Association, the Westark Christian Action Council, the National Right to Life Committee, the Eagle Forum, the Family Research Council, the Traditional Values Coalition, and the Christian Coalition. From where I sit the very existence of these groups suggests that right wingers have more money and organizations than they do good sense, these well-financed extremists who are concerned with the quality of life only until the moment of birth.

Furthermore, comparisons between the published statements of the much-loved former Surgeon General Dr. Everett Koop and current nominee Dr. Jocelyn Elders reveals little difference. The Reagan appointee was an advocate who favored sex education, who agreed with Dr. Elders that issues of abortion are often lost in emotional debate, and agreed with her that abortion could be reduced by preventing unwanted pregnancies. Like Elders, Koop stated that education and information are among the few weapons against AIDS. The far right would paint Dr. Jocelyn Elders as a revolutionary, but the man Reagan appointed was no revolutionary, simply someone who was motivated by health statistics to speak his mind.

But here's the bottom line – the United States Senate needs to hear that people support Jocelyn Elders. So does the White House. Pick up a telephone and make some calls and raise some hell. Start with our local Senators, neither of who, if the truth is told, had Lani Guinier's back. Move on to the President. Make a phone call, write a letter, send some fax.

Last time there was a Clinton shuffle, we didn't even notice it starting until it was almost over. This time, the eyes of the nation are on the President. Will another black woman be slam dunked in the name of political expediency? Or will President Clinton find his backbone?

We can help him find his backbone if we let him and the Senate know we are watching. Dr. Jocelyn Elders is a wonderful, principled woman who deserves confirmation, and the opportunity to shape our nation's health policy. She doesn't deserve to be caricatured by the Limbaughs of the world. Shuffle or backbone? Stay tuned to Friday's confirmation hearings.

Sun Reporter, June, 1993

BLACK WOMEN HEADING HOUSEHOLDS: A TRIBUTE TO TENACITY

To let some mainstream policy analysts tell it, households headed by black women are the root cause of many of Black America's social problems. These folks look at our community with a view that is narrow and biased, and one of the things they have clearly failed to do is to consider the alternatives.

It is true that almost half of all black families are headed by black women, and that more than half of all black children live in these households. Instead of scapegoating the black woman who raises her children alone, why don't we celebrate her? After all, if this woman chose **not** to raise her children alone, who would take care of them? There would be more black children in the foster care pipeline, more children abandoned, more children alone. Instead of pointing fingers at the black woman who heads her household, perhaps it is time for us to look at ways to make this woman's job a bit easier.

For example, we know that the majority of children in households headed by women live in poverty. Why? Because typically female jobs pay poverty wages. A third of all black working women hold clerical jobs, where wages average about $350 a week. The average black women working full time earned just $324 per week in 1991, or less than $15,000 a year. If these women were raising children, they were doing a great job on a little bit of money!

Education improves a black woman's earnings, but a

black woman with a college degree earns, on average, the same amount as a white man with a high school diploma. Even still, many black women are persistent in persuing their educational goals. Many are enrolled in community colleges, night schools, and other degree programs so that they can earn enough money to feed their children. Some run from work to school to babysitter studying on the run. These black women are inspirations, not objects of scorn. There is something terribly warped about Presidents and candidates describing this single mother in terrible terms, even as she works to improve her lot.

It takes more than hard work. Our society must provide the child care, health care, affirmative action, and equal employment opportunity initiatives necessary to reward the work of the mother with her shoulder to the grindstone. Where are the after school programs, summer jobs, and library hours for her offspring. All of these things have bit the dust as budget cuts have become more the exception than the rule.

Granted, every single mother doesn't chase an educational dream. But those who do their best are often strangled by the stereotypes, stereotypes that are a long way from the truth. I've got a special stake in debunking these stereotypes - my mom raised five children on her own after my parents were divorced; now my sister, Mariette, is raising two rambunctious boys after her divorce. Both women give 110 percent, as do many of the women in our community who pick themselves up and dust themselves off when they have the responsibility of raising children alone. They don't analyze it, they just do it, despite the nonsense they hear about "single mothers."

Indeed, my sister told me one day, "I really don't know the meaning of the term leisure time." I had to think about it and agree. When she isn't working or going to school, she's shuttling her boys to an array of cultural activities. They go to Marine World, Disneyland, museums, zoos. "We were exposed to everything, my kids will be, too," Mariette

Malveaux, says determined. When something's got to give, it is her free time.

If more than half of black children are being raised by black women, then these mothers hold Black America's future in their hands and in their households. Instead of "dissing" these women, let's pay tribute to them. They do their best with a lot less than many two parent families have! What, indeed, would we do without them.

Sun Reporter, May, 1991

CLARENCE THOMAS AND THE GENDER THING

"She gets mad when the mailman is late with her welfare check, that's how dependent she is," said Clarence Thomas to his sister, Emma Mae in a 1980 speech that he delivered to a group of black conservatives. That speech marked his induction into the Hall of Shame, the group of men who cross women's backs to gain a place of prominence. Republicans took note of Thomas after he skewered his sister in public, but the rest of us should take note, too, to the way this man fails to understand the way gender affects life chances and opportunities.

One might argue that had Emma Mae Thomas been a man she, too, would have had the benefit of the Catholic education that Myers Anderson provided grandsons Clarence and Myers. Girl that she was, she remained home with her mother and started a career of low-wage work. Indeed, the record may well show that Emma Mae Thomas is the firmer believer of responsibility and self-help than her male siblings. It was she, after all, who provided care for an aging aunt, and it was she whose path away from public assistance was paved by two part-time jobs.

Emma Mae Martin seems to be as hard a worker as her brother, but women's work has always been less well renumerated than that of men. While Clarence Thomas earns more than $110,000 as a federal judge, most hospital aides like his sister earn less than $5 an hour. Instead of holding a hardworking woman up for ridicule, Thomas might try practicing some of the self-help he preaches by offering some of the same assistance to his sister that his grandfather once offered him.

Some say the Clarence Thomas story is one of hard work and bootstrap pulling. From where I sit, though, this is a story of the way gender shapes opportunities within families. Judge Thomas cannot help the fact that, as the male offspring of the grandfather he revered, he had advantages that his sister missed. But it is disappointing that he seems insensitive to the gender basis of his advantages. His supporters speak of his hard work, but did his mother or sister work less hard, or was their work merely less well rewarded?

Economic reality dictates most women's workforce participation, but the absence of family and medical leave policy in our society means that our society depends on the unpaid work of women. Women are often pressed to drop out of the labor force when a family member—a parent, older relative, or child—needs care. For providing that kind of support in her family, Emma Mae Martin earned her brother's public scorn. What can the rest of us women expect from Supreme Court Justice Clarence Thomas as issues of pay equity and family policy come before this court?

USA Today, September, 1991

WHERE DO WOMEN GO FROM HERE?

When women commemorated the anniversary of suffrage a year ago, many pointed out how much women had lost, especially when the important issue of choice is concerned. But with a stroke of a pen, President Clinton balanced the scales on many choice issues. Two days after he took office, and twenty years after abortion was legalized, President Clinton lifted the "gag rule" in federally funded clinics, removed the moratorium on fetal tissue research, agreed to allow privately funded abortions in military hospitals, and overturned the ban on importing RU486. His decisions don't completely turn the clock back — the Hyde Amendment prevents poor women from receiving publicly funded abortions, and the far right has been so effective in intimidating physicians that fewer offer abortions now than a decade or so ago.

By removing the threat to legal abortion, President Clinton has also removed the issue that generated heat and headlines and pulled women together. That's why I couldn't wait to read the August issue of *Social Policy Magazine*. Its theme is the "Women's Movement at the Crossroads," and takes a look at some of the reasons so many women look askance when they hear the words "women's movement."

How big is the organized women's movement, anyway? There probably aren't more than 200,000 members of the National Organization for Women, as organization that clings to a white middle class and extremist fringe that repels many women. The National Women's Political Caucus is smaller but more focused on electoral work, with about 35,000 dues paying members. Neither group represents a majority of our nation's 93 million adult women. Indeed, most women run from the title "feminist" and have little or nothing to do with the women's movement.

Why? Linda Tarr-Whelan asks the question directly in her article "Realigning Priorities." On the basis of the Women's Voice poll her organization, the Center for Policy Alternatives, administered with the Ms. Foundation, she says women of all incomes, races, ages, educational levels and political party agree on the need for universal health care (86 percent), equal pay (78 percent) and flex-time, the top concern of working women.

Women may agree on economic issues, but the Clinton Administration's economic agenda has served only a subset of women. The Family and Medical Leave Act, for example, excludes those who work for "small" businesses. Fully half of the workforce does not have the benefit of family leave because they work for firms with fewer than 50 employees. Others can't take advantage of the benefits because the Family and Medical Leave Act only provides for unpaid leave.

Similarly, much ado was made of the inclusion of the Earned Income Tax Credit in the budget package. Designed to help low-income, full time working people (mostly women) with children, the EITC is based on the premise that no one who works forty hours a week or more should live in poverty. The credit will be provided to the working poor whether they owe taxes or not, and will make up the difference between full-time work and the poverty line. But part-time and temporary employment is a growing feature of our downsizing economy, and those who hold these jobs will not qualify for the EITC.

Finally, Tarr-Whelan and the others who have written about women at the crossroads fail to answer an important question — why has public assistance never been defined as a feminist issue? Since most of the children who receive Aid to Families with Dependent Children (AFDC) are women, why has the organized women's movement been so silent about the controversial issue of welfare reform?

On the 73rd anniversary of women's suffrage, it is useful to remember that it is easier to come together around suffrage and abortion than economic equity. The women whose lots have improved since President Clinton took office may well ask about the women's movement at the crossroads. Those with economic status as part-time or peripheral workers may be tempted to ask what the women's movement has done for them lately.

King Features, August, 1993

ABOUT THE AUTHOR

JULIANNE MALVEAUX is an economist, columnist, and television/radio commentator. Her twice-weekly syndicated column is available through the King Features Syndicate. Her work has also appeared in *USA Today, Black Issues in Higher Education, Essence, Emerge, Ms.* and other magazines. Her research has been published in a number of academic journals and collections of essays. With Margaret Simms, she co-edited *Slipping Through the Cracks: The Status of Black Women.* She is a regular panelist on the PBS show, "To The Contrary," and appears on CNN's "CNN and Company" and other programs. Malveaux earned her Bachelor of Arts and Master of Arts degree from Boston University and a Ph.D. in Economics from Massachusetts Institute of Technology. A former college professor, Malveaux speaks to civic and college groups about economic and public policy, the labor market, gender, and race. Malveaux is a native San Franciscan. She is active in local and national civic groups, and serves as Vice President of the National Association of Negro Business and Professional Women's Clubs.

PUBLISHER'S NOTE

Copies of this book are available from the publisher.

To order, write to: Pines One Publishing Sales Department, 3870 Crenshaw Blvd., Suite 391, Los Angeles, CA 90008, or call (213) 290-1182; Fax (213) 291-0900. A limited number of copies signed by Julianne Malveaux are available for $14.95

Please note that we give a discount for bulk orders of three or more books. When ordering, add $2.00 postage and handling for the first book and .50 for each additional book. California residents please add 7.75 percent sales tax ($1.16).

*Also available from our backlist:

Just A Thought, The Smiley Report
by Tavis Smiley (paper) $9.95

❏ Please add my name to the Malveaux Report newsletter so that I may receive one free copy.

❏ Please send information on arranging speaking engagements with Julianne Malveaux.

Name: _____

Company Name: _____

Address: _____

City: _____

State: _____ Zip: _____

Phone: _____
